ECONOMICS

ECONOMICS

Making Sense of the Modern Economy

4th edition

Edited by Richard Davies

PUBLICAFFAIRS
New York

Typeset in EcoType by MacGuru Ltd
info@macguru.org.uk

Library of Congress Control Number: 2015948025
ISBN 978-1-61039-615-8 (PB)
ISBN 978-1-61039-616-5 (EB)

First Edition

10 9 8 7 6 5 4 3 2 1

Contents

About the editor

RICHARD DAVIES was *The Economist*'s Economics Editor until July 2015, when he left to become special economics adviser to the UK Chancellor of the Exchequer, George Osborne. Before joining the newspaper, he worked at the Bank of England, where he managed teams covering international economics and the financial sector. He was a lead author of the bank's *Financial Stability Report*, covering the stability of the banking sector. He also worked on secondment at the Bank of Canada in Ottawa. He began his career as a microeconomist, working for a private-sector consultancy, and then as a government antitrust economist at the UK Competition Commission. His academic research has been published in the *Journal of Money, Credit and Banking* and the *Journal of Financial Stability*, and he has held a lectureship at Lincoln College, Oxford, where he taught economics.

Contributors

Ryan Avent is *The Economist's* news editor.

Henry Curr was *The Economist's* Britain economics correspondent and is now US economics correspondent, based in Washington, DC.

Greg Ip was *The Economist's* US economics editor, based in Washington, DC.

Zanny Minton Beddoes was *The Economist's* economics editor until 2014 and has been the newspaper's editor-in-chief since 2015.

Simon Rabinovitch is Asia economics editor of *The Economist*, based in Shanghai.

Paul Wallace is *The Economist's* Europe economics editor.

Callum Williams is *The Economist's* economics correspondent.

Introduction: the everday science

LIFE'S BIGGEST PROBLEM is a simple one: we cannot do everything. Sometimes it is nature that holds us back. Millions of children dream of life as an astronaut, but the truth is that even the hardest working will find their physical and mental capabilities mean they fall short of NASA's requirements. Sometimes it is low income or wealth that stops us getting what we want: desires for the latest gadget, outfit or car are stymied when wages are meagre and credit scarce; buying a house is tough without a big deposit. Some face far fewer constraints, but in the end even those with the sharpest minds, rudest health and fattest wallets will run out of time. Whatever the reason, scarcity of natural and economic resources is unavoidable. Dealing with these shortages is a task every human shares.

Scarcity means that to do our best we must make decisions that involve trade-offs. Take education. Teenagers must decide whether a university degree and the debts that it will bring justify gains received in the distant future. Business is a game of trade-offs too. A shopkeeper deciding what to do with the monthly takings must choose between the comfort of a healthy cash cushion and the riskier choices – building up inventory or hiring new staff – needed to win more customers. Running a home means facing a series of finely balanced decisions: whether to spend or save, to work or take a holiday, to choose a fixed or floating-rate mortgage.

Economics is the study of trade-offs. A mongrel subject that has borrowed from hard disciplines like mathematics and physics, and from softer ones like history and psychology, it can be hard to pin down. As this book makes clear, what unifies economics is the problem of scarcity, the trade-offs scarcity forces us to make, and how

– when they work well – markets can help allocate scarce resources efficiently. The articles in this collection cover everyday puzzles, from how best to play the lottery to why people talk in quiet carriages. They also cover problems facing states, from whether fines or prison are the best way to deter crime to why we seem unable to avoid bank crashes. The common thread is why, when faced with a tricky trade-off, people make the choices they do and how they might make them more wisely.

Economies in crisis

Perhaps the most pressing global shortfall is a scarcity of income. In 2014 the value of output across the world – global gross domestic product (GDP) – was around $75 trillion. With the world's population estimated at a little over 7 billion, each person would get around $10,700 if GDP were divvied up equally. Yet for many that amount is a dream. Around one in seven people live in extreme poverty. For those 1 billion, economic constraints are sharp: they survive on less than $1.25 a day, or $450 per year. At this level scarce resources become a constraint on life. In low-income countries 40% of recorded deaths are of children under the age of 15, whereas in advanced countries just 1% die so young. Poverty-stricken people lose their lives in avoidable ways, with AIDS, malaria, tuberculosis and diarrhoeal illness killing 6 million people in low-income countries in 2012.

Much of this is a problem of resource allocation. Extreme poverty often means a lack of food: of the 805 million undernourished people in 2012–14, 791 million live in developing countries. Their diet, short on calories and protein, saps energy, destroys muscles and makes them susceptible to disease. At the same time, those living in advanced countries throw away 222 million tonnes of food a year. The binned meals are worth an estimated $400 billion, more than the entire food production of sub-Saharan Africa. If that money were sent to the world's poorest, it could provide $400 a year or $1.10 a day. Extreme poverty would be eradicated. If the global economy is a machine for allocating scarce resources, the economics of food suggest something is badly wrong with it.

Disparities are just as sharp within countries. Over the past 30 years, the incomes of the bottom tenth of workers has fallen by 5% in

America when adjusted for inflation. For the top tenth, real incomes have increased by 50%. Widening income inequality is not just a rich-world phenomenon. In emerging-market economies like India and Russia inequality is more acute. In China, the world's second largest economy, it is staggering: in 1980 the top tenth of workers earned 6.5 times the bottom tenth; by 2012 they earned 62 times as much. Of the G20 group of large economies, only Brazil has experienced falling income inequality over the past ten years.

The world's wealth is even more concentrated. In America the richest 0.1% of families' share of wealth rose from 7% in the late 1970s to 22% in 2012. Just 160,000 families boast net assets of over $20 million; the $3.2 trillion they jointly own is around the size of Germany's economy. Differences in effort, talent and luck will always mean people end up unequal, but many worry that disparities are becoming entrenched. In America the vast wealth held by family foundations has created a new aristocracy that blends wealth with philanthropy and ensures that heirs to fortunes also inherit access to top-tier universities.

New economic dividing lines are cropping up. The major economic battle of the next decade may not be between rich and poor, but between the old and the young. The current cohort of retirees poses a major challenge. There are lots of them: between 1946 and 1965, 76 million babies were born in America, around 30 million more than in 1925–45 and 20 million more than in 1965–85. The same pattern appears in many rich countries. These baby-boomers, now between 49 and 69 years old, will be around for a long time – male life expectancy was less than 60 years in 1940, today is it close to 80. Many will receive pensions for more years than they worked.

Today's under-50s have been groomed to foot the bill. There is a commonly held view that state pensions are paid from a pot built up during a worker's years of toil, but in truth no such pot exists. They are "pay as you go" systems with pensioners' grants coming from taxes on people of working age. The tab will become increasingly painful: pensions have risen from 13% to 15% of public spending in Britain in 2009–14 as the baby boomers have started to retire. Unsustainably generous pension systems, from Britain to Brazil, will be tough to reform: because the over-65s tend to vote, chipping away at their benefits can lose an election. Unless this changes the global pension bill will balloon.

Funding will be tough. Many workers' prospects are flaky at best. Across the OECD group of rich countries a 7% unemployment rate means there were 46 million unemployed workers in 2014. That is a benefits queue 50% bigger than the entire British workforce. In some countries things are worse: in Spain and Greece more than 20% are out of work. Across the rich world the number of long-term unemployed has almost doubled since 2007. Just as worrying is the rise in inactivity: the number of people out of work but not looking for it either. In America this trend has been marked, with those unfit to work jumping from 7 million to 9 million between 2007 and 2014.

For those with jobs life is hardly rosy. Meagre pay rises mean that inflation has eroded buying power. Between 2009 and 2013 inflation-adjusted pay fell or was flat in 21 of the 27 advanced countries assessed by the OECD. When inflation is taken into account, many rich-world countries are still far below their previous peaks in terms of income per head. Even those in countries that are growing have suffered: in Britain pay dropped by 8% between 2007 and 2014, with the median worker suffering the biggest drop in buying power since Victorian times. In America median workers' inflation-adjusted pay has hardly budged for 40 years.

Hoping it's a hangover

With any luck, some of these woes can be put down to a terrible economic hangover. History shows that recoveries from banking crashes take much longer than recoveries from normal recessions. Proponents of the hangover theory argue that, in the end, it will lift. This would mean sunnier times ahead: between 1992 and 2007 advanced economies expanded by an average of 3% per year – more than 55% in 15 years. Large emerging economies did even better, with Brazil, Russia, India and South Africa expanding by 90%. A return to such buoyant growth would cut joblessness and lift wages.

Others worry that that golden period will never return. Of the advanced economies only America, Britain and Canada are growing at anywhere near pre-crisis rates, and another 20 rich nations managed an average expansion of less than 1.5% in 2014. Performance has been so bad for so long that many now worry that the rich world's debt hangover has morphed into something worse: a "secular stagnation" of low growth, rock-bottom interest rates and anaemic investment. Emerging markets have lost their vigour too. Apart from India, the BRICs' vim has gone. As China slows, fears of a property bubble and murky shadow banks are on the rise. Brazil and South Africa, with runaway inflation and hefty debts, are badly mismanaged. Russia has become a pariah, with Western sanctions locking it out of global finance and its own retaliation shutting it out of world trade. A return to the growth of the past seems a distant hope.

Despite all this, many are making big bets on a bright future. Governments are still spending more than they earn in taxes and are issuing debt to cover the shortfall. Firms are paying dividends despite dwindling profits, and some are selling bonds to fill the gap. Workers toiling on low wages are still managing to shop. Far from being stung by the experience of 2008, the world is taking on yet more debt: since 2007 it has grown by $57 billion. The global debt-to-GDP ratio has risen by 17 percentage points, as household sectors in four-fifths of countries have piled up more debt. Even if growth returns to pre-crisis levels, paying these dues will be hard. If it does not, the future could be one of cuts – to state payouts, firms' dividends, workers' pay and the weekly shop. In a world living beyond its means the future need not be better than the past: it could be a lot worse.

Economics from the ashes

Can economics help? Many would say no. Ever since Thomas Carlyle dubbed it the "dismal science", economics has had fierce critics. Carlyle's objection had two prongs. First, he simply didn't like the way economists think, arguing that their obsession with questions of supply and demand meant a narrow view of life. Second, he found economists' predictions dismal. This argument – that economics is the wrong way to look at life's problems and its forecasts are inaccurate – is one that has strong currency today.

The articles in this book show why Carlyle was wrong. Written between 2012 and 2015, they are grouped into three parts. Part 1 looks at the economics of money and the role – both good and evil – that banks play in the modern economy. Part 2 investigates the changing world of work, covering the rise of the megafirm, the problem of low pay and inequality. Part 3 considers the economic challenges of the future, and asks whether robots and innovation can help overcome the grinding rise in health-care and education costs. (Note that the titles of some articles have been edited for clarity.)

Readers should find some reasons for optimism. The articles make clear that those at the cutting edge of economics understand the world better than ever before. And many more stand to gain from this knowledge, with a rush of new economists in the pipeline. In America, 36,540 new economists graduated in 2013, 15% more than in 2008. In Britain, government statistics show a 25% increase in economics students over the same period, despite the fact that the overall number of university students fell by 2%. In China there are close to 1 million students enrolled in economics courses.

Those opting to study economics are demanding change. From Britain to India, groups of students are pushing for reform and a redesign of the economics curriculum to better capture the realities of modern life. Economics is a subject that has a history of evolution and change, suggesting these reformers are likely to have an impact. The magpie subject will steal a little less from mathematics, a little more from history and philosophy.

It is crucial that economics evolves and improves. Despite poor economic performance, economists have become far more powerful over the past 20 years. Central banks led the charge, with a move to make them independent of political control sweeping the globe. And economists have come to regulate huge chunks of the corporate world, overseeing not just banking but also water, energy and telecoms markets. Fiscal decisions are always a mixture of politics and economics, but the balance is tipping in economists' favour, with many countries setting up independent bodies to oversee their budgets in an attempt to prevent pre-election splurges. The quiet rise of the technocrat economist shows no signs of slowing.

Economics is extending into new areas. The economics of charity is one example. As charities compete for scarce donor funding, many are being asked to calculate the impact of their work and are turning to economists to help them. Health care is another. In Britain, the National Institute for Clinical Excellence, an independent group, decides whether the National Health Service should pay for recently invented drugs. Its decisions are based on a quantitative analysis of the trade-off between spending more cash and the number of extra days a patient might live. With economic hands on myriad policy decisions, many of them in areas not typically regarded as being relevant to economics, it is important to understand what economists are up to and whether they are any good.

The rise of economics extends far beyond public policy. The smartphone has allowed a new assortment of firms to flower, many of them run on economic principles. The world's best-known search engine, Google, runs 3.5 billion searches per day, with each one of them selling adverts using a lightning-quick auction designed by its chief economist. By auctioning its adverts Google makes sure it finds the right price. Upstarts like Uber, a firm that is revolutionising taxi markets, are pricing specialists too: by rapidly adjusting its prices, Uber attracts more drivers during periods of acute scarcity (Friday nights). In the world of information technology, economists' obsession with supply and demand can prove highly lucrative.

Smartphones give their users new economic roles. An eBay user can become an online shopkeeper overnight; Airbnb "hosts" can suddenly find themselves acting as mini hoteliers. This brings unfamiliar trade-offs: how to set the right reserve price for an auction, or how to set room-rental rates to balance returns and occupancy. Since dealing with these new choices can be tough, the new firms, often designed by economists, guide their users towards the best choices. Easy to access and nudged towards efficiency by the world's leading economists, these new markets are major reasons for optimism.

New markets are not the only reason for hope. Better measurement of GDP means the role that important activities – including the arts, and research and development (R&D) – play in economic growth can be identified more accurately. Understanding the economy better should lead to improved policies. An economic approach to crime is prioritising fines over prison, helping to deter criminals and keep the prison bill down. The privatisation of state-owned infrastructure, including ports, has resulted in huge efficiency gains. Clever use of internet search data can help identify cities at risk of acute unemployment long before official statistics do, helping policymakers to react quickly. And the use of robots in manufacturing can provide a huge productivity boost.

But any optimism about economics must be tempered by frustration. In a resource-stretched world there are many natural constraints we can do little about. But the biggest hurdles are not a lack of land, water or time: they are man-made. Japan's 780% tariff on rice imports cripples trade and protects inefficient producers. The EU's tariffs on food imports are worse: by penalising processed foods such as canned fruit or refined coffee and chocolate, rich EU countries ensure that African nations export mainly low-value-added raw foodstuffs. The world's largest economy, America, is a land of protectionism and public-sector unionisation, keeping foreigners and outsiders in their place. The economic giant of the future, China, has fattened itself by subsidising heavy industry and distorting its exchange rate.

All this means that the problems the world faces are not of pure economics, but of political economy. Taken on its own, economics is in good shape, moving on from the 2008 crash, reinventing itself and offering great gains to those at its cutting edge. The problem is that economic lessons are not learned. The global economy is not as economists would have it; it is a system of entrenched interests, powerful lobby groups and distorted markets. This often results in prices that are too high, and a supply of goods that is too low. In other words, things are scarcer than they need to be. If economics is the study of trade-offs, understanding the modern economy means admitting a nasty truth: that the toughest trade-offs are man-made.

PART 1

Money, banks and crashes

From evil roots to green shoots

The crash of 2008 was a seismic event in economics. Despite the time that has passed and the efforts that have been made to fix the global economy, the world's problems – from dodgy banks to indebted states – still haunt it. The first part of this book asks how and why we ended up here. Why is debt so tempting to shoppers and governments alike? Why do banks take such extraordinary risks? And what can the euro zone do to get out of its catastrophic slump?

Some answers come from what seems the simplest of things: money. A human invention, money is sometimes called "the root of all evil". In fact, as, Nobuhiro Kiyotaki, a Princeton University economist, has pointed out, the saying is the wrong way round. If anything, evil is the root of all money. The evil Mr Kiyotaki had in mind was a lack of trust. If you are unsure of those you trade with, money soothes the problem. Chapter 1 tracks how money has morphed from its earliest roots, and looks at the weird forms of money from cash substitutes used in prisons to mobile money used in Africa. It ends with an assessment of the two types of money we will use in the future: digital currencies such as Bitcoin and the Chinese yuan. The rise of both brings opportunities and challenges.

Just as money goes back centuries, so do financial crashes. Chapter 2 argues that five economic crises, starting in 1792 and ending in 1933 can help us understand why we ended up with the current financial system. It tracks the activities of the bankers, regulators and criminals behind the slumps. It is a reminder that financiers have been making the same mistakes – allowing leverage to get too high, or liquidity to get too low – for centuries.

Sadly the lessons of history were not learned, resulting in another leverage-fuelled crash. Although Britain and America were bellwethers for the crisis, it is the euro zone that has been hardest hit. Chapter 3 tracks the euro zone's slump, starting with the stunning build-up of debt in the currency zone. It explains how the depth of the crash has revolutionised monetary policy. And it provides a balanced view of the arguments for and against austerity and how quickly governments can cut spending without killing the economy.

The biggest hope for the euro zone is that its competitiveness is so poor there are big improvements to make. The single market should bring huge opportunities for its members. Grabbing them will require tough choices, often pitting entrepreneurs against insiders: from Portugal's port unions to those across Europe who gum up labour markets. Despite the region's woes, there are reasons for optimism. When the private sector is unleashed prices tumble and output soars, as the articles on taxis and ports show.

1　Money

Monetary beginnings: on the origin of specie

Theories on where money comes from say something about where the dollar and euro will go

MONEY IS PERHAPS the most basic building-block in economics. It helps states collect taxes to fund public goods. It allows producers to specialise and reap gains from trade. It is clear what it does, but its origins are a mystery. Some argue that money has its roots in the power of the state. Others claim the origin of money is a purely private matter: it would exist even if governments did not. This debate is long-running but it informs some of the most pressing monetary questions of today.

Money fulfils three main functions. First, it must be a medium of exchange, easily traded for goods and services. Second, it must be a store of value, so that it can be saved and used for consumption in the future. Third, it must be a unit of account, a useful measuring-stick. Lots of things can do these jobs. Tea, salt and cattle have all been used as money. In Britain's prisons, inmates currently favour shower-gel capsules or rosary beads.

The use of money stretches back millennia. Electrum, an alloy of gold and silver, was used to make coins in Lydia (now western Turkey) in around 650BC. The first paper money circulated in China in around 1000AD. The Aztecs used cocoa beans as cash until the 12th century. The puzzle is how people agreed what to use.

Carl Menger, an Austrian economist, set out one school of thought as long ago as 1892. In his version of events, the monetisation of an economy starts when agricultural communities move away from subsistence farming and start to specialise. This brings efficiency gains but means that trade with others becomes necessary. The problem is that operating markets on the basis of barter is a pain: you have to scout around looking for the rare person who wants what you have and has what you want.

Money evolves to reduce barter costs, with some things working better than others. The commodity used as money should not lose value when it is bought and sold. So clothing is a bad money, since no one places the same value on second-hand clothes as new ones. Instead, something that is portable, durable (fruit and vegetables are out) and divisible into smaller pieces is needed. Menger called this property "saleableness". Spices and shells are highly saleable, explaining their use as money. Government plays no role here. The origin of money is a market-led response to barter costs, in which the best money is that which minimises the costs of trade. Menger's is a good description of how informal monies, such as those used by prisoners, originate.

But the story just doesn't match the facts in most monetary economies, according to a 1998 paper by Charles Goodhart of the London School of Economics. Take the widespread use of precious metals as money. A Mengerian would say that this happens because metals are durable, divisible and portable: that makes them an ideal medium of exchange. But it is incredibly hard to value raw metals, Mr Goodhart argued, so the cost of using them in trade is high. It is much easier to assess the value of a bag of salt or a cow than a lump of metal. Raw metals fail Menger's own saleableness test.

This problem explains why metal money has circulated not in lumps but as coins, with a regulated amount of metal in each coin. But history shows that minting developed not as a private-sector attempt to minimise the costs of trading, but as a government operation. It was state intervention, not the private market, that made metal specie work as money.

That suggests another theory is needed, in which the state plays a bigger role in the origin of money. Mr Goodhart called this the "Cartalist" theory. The fiscal wing of government has a huge incentive to move its economy away from barter. Once money exists, income and expenditure can be measured. That means they can be taxed. And the public purse gets a second boost from seigniorage, the difference between the value of the coins and the cost of producing them. On this account, governments impose taxes payable only in money, creating a demand for money that means it will be widely accepted as payment for goods. The state forces the economy away from barter for its own fiscal purposes.

Mr Goodhart used monetary history to test these competing theories. He examined the overthrow of Rome and a period in the tenth century when the Japanese government stopped minting coins. If the origin of money were purely private, these shocks should have had no monetary effects. But after Rome's collapse, traders resorted to barter; in Japan they started to use rice instead of coins. There is a clear link between fiscal power and money.

The struggle for life

The evidence suggests that only "informal" monies can spring up purely privately. But informal money can exist on the grandest scale. The dollar's position as the world's reserve currency is not mandated by any government, for example. Its pre-eminence outside America rests on it being the best option for international transactions. Once a competitor currency becomes preferable, firms and other governments will move on. The good news for the dollar is that the Chinese yuan is not yet widely accepted and suffers from higher inflation, reducing its usefulness. But a shift in the world's reserve currency could be swifter than many assume.

The dollar's other competitor, the euro, has deeper problems. Its origins were not private. Nor is it a proper Cartalist money, backed by a nation state. This means it lacks a foundation in the power of either the market or the state. In his paper, written a year before the euro was introduced, Mr Goodhart was prescient, highlighting "an unprecedented divorce between the main monetary and fiscal authorities". Cartalists, he said "worry whether the divorce may not have some unforeseen side effects".

Strange money: shillings, cows and mobile phones

Somalia's mighty shilling: hard to kill

A currency issued in the name of a central bank that no longer exists

USE OF A PAPER CURRENCY is normally taken to be an expression of faith in the government that issues it. Once the solvency of the issuer is in doubt, anyone holding its notes will quickly try to trade them in for dollars, jewellery or, failing that, some commodity with enduring value (when the rouble collapsed in 1998 some factory workers in Russia were paid in pickles). The Somali shilling, now entering its second decade with no real government or monetary authority to speak of, is a splendid exception to this rule.

Somalia's long civil war has ripped apart what institutions it once had. In 2011 the country acquired a notional central bank under the remit of the Transitional Federal Government. But the government's authority does not extend far beyond the capital, Mogadishu. The presence of the Shabab, a murderous fundamentalist militia, in the south and centre of the country, makes it unlikely that Somalia will become whole anytime soon. Meanwhile, 2.3 million people are in need of edible aid. Why, then, are Somali shillings, issued in the name of a government that ceased to exist long ago and backed by no reserves of any kind, still in use?

One reason may be that the supply of shillings has remained fairly fixed. Rival warlords issued their own shillings for a while and there are a fair number of fakes in circulation. But the lack of an official printing press able to expand the money supply has given the pre-1992 shilling a certain cachet. Even the forgeries do it the honour of declaring they were printed before the central bank collapsed: implausibly crisp red 1,000-shilling notes, with their basket weavers on the front and orderly docks on the back, declare they were printed in the capital in 1990.

Abdirashid Duale, boss of Dahabshiil, the largest network of banks in Somalia, says that his staff are trained to distinguish good fakes from the real thing before exchanging them for dollars. Others accept the risk of holding a few fakes as a cost of doing business (shillings are often handed over in thick bundles of 100 notes). By this alchemy, an imitation of a thing which is already of notional value turns out to be worth something.

Shelling out shillings

A second reason for the shilling's longevity is that it is too useful to do away with. Large transactions, such as the purchase of a house, a car, or even livestock, are dollarised. But Somalis need small change with which to buy tea, sugar, qat (a herbal stimulant) and so on. Many staples are not produced domestically, making barter impractical. The shilling serves as well as shells or beads would as a medium of exchange. It also has a role as a secondary store of value. Once a year the economy gets an injection of dollars when goats are sold to Saudi Arabia to feed pilgrims undertaking the haj. Herders need to find ways to save money received then for spending over the next year. The shilling is one of them.

The shilling has a further source of strength. Since each party to a transaction is likely to be able to place the other within Somalia's system of kinship, the shilling is underpinned by a strong social glue. Paper currencies always need tacit consent from their users that they will exchange bills for actual stuff. But in Somalia this pact is rather stronger: an individual who flouts the system risks jeopardising trust in both himself and his clan.

Having survived against great odds, the shilling now faces a serious challenge in the form of dollars transferred by mobile phone. Zaad, a mobile-money service, allows users to pay for goods by texting small amounts of money to a merchant's account, and is proving popular in Mogadishu. But the shilling's endurance suggests it should not be counted out. If it can survive without a government, it can probably brush off modern technology, too.

The economics of cow ownership: udder people's money

Cattle may be a terrible investment but a decent savings vehicle

IN INDIA THERE ARE about 280 million cows. They produce valuable things – milk, dung and calves. But cattle are expensive to keep. The biggest outlay is food – the average cow consumes fodder worth about 10,000 rupees ($160) a year. Veterinary costs also add up.

These expenses are so high that cows are often a poor investment. According to a splendidly titled NBER paper, "Continued Existence of Cows Disproves Central Tenets of Capitalism?", which looks at cow and buffalo ownership in rural areas of northern India, the average return on a cow is –64% once you factor in the cost of labour.

If returns on cattle are so bad, why do households buy them? People may not be thinking about economics, of course. Hindus may derive spiritual fulfilment from cow ownership. Households may prefer to produce high-quality milk at home, even if doing so costs more.

But the authors suggest that there may also be sound economic reasoning behind cow ownership. According to ICRIER, a think-tank, only 7% of Indian villages have a bank branch. That means people lack a formal savings mechanism for their spare cash. And although there are informal ways to save – joining a local savings club, for example, or simply stuffing money under the mattress – owning a cow may be a better option.

That is because most people find spending easier than saving. Immediate pleasures are easier to grasp than future joys – and so people make spending decisions that they later regret. Economists refer to this as "myopia". Cows force people not to be myopic. Compared with money held in savings accounts, cattle are illiquid assets. Taking cash from a cow is harder than taking money from an account. As a result, temptation spending is trickier.

The paper has implications for poverty-alleviation strategies and for financial services in developing countries. Aid programmes that try to reduce poverty by distributing livestock may be ineffective at raising incomes, if the returns from owning them are so poor. If cows are used as a means of saving, the spread of mobile banking in places like India will provide another, better option. Even then the problem of temptation spending arises. Dean Karlan, one of the authors, is interested in the idea of "commitment savings accounts", whereby people forgo their right to withdraw funds until they reach a specified level.

October 2013

Airtime is money
The use of pre-paid mobile-phone minutes as a currency

MOBILE MONEY IN AFRICA comes in different flavours. The sophisticated sort, exemplified by services such as M-Pesa in Kenya, allows account-holders to transfer legal tender electronically to fellow account-holders by entering commands on a mobile phone. Popular though such services are, they have not stopped an older form of mobile money flourishing. This sort uses pre-paid mobile-airtime minutes as a de facto currency that can be transferred between phones, exchanged for cash with dealers who rent out phones, or bartered for goods and services.

Pre-paid minutes can be swapped for cash or spent in shops most easily in Côte d'Ivoire, Egypt, Ghana and Uganda, says Chris Chan of Tranglo, a Malaysian firm that facilitates "airtime remittances" to mobile phones. Airtime is commonly used as money in Nigeria, too. Hannes Van Rensburg, Visa's boss for sub-Saharan Africa, says this is partly because regulators there have made it difficult for banks to offer the newer form of mobile money.

But even in places like Kenya, airtime minutes are still being used as currency. Unlike mobile money, airtime's value does not rely directly on a government's stability or ability to hold down inflation by, say, showing restraint printing money. Opening a mobile-money account typically requires waiting for days after showing your ID. In contrast, airtime can often be purchased and sent immediately and anonymously. Because many telecoms firms in Africa and elsewhere transfer minutes nationwide free of charge, airtime is especially useful for settling small debts.

In Zimbabwe, for example, American banknotes have largely replaced the hyperinflation-ravaged Zimbabwean dollar. American coins are scarce, however, so pretty much everybody in Zimbabwe transfers airtime in their place at least occasionally, says Oswell Binha, president of the Zimbabwe National Chamber of Commerce in Harare. Zimbabwean shoppers are tired of being given sweets in lieu of change, so shopkeepers who give airtime rather than yet another "$0.63-worth of chocolates" have a competitive advantage, Mr Binha says. By the end of 2012, Yo! Time, a Harare-based start-up that simplifies these retailer-to-shopper airtime payouts, was processing more than 9,000 payouts a day for clients; in the middle of that year the figure was 2,000.

The use of airtime as currency is fuelled by the growing ease of sending minutes abroad. A Dublin firm called ezetop (now called ding*), for example, sells airtime for 238 telecoms firms via the web, text messaging and about 450,000 shops in 20 countries. The value of international airtime transfers doubled from $350 million in 2011 to $700 million in 2012, estimates Berg Insight, a consultancy.

Some authorities are concerned about airtime's use as money. As one industry executive puts it, network operators are, in effect, "issuing their own currency" and setting its exchange rate; central banks tend to dislike such things. Others worry that airtime could be used by criminal or extremist groups to move money covertly. According to a senior official at the Financial Action Task Force (FATF), an intergovernmental body in Paris, it appears that some groups buy top-up scratch cards in one country and sell the airtime in another. Regulations will surely follow, but such rules must be set against the good that tradable airtime does.

The dollar: the once and future currency

The world's love/hate relationship with the dollar

"LUMPY, UNPREDICTABLE, POTENTIALLY large": that was how Tim Geithner, then head of the New York Federal Reserve, described the need for dollars in emerging economies in the dark days of October 2008, according to transcripts of a Fed meeting released in February 2014. To help smooth out those lumps, the Fed offered to "swap" currencies with four favoured central banks, as far off as South Korea and Singapore. They could exchange their own money for dollars at the prevailing exchange rate (on condition that they later swap them back again at the same rate). Why did the Fed decide to reach so far beyond its shores? It worried that stress in a financially connected emerging economy could eventually hurt America. But Mr Geithner also hinted at another motive. "The privilege of being the reserve currency of the world comes with some burdens," he said.

That privilege is the subject of a book, *The Dollar Trap*, by Eswar Prasad of Cornell University, who shares the world's ambivalence towards the currency. The 2008 financial crisis might have been expected to erode the dollar's global prominence. Instead, he argues, it cemented it. America's fragility was, paradoxically, a source of strength for its currency.

In the last four months of 2008 America attracted net capital inflows of half a trillion dollars. The dollar was a haven in tumultuous times, even when the tumult originated in America itself. The crisis also "shattered conventional views" about the adequate level of foreign-exchange reserves, prompting emerging economies with large dollar hoards to hoard even more. Finally, America's slump forced the Fed to ease monetary policy dramatically. In response, central banks in emerging economies bought dollars to stop their own currencies rising too fast.

Could Fed swap lines serve as a less costly alternative to rampant reserve accumulation? If central banks could obtain dollars from the Fed whenever the need arose, they would not need to husband their own supplies. The demand is there: India, Indonesia, the Dominican Republic and Peru have all made inquiries. The swap lines are good business: the Fed keeps the interest from the foreign central bank's loans to banks, even though the other central bank bears the credit risk. The Fed earned 6.84% from South Korea's first swap, for example. But it is not a business the Fed wants to be in. As one official said, "We're not advertising."

Swap lines would help emerging economies endure the dollar's reign. But will that reign endure? Mr Prasad thinks so. The dollar's position is "suboptimal but stable and self-reinforcing," he writes. Much as Mr Prasad finds America's privileges distasteful, his book points to the country's qualifications for the job.

America is not only the world's biggest economy, but also among the most sophisticated. Size and sophistication do not always go together. In the 1900s the pound was the global reserve currency and Britain's financial system had the widest reach. But America was the bigger economy. In the 2020s China will probably be the world's biggest economy, but not the most advanced.

America's sophistication is reflected in the depth of its financial markets. It is unusually good at creating tradeable claims on the profits and revenues that its economy generates. In a more primitive system, these spoils would mostly accrue to the state or tycoons; in America, they back a vast range of financial assets.

Mr Prasad draws the obvious contrast with China and its currency, the yuan, a "widely hyped" alternative to the dollar. China's GDP is now over half the size of America's. But its debt markets are one-eighth as big, and foreigners are permitted to own only a tiny fraction of them. China's low central-government debt should be a source of strength for its currency. But it also limits the volume of financial instruments on offer.

America has a big external balance-sheet, if not an obviously strong one. Its foreign liabilities exceed its overseas assets. But this worrying fact conceals a saving grace: its foreign assets are unusually adventurous and lucrative. Its liabilities, on the other hand, are largely liquid, safe and low-yielding. America therefore earns more on its foreign assets than it pays on its foreign liabilities.

Alongside its economic maturity, America also has a greying

population. This ageing is a source of economic weakness. But, Mr Prasad argues, it may be another reason for the dollar's global appeal. America's pensioners hold a big chunk of the government debt that is not held by foreigners. A formidable political constituency, they will not allow the government to inflate away the value of these claims. Thus America's powerful pensioners serve to protect the interests of its generous foreign creditors.

America's sophistication has one final implication: the dollar has no long-term tendency to strengthen. That again contrasts with its principal long-run rival. China is still a catch-up economy. As it narrows the productivity gap with America, its exchange rate, adjusted for inflation, will tend to rise. The yuan appreciated by about 35% against the dollar between mid-2005 and mid-2014.

A self-deprecating currency

The dollar's depreciation over that period is, of course, bad for anyone holding American assets. But the dollar is not merely a store of value. It has also become a popular "funding" currency. Banks and multinational firms borrow in dollars, even as they accumulate assets in other denominations. Since no one wants to borrow in a currency that only goes up, this is not a role that China's currency could easily play. Moreover, because of its role as a funding currency, the dollar tends to strengthen in times of crisis. That explains why emerging economies feel a "lumpy", "unpredictable" need for dollars. America's currency may not hold its value against others. But in times of stress, the appeal of a dollar asset is that it always holds its value against a dollar debt. The dollar is a global hegemon partly because it is also a global hedge.

March 2014

Bitcoin and digital currencies: a new specie

Regulators should keep their hands off new forms of digital money such as Bitcoin

SMALL TRIBES have often used unique forms of money. Until recently, west Africa's Ashanti had perhaps the oddest. Eschewing the convenience of metal discs, stones or shells, they used metal painstakingly moulded into the shape of small chairs, representing the tribal chief's throne. But the latest cult currency – Bitcoin – is stranger still. Invented in 2009, this computerised money exists only as strings of digital code.

The Bitcoin tribe is still a small one, and consists mainly of computer geeks, drug-dealers, gold bugs and libertarians. But wild fluctuations in the value of a Bitcoin, from under $20 at the start of 2013 to over $200 at one point in April, has won the currency wider attention. The price may yet crash to earth. But whatever happens to Bitcoin, it shows how useful a widely accepted digital currency could be.

Bitcoins are a store of value, whose purchasing power is protected not by a central bank but by a hard limit (21 million) on the number of coins that can exist. Because each coin can be split into smaller parts Bitcoins can be used for small transactions, even if the value of a single coin rockets. And a unique digital signature makes them impossible to forge. This is a big advance: almost 3% of Britain's pound coins are fakes.

As a result more and more people and businesses are prepared to accept Bitcoins as a way to make and receive payments. It is here that digital currencies' real value lies. To see why, think of peer-to-peer markets such as eBay, Alibaba and Airbnb. These enable buyers and sellers to meet, exchanging goods and services directly. Bitcoins mean that the other side of the deal – the transfer of cash as payment – can work in the same direct way.

Sceptics will retort that the dollar already plays this role. But using greenbacks for small purchases is a pain. Because all dollar transactions are cleared via the American banking system, a dollar payment from, say, a British buyer to a Chinese seller could involve a British and Chinese bank, plus two American ones. Add in foreign-exchange fees, and an internationally accepted digital currency starts to look cheaper and more elegant. Buying foreign goods online with Bitcoins is just like paying cash at home: instant, direct and untraceable.

These features are also red flags to regulators. Because it is anonymous, drug-dealers love Bitcoin. Even those not using Bitcoin to buy illegal goods may be using it to skip tax payments. But the urge to dole out digital red tape should be resisted. Drug-dealing is illegal whether in dollars, Bitcoins or barter. Tax avoidance is just as easy using cash. The criminal activity, not the new technology, should be targeted.

The case for regulation will get stronger as the infrastructure supporting Bitcoin (or its successors) becomes more sophisticated. There are already Bitcoin banks, for instance. If digital banks start to mimic conventional lenders and make loans that exceed the amount of deposits they keep on hand, the system will become prone to runs. Banking regulators will need to step in (after hiring some computer whizzes).

Your network, or mine?

For Bitcoin itself, the biggest risk is not regulation but competition. Like any currency its value is dependent on the number of users. Being the first to build a network can be an advantage. But networks can also be supplanted as users suddenly switch to an even better competitor. As markets like eBay and Airbnb grow, for example, their user fees start to become a necessary payment, a bit like a tax. If those charges could be paid in a new form of digital money, the demand for that cash would be much more stable. Bitcoin might end up like MySpace, the now moribund precursor to Facebook.

There is a limit to how far digital currencies like Bitcoin can spread. Long-term demand for the dollar is guaranteed by the fact that American citizens must pay taxes in dollars. Governments will never confer the status of legal tender on a private currency. But Bitcoin and its kind are more than a passing frenzy: the digital-currency tribe is small but it will grow.

China's currency future: trading the yuan

Buzz about the rise of China's currency has run far ahead of sedate reality

IF HEADLINES TRANSLATED into trading volumes, the yuan would be well on its way to dominating the world's currency markets. It once again graced front pages in June 2014 after moves to lift its status in London, the world's biggest foreign-exchange market. This was the latest instalment of a five-year-long public-relations campaign. Since 2009, when China first declared its intention to promote the yuan internationally, a string of announcements and milestones has cast the Chinese currency as a putative rival to the dollar.

The hype rests on several seemingly impressive numbers. Yuan deposits beyond China's borders increased tenfold in between 2009 and 2014. The "dim sum" bond market for yuan-denominated debt issued outside China has gone from non-existence to a dozen issuances a month. And the yuan is the second-most-used currency in the world for trade finance.

Adding to the impression that something big is afoot is the competition between cities around the world to establish themselves as yuan-trading hubs. London puffed up its chest in June 2014 after the Chinese government designated China Construction Bank as the official clearing bank for yuan-denominated transactions in Britain and agreed to launch direct trading between the pound and the yuan in China. These announcements were made to coincide with a trip to London by Li Keqiang, China's prime minister.

The designation of a clearing bank creates a channel for yuan held in Britain to flow into Chinese capital markets, boosting London's appeal as a trading centre for the currency. Other cities such as Frankfurt and Singapore have also been awarded clearing banks, but London already controls nearly 60% of yuan-denominated trade payments between Asia and Europe, and this agreement will shore up its position.

London's currency traders, however, will not be hyperventilating. The rapid growth in the use of the yuan outside China, whether for trade settlement or investment, has been from a minuscule base. The yuan is the seventh-most-used currency in international payments, according to SWIFT, a global transfer system. That is up from 20th place at the start of 2012. However, the Chinese currency still accounts for a mere 1.4% of global payments, compared with the dollar's 42.5%. Given that many of those deals just shuffle cash between Chinese companies and their subsidiaries in Hong Kong, there is much less than meets the eye to the yuan's stature as a trade-settlement currency.

Even more telling is the yuan's standing as an investment currency. The dollar's biggest selling point as a global reserve currency is the deep, liquid pool of American assets open to international buyers. Despite the barrage of reports in recent years about the dim-sum bond market, China's offerings are much sparser. Jonathan Anderson of Emerging Advisors Group calculates that global investors have access to $56 trillion of American assets, including bonds and stocks. They can also get their hands on $29 trillion of euro-denominated assets and $17 trillion of Japanese ones. But when it comes to Chinese assets, just $0.3 trillion or so are open to foreign investors. This puts the yuan on a par with the Philippine peso and a bit above the Peruvian nuevo sol, Mr Anderson notes.

What is holding the yuan back? The answer is China itself – both by circumstance and, more importantly, by design. For a currency to go global, there has to be a path for it to leave its country of origin. The easiest route is via a trade deficit. For example, since the United States imports more than it exports, it in effect adds to global holdings of dollars on a daily basis. That does not work for China, which almost always runs a large trade surplus. It has tried to solve this problem by offering to pay for imports in yuan, while still accepting dollars for its exports.

Yet this approach can go only so far, because of the design of the Chinese system. Foreigners paid in yuan cannot do much with the currency and thus look askance at it. China could change this at a stroke by flinging open its capital account. There is speculation that it might do just that as debate about financial reform intensifies in Beijing. But Yu Yongding, a former adviser to the central bank, predicts that caution will prevail, with the government slowly lowering its wall of capital controls rather than demolishing it. That would be far better for China's financial stability. But it also means that the chasm between the hype about the yuan and the mundane reality is likely to widen.

June 2014

2   A short history of financial crashes

The slumps that shaped modern finance

Finance is not merely prone to crises, it is shaped by them. Five historical crises show how aspects of today's financial system originated – and offer lessons for today's regulators

WHAT IS MANKIND'S greatest invention? Ask people this question and they are likely to pick familiar technologies such as printing or electricity. They are unlikely to suggest an innovation that is just as significant: the financial contract. Widely disliked and often considered grubby, it has nonetheless played an indispensable role in human development for at least 7,000 years.

At its core, finance does just two simple things. It can act as an economic time machine, helping savers transport today's surplus income into the future, or giving borrowers access to future earnings now. It can also act as a safety net, insuring against floods, fires or illness. By providing these two kinds of service, a well-tuned financial system smooths away life's sharpest ups and downs, making an uncertain world more predictable. In addition, as investors seek out people and companies with the best ideas, finance acts as an engine of growth.

Yet finance can also terrorise. When bubbles burst and markets crash, plans paved years into the future can be destroyed. As the impact of the crisis of 2008 subsides, leaving its legacy of unemployment and debt, it is worth asking if the right things are being done to support what is good about finance, and to remove what is poisonous.

History is a good place to look for answers. Five devastating slumps – starting with America's first crash, in 1792, and ending with the world's biggest, in 1929 – highlight two big trends in financial evolution. The first is that institutions that enhance people's economic lives, such as central banks, deposit insurance and stock exchanges, are not the products of careful design in calm times, but are cobbled together at the bottom of financial cliffs. Often what starts out as a post-crisis sticking plaster becomes a permanent feature of the system. If history is any guide, decisions taken now will reverberate for decades.

This makes the second trend more troubling. The response to a crisis follows a familiar pattern. It starts with blame. New parts of the financial system are vilified: a new type of bank, investor or asset is identified as the culprit and is then banned or regulated out of existence. It ends by entrenching public backing for private markets: other parts of finance deemed essential are given more state support. It is an approach that seems sensible and reassuring.

But it is corrosive. Walter Bagehot, editor of *The Economist* between 1860 and 1877, argued that financial panics occur when the "blind capital" of the public floods into unwise speculative investments. Yet well-intentioned reforms have made this problem worse. The sight of Britons stuffing Icelandic banks with sterling, safe in the knowledge that £35,000 of deposits were insured by the state, would have made Bagehot nervous. The fact that professional investors can lean on the state would have made him angry.

These five crises reveal where the titans of modern finance – the New York Stock Exchange, the Federal Reserve, Britain's giant banks – come from. But they also highlight the way in which successive reforms have tended to insulate investors from risk, and thus offer lessons to regulators in the current post-crisis era.

1792: the origins of modern finance

If one man deserves credit for both the brilliance and the horrors of modern finance it is Alexander Hamilton, the first Treasury secretary of the United States. In financial terms the young country was a blank canvas: in 1790, just 14 years after the Declaration of Independence, it had five banks and few insurers. Hamilton wanted a state-of-the-art

FIG 2.1 **Federal frothiness**
Security prices, 100=par value of US bond, $

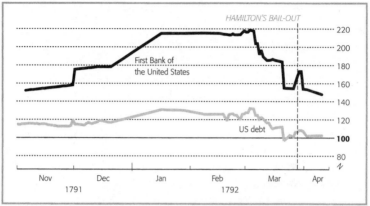

Source: *America's First Securities Markets, 1787–1836: Emergence,
Development, Integration* by R.E. Sylla, J. Wilson and R.E. Wright

financial set-up, like that of Britain or Holland. That meant a federal
debt that would pull together individual states' IOUs. America's new
bonds would be traded in open markets, allowing the government to
borrow cheaply. And America would also need a central bank, the
First Bank of the United States (BUS), which would be publicly owned.

This new bank was an exciting investment opportunity. Of the $10
million in BUS shares, $8 million were made available to the public.
The initial auction, in July 1791, went well and was oversubscribed
within an hour. This was great news for Hamilton, because the two
pillars of his system – the bank and the debt – had been designed to
support each other. To get hold of a $400 BUS share, investors had
to buy a $25 share certificate or "scrip", and pay three-quarters of the
remainder not in cash, but with federal bonds. The plan therefore
stoked demand for government debt, while also furnishing the bank
with a healthy wedge of safe assets. It was seen as a great deal: scrip
prices shot up from $25 to reach more than $300 in August 1791. The
bank opened that December.

Two things put Hamilton's plan at risk. The first was an old friend
gone bad, William Duer. The scheming old Etonian was the first
Englishman to be blamed for an American financial crisis, but would

not be the last. Duer and his accomplices knew that investors needed federal bonds to pay for their BUS shares, so they tried to corner the market. To fund this scheme Duer borrowed from wealthy friends and, by issuing personal IOUs, from the public. He also embezzled from companies he ran.

The other problem was the bank itself. On the day it opened it dwarfed the nation's other lenders. Already massive, it then ballooned, making almost $2.7 million in new loans in its first two months. Awash with credit, the residents of Philadelphia and New York were gripped by speculative fever. Markets for short sales and futures contracts sprang up. As many as 20 carriages a week raced between the two cities to exploit opportunities for arbitrage.

The jitters began in March 1792. The BUS began to run low on the hard currency that backed its paper notes. It cut the supply of credit almost as quickly as it had expanded it, with loans down by 25% between the end of January and March. As credit tightened, Duer and his cabal, who often took on new debts in order to repay old ones, started to feel the pinch.

Rumours of Duer's troubles, combined with the tightening of credit by the BUS, sent America's markets into sharp descent. Prices of government debt, BUS shares and the stocks of the handful of other traded companies plunged by almost 25% in two weeks. By March 23rd Duer was in prison. But that did not stop the contagion, and firms started to fail. As the pain spread, so did the anger. A mob of angry investors pounded the New York jail where Duer was being held with stones.

Hamilton knew what was at stake. A student of financial history, he was aware that France's crash in 1720 had hobbled its financial system for years. And he knew Thomas Jefferson was waiting in the wings to dismantle all he had built. His response, as described in a 2007 paper by Richard Sylla of New York University, was America's first bank bail-out. Hamilton attacked on many fronts: he used public money to buy federal bonds and pep up their prices, helping protect the bank and speculators who had bought at inflated prices. He funnelled cash to troubled lenders. And he ensured that banks with collateral could borrow as much as they wanted, at a penalty rate of 7% (then the usury ceiling).

FIG 2.2 **Alexander's legacy**

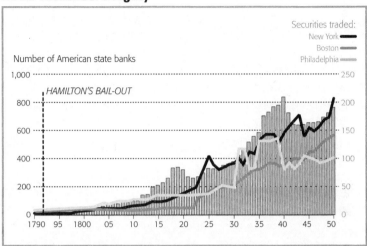

Source: *Emerging Financial Markets and Early US Growth* by P.L. Rousseau and R. Sylla, 2005

The Buttonwood agreement

Even as the medicine was taking effect, arguments about how to prevent future slumps had started. Everyone agreed that finance had become too frothy. Seeking to protect naive amateurs from risky investments, lawmakers sought outright bans, with rules passed in New York in April 1792 outlawing public futures trading. In response to this aggressive regulation a group of 24 traders met on Wall Street – under a Buttonwood tree, the story goes – to set up their own private trading club. That group was the precursor of the New York Stock Exchange.

Hamilton's bail-out worked brilliantly. With confidence restored, finance flowered. Within half a century New York was a financial superpower: the number of banks and markets shot up, as did GDP. But the rescue had done something else too. By bailing out the banking system, Hamilton had set a precedent. Subsequent crises caused the financial system to become steadily more reliant on state support.

1825: the original emerging-markets crisis

Crises always start with a new hope. In the 1820s the excitement was over the newly independent Latin American countries that had broken free from Spain. Investors were especially keen in Britain, which was booming at the time, with exports a particular strength. Wales was a source of raw materials, cutting 3 million tonnes of coal a year, and sending pig iron across the globe. Manchester was becoming the world's first industrial city, refining raw inputs into higher-value wares like chemicals and machinery. Industrial production grew by 34% between 1820 and 1825.

As a result, cash-rich Britons wanted somewhere to invest their funds. Government bonds were in plentiful supply given the recent Napoleonic wars, but with hostilities over (and risks lower) the exchequer was able to reduce its rates. The 5% return paid on government debt in 1822 had fallen to 3.3% by 1824. With inflation at around 1% between 1820 and 1825 gilts offered only a modest return in real terms. They were safe but boring.

Luckily investors had a host of exotic new options. By the 1820s London had displaced Amsterdam as Europe's main financial hub, quickly becoming the place where foreign governments sought funds. The rise of the new global bond market was incredibly rapid. In 1820 there was just one foreign bond on the London market; by 1826 there were 23. Debt issued by Russia, Prussia and Denmark paid well and was snapped up.

But the really exciting investments were those in the new world. The crumbling Spanish empire had left former colonies free to set up as independent nations. Between 1822 and 1825 Colombia, Chile, Peru, Mexico and Guatemala successfully sold bonds worth £21 million ($2.8 billion in today's prices) in London. And there were other ways to cash in: the shares of British mining firms planning to explore the new world were popular. The share price of one of them, Anglo Mexican, went from £33 to £158 in a month.

The big problem with all this was simple: distance. To get to South America and back in six months was good going, so deals were struck on the basis of information that was scratchy at best. The starkest example was the "Poyais" bonds sold by Gregor MacGregor on behalf

FIG 2.3 **Latin languish**
Government bond prices

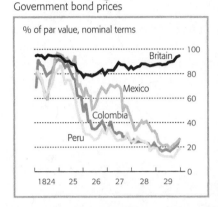

Source: *Bonds and Brands* by Marc Flandreau and Juan H. Flore

of a new country that did not, in fact, exist. This shocking fraud was symptomatic of a deeper rot. Investors were not carrying out proper checks. Much of the information about new countries came from journalists paid to promote them. More discerning savers would have asked tougher questions: Mexico and Colombia were indeed real countries, but had only rudimentary tax systems, so they stood little chance of raising the money to make the interest payments on their new debt.

Investors were also making outlandish assumptions. Everyone knew that rivalry with Spain meant that Britain's government supported Latin American independence. But the money men took another step. Because Madrid's enemy was London's friend, they reasoned, the new countries would surely be able to lean on Britain for financial backing. With that backstop in place the Mexican and Colombian bonds, which paid 6%, seemed little more risky than 3% British gilts. Deciding which to buy was simple.

But there would be no British support for these new countries. In the summer of 1823 it became clear that Spain was on the verge of default. As anxiety spread, bond prices started to plummet. Research by Marc Flandreau of the Geneva Graduate Institute and Juan Flores of the University of Geneva shows that by the end of 1825 Peru's bonds had fallen to 40% of their face value, with others following them down.

Britain's banks, exposed to the debt and to mining firms, were hit hard. Depositors began to scramble for cash: by December 1825 there were bank runs. The Bank of England jumped to provide funds both to crumbling lenders and directly to firms in a bail-out that Bagehot later regarded as the model for crisis-mode central banking. Despite

FIG 2.4 **Rise of the megabanks**
Banks in England and Wales, number

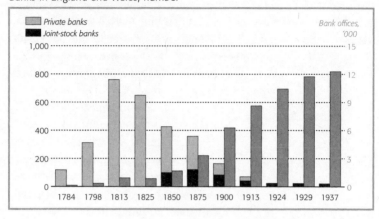

Sources: *Money and banking in the UK* by M. Collins, 1998;
Country banking in the industrial revolution by L.S. Pressnell, 1956; Bank of England

this many banks were unable to meet depositors' demands. In 1826 more than 10% of the banks in England and Wales failed. Britain's response to the crash would change the shape of banking.

The most remarkable thing about the crisis of 1825 was the sharp divergence in views on what should be done about it. Some blamed investors' sloppiness: they had invested in unknown countries' debt, or in mining outfits set up to explore countries that contained no ores. A natural reaction to this emerging-markets crisis might have been to demand that investors conduct proper checks before putting money at risk.

But Britain's financial chiefs, including the Bank of England, blamed the banks instead. Small private partnerships akin to modern private-equity houses, they were accused of stoking up the speculative bubble with lax lending. Banking laws at the time specified that a maximum of six partners could supply the equity, which ensured that banks were numerous but small. Had they only been bigger, it was argued, they would have had sufficient heft to have survived the inevitable bust.

Mulling over what to do, the committees of Westminster and Threadneedle Street looked north, to Scotland. Its banks were "joint stock" lenders that could have as many partners as they wanted, issuing equity to whoever would buy it. The Scottish lenders had fared much better in the crisis. Parliament passed a new banking act copying this set-up in 1826. England was already the global hub for bonds. With ownership restrictions lifted, banks like National Provincial, now part of Royal Bank of Scotland (RBS), started gobbling up rivals, a process that has continued ever since.

The shift to joint-stock banking is a bittersweet moment in British financial history. It had big upsides: the ancestors of the modern megabank had been born, and Britain became a world leader in banking as well as bonds. But the long chain of mergers it triggered explains why RBS ended up becoming the world's largest bank – and, in 2009, the largest one to fail. Today Britain's big four banks hold around 75% of the country's deposits, and the failure of any one of them would still pose a systemic risk to the economy.

1857: the first global crash

By the mid-19th century the world was getting used to financial crises. Britain seemed to operate on a one-crash-per-decade rule: the crisis of 1825–26 was followed by panics in 1837 and 1847. To those aware of the pattern, the crash of 1857 seemed like more of the same. But this time things were different. A shock in America's Midwest tore across the country and jumped from New York to Liverpool and Glasgow, and then London. From there it led to crashes in Paris, Hamburg, Copenhagen and Vienna. Financial collapses were not merely regular – now they were global, too.

On the surface, Britain was doing well in the 1850s. Exports to the rest of the world were booming, and resources increased with gold discoveries in Australia. But beneath the surface two big changes were taking place. Together they would create what *The Economist*, writing in 1857, called "a crisis more severe and more extensive than any which had preceded it".

The first big change was that a web of new economic links had formed. In part, they were down to trade. By 1857 America was running a $26 million current-account deficit, with Britain and its colonies as its major trading partners. Americans bought more goods

FIG 2.5 **The dotcoms of their day**
1857 railroad stocks, average regional price, par value = 100

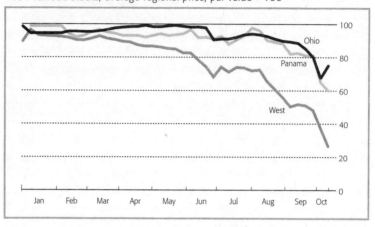

Sources: J. Wahl, 2009; R. Sylla *et al.*, 2002

than they sold, with Britain buying American assets to provide the funds, just as China does today. By the mid-1850s Britain held an estimated $80 million in American stocks and bonds.

Railway companies were a popular investment. Shares of American railway firms such as the Illinois Central and the Philadelphia and Reading were so widely held by British investors that Britons sat on their boards. That their earnings did not justify their valuations did not matter much: they were a bet on future growth.

The second big change was a burst of financial innovation. As Britain's aggressive joint-stock banks gobbled up rivals, deposits grew by almost 400% between 1847 and 1857. And a new type of lender – the discount house – was mushrooming in London. These outfits started out as middlemen, matching investors with firms that needed cash. But as finance flowered the discount houses morphed, taking in investors' cash with the promise that it could be withdrawn at will, and hunting for firms to lend to. In short, they were banks in all but name.

Competition was fierce. Because joint-stock banks paid depositors the Bank of England's rate less one percentage point, any discount house paying less than this would fail to attract funds. But because the central bank was also an active lender, discounting the best bills, its rate put a cap on what the discount houses could charge borrowers. With just one percentage point to play with, the discount houses had to be lean. Since cash paid zero interest, they cut their reserves close to zero, relying on the fact that they could always borrow from the Bank of England if they faced large depositor withdrawals. Perennially facing the squeeze, London's new financiers trimmed away their capital buffers.

Meanwhile in America, Edward Ludlow, the manager of Ohio Life, an insurance company, became caught up in railway fever. New lines were being built to link eastern cities with new frontier towns. Many invested heavily but Ludlow went all in, betting $3 million of Ohio Life's $4.8 million on railway companies. One investment alone, in the Cleveland and Pittsburgh line, accounted for a quarter of the insurer's capital.

In late spring 1857, railroad stocks began to drop. Ohio Life, highly leveraged and overexposed, fell faster, failing on August 24th. As research by Charles Calomiris of Columbia University and Larry Schweikart of Dayton University shows, problems spread eastwards, dragging down stockbrokers that had invested in railways. When banks dumped their stock, prices fell further, magnifying losses. By October 13th Wall Street was packed with depositors demanding their money. The banks refused to convert deposits into currency. America's financial system had failed.

As the financial dominoes continued to topple, the first British cities to suffer were Glasgow and Liverpool. Merchants who traded with American firms began to fail in October. There were direct financial links, too. Dennistoun, Cross and Co., an American bank that had branches in Liverpool, Glasgow, New York and New Orleans, collapsed on November 7th, taking with it the Western Bank of Scotland. That made the British crisis systemic: the bank had 98 branches and held £6 million in deposits. There was "wild panic" with troops needed to calm the crowds.

The discount houses magnified the problem. They had become a vital source of credit for firms. But investors were suspicious of their balance-sheets. They were right to be: one reported £10,000 of capital supporting risky loans of £900,000, a leverage ratio that beats even modern excesses. As the discount houses failed, so did ordinary firms. In the last three months of 1857 there were 135 bankruptcies, wiping out investor capital of £42 million. Britain's far-reaching economic and financial tentacles meant this caused panics across Europe.

As well as being global, the crash of 1857 marked another first: the recognition that financial safety nets can create excessive risk-taking. The discount houses had acted in a risky way, holding few liquid assets and small capital buffers in part because they knew they could always borrow from the Bank of England. Unhappy with this, the Bank changed its policies in 1858. Discount houses could no longer borrow on a whim. They would have to self-insure, keeping their own cash reserves, rather than relying on the central bank as a backstop. That step made the 1857 crisis an all-too-rare example of the state attempting to dial back its support. It also shows how unpopular cutting subsidies can be.

The Bank of England was seen to be "obsessed" by the way discount houses relied on it, and to have rushed into its reforms. *The Economist* thought its tougher lending policy unprincipled: it argued that decisions should be made on a case-by-case basis, rather than applying blanket bans. Others thought the central bank lacked credibility, as it would never allow a big discount house to fail. They were wrong. In 1866 Overend & Gurney, by then a huge lender, needed emergency cash. The Bank of England refused to rescue it, wiping out its shareholders. Britain then enjoyed 50 years of financial calm, a fact that some historians reckon was due to the prudence of a banking sector stripped of moral hazard.

1907: the bankers' panic

As the 20th century dawned America and Britain had very different approaches to banking. The Bank of England was all-powerful, a tough overseer of a banking system it had helped design. America was the polar opposite. Hamilton's BUS had closed in 1811 and its replacement, just around the corner in Philadelphia, was shut down in 1836. An atomised, decentralised system developed. Americans thought banks could look after themselves – until the crisis of 1907.

The absence of a lender of last resort had certainly not crimped the expansion of banking. The period after the civil war saw an explosion in the number of banks. By 1907 America had 22,000 banks – one for

FIG 2.6 **Breakdown of trust**
Deposits at New York trust companies, $ million

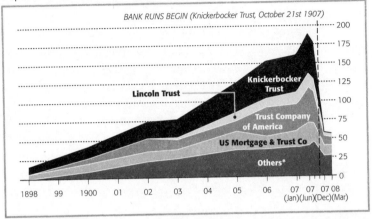

*Seven other trust companies.
Source: Annual Report of the Superintendent of Banks, New York

every 4,000 people. In most towns, there was a choice of local banks or state-owned lenders.

Despite all these options, savvy metropolitan investors tended to go elsewhere – to the trust companies. These outfits appeared in the early 1890s to act as "trustees", holding their customers' investments in bonds and stocks. By 1907 they were combining this safe-house role with riskier activities: underwriting and distributing shares, and owning and managing property and railways. They also took in deposits. The trust companies had, in short, become banks.

And they were booming. Compared with ordinary banks, they invested in spicier assets and were more lightly regulated. Whereas banks had to hold 25% of their assets as cash (in case of sudden depositor demands), the trusts faced a 5% minimum. Able to pay higher rates of interest to depositors, they became a favourite place to park large sums. By 1907 they were almost as big as the national banks, having grown by nearly 250% in ten years.

America was buzzing too. Between 1896 and 1906 its average annual growth rate was almost 5%. This was extraordinary, given that America faced catastrophes such as the Baltimore fire of 1904 and the

San Francisco earthquake of 1906, which alone wiped out around 2% of GDP. All Americans, you might think, would have been grateful that things stayed on track.

But two greedy scammers – Augustus Heinze and Charles Morse – wanted more, as a 1990 paper by Federal Reserve economists Ellis Tallman and Jon Moen shows. The two bankers had borrowed and embezzled vast sums in an attempt to corner the market in the shares of United Copper. But the economy started to slow a little in 1907, depressing the prices of raw materials, including metals. United Copper's shares fell in response. With the prices of their stocks falling, Heinze and Morse faced losses magnified by their huge leverage. To prop up the market, they began to tap funds from the banks they ran. This whipped up trouble for a host of smaller lenders, sparking a chain of losses that eventually embroiled a trust company, the Knickerbocker Trust.

A Manhattan favourite located on the corner of 34th Street and 5th Avenue, its deposits had soared from $10 million in 1897 to over $60 million in 1907, making it the third-largest trust in America. Its Corinthian columns stood out even alongside its neighbour, the Waldorf Astoria. The exterior marble was from Vermont; the interior marble was from Norway. It was a picture of wealth and solidity.

Yet on the morning of October 22nd the Knickerbocker might as well have been a tin shack. When news emerged that it was caught up in the Heinze-Morse financial contagion, depositors lined the street demanding cash. The Knickerbocker paid out $8 million in less than a day, but had to refuse some demands, casting a pall over other trusts. The Trust Company of America was the next to suffer a depositor run, followed by the Lincoln Trust. Some New Yorkers moved cash from one trust to another as they toppled. When it became clear that the financial system was unsafe, Americans began to hoard cash at home.

For a while it looked as though the crisis could be nipped in the bud. After all, the economic slowdown had been small, with GDP still growing by 1.9% in 1907. And although there were crooks like Heinze and Morse causing trouble, titans like John Pierpont Morgan sat on the other side of the ledger. As the panic spread and interest rates spiked to 125%, Morgan stepped in, organising pools of cash to help ease the strain. At one point he locked the entire New York banking community in his library until a $25m bail-out fund had been agreed.

But it was not enough. Depositors across the country began runs on their banks. Sensing imminent collapse, states declared emergency holidays. Those that remained open limited withdrawals. Despite the robust economy, the crash in New York led to a nationwide shortage of money. This hit business hard, with national output dropping a staggering 11% between 1907 and 1908.

With legal tender so scarce alternatives quickly sprang up. In close to half of America's large towns and cities, cash substitutes started to circulate. These included cheques and small-denomination IOUs written by banks. The total value of this private-sector emergency cash – all of it illegal – was around $500 million, far bigger than the Morgan bail-out. It did the trick, and by 1909 the American economy was growing again.

The earliest proposals for reform followed naturally from the cash shortage. A plan for $500 million of official emergency money was quickly put together. But the emergency-money plan had a much longer-lasting impact. The new currency laws included a clause to set up a committee – the National Monetary Commission – that would discuss the way America's money worked. The NMC sat for four years, examining evidence from around the world on how best to reshape the system. It concluded that a proper lender of last resort was needed. The result was the 1913 Federal Reserve Act, which established America's third central bank in December that year. Hamilton had belatedly got his way after all.

1929–33: the big one

Until the eve of the 1929 slump – the worst America has ever faced – things were rosy. Cars and construction thrived in the roaring 1920s, and solid jobs in both industries helped lift wages and consumption. Ford was making 9,000 of its Model T cars a day, and spending on new-build homes hit $5 billion in 1925. There were bumps along the way (1923 and 1926 saw slowdowns) but momentum was strong.

Banks looked good, too. By 1929 the combined balance-sheets of America's 25,000 lenders stood at $60 billion. The assets they held seemed prudent: just 60% were loans, with 15% held as cash. Even the 20% made up by investment securities seemed sensible: the lion's share of holdings comprised bonds, with ultra-safe government

FIG 2.7 **The long climb back**
Share prices, December 1925=100, real terms

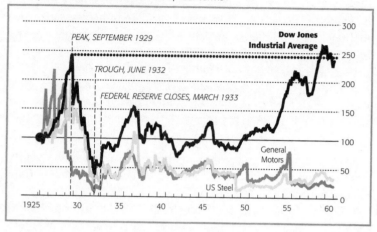

Sources: Federal Reserve Bank of St Louis; Centre for Research in Security Prices

bonds making up more than half. With assets of such high quality the banks allowed the capital buffers that protected them from losses to dwindle.

But as the 1920s wore on the young Federal Reserve faced a conundrum: share prices and prices in the shops started to move in opposite directions. Markets were booming, with the shares of firms exploiting new technologies – radios, aluminium and aeroplanes – particularly popular. But few of these new outfits had any record of dividend payments, and investors piled into their shares in the hope that they would continue to increase in value. At the same time established businesses were looking weaker as consumer prices fell. For a time the puzzle – whether to raise rates to slow markets, or cut them to help the economy – paralysed the Fed. In the end the market-watchers won and the central bank raised rates in 1928.

It was a catastrophic error. The increase, from 3.5% to 5%, was too small to blunt the market rally: share prices soared until September 1929, with the Dow Jones index hitting a high of 381. But it hurt America's flagging industries. By late summer industrial production was falling at an annualised rate of 45%. Adding to the domestic woes came bad news from abroad. In September the London Stock Exchange crashed when Clarence Hatry, a fraudulent financier, was arrested. A sell-off was coming. It was huge: over just two days, October 28th and 29th, the Dow lost close to 25%. By November 13th it was at 198, down 45% in two months.

Worse was to come. Bank failures came in waves. The first, in 1930, began with bank runs in agricultural states such as Arkansas, Illinois and Missouri. A total of 1,350 banks failed that year. Then a second wave hit Chicago, Cleveland and Philadelphia in April 1931. External pressure worsened the domestic worries. As Britain dumped the Gold Standard its exchange rate dropped, putting pressure on American exporters. There were banking panics in Austria and Germany. As public confidence evaporated, Americans again began to hoard currency. A bond-buying campaign by the Federal Reserve brought only temporary respite, because the surviving banks were in such bad shape.

This became clear in February 1933. A final panic, this time national, began to force more emergency bank holidays, with lenders in Nevada, Iowa, Louisiana and Michigan the first to shut their doors. The inland banks called in inter-bank deposits placed with New York lenders, stripping them of $760 million in February 1933 alone. Naturally the city bankers turned to their new backstop, the Federal Reserve. But the unthinkable happened. On March 4th the central bank did exactly what it had been set up to prevent. It refused to lend and shut its doors. In its mission to act as a source of funds in all emergencies, the Federal Reserve had failed. A week-long bank holiday was called across the nation.

It was the blackest week in the darkest period of American finance. Regulators examined banks' books, and more than 2,000 banks that closed that week never opened again. After this low, things started to improve. Nearly 11,000 banks had failed between 1929 and 1933, and the money supply dropped by over 30%. Unemployment, just 3.2% on the eve of the crisis, rose to more than 25%; it would not return to its previous lows until the early 1940s. It took more than 25 years for the Dow to reclaim its peak in 1929.

Reform was clearly needed. The first step was to de-risk the system. In the short term this was done through a massive injection of publicly supplied capital. The $1 billion boost – a third of the system's existing equity – went to more than 6,000 of the remaining 14,000 banks. Future risks were to be neutralised by new legislation, the Glass-Steagall rules that separated stockmarket operations from more mundane lending and gave the Fed new powers to regulate banks whose customers used credit for investment.

A new government body was set up to deal with bank runs once and for all: the Federal Deposit Insurance Commission (FDIC), established on January 1st 1934. By protecting $2,500 of deposits per customer it aimed to reduce the costs of bank failure. Limiting depositor losses would protect income, the money supply and buying power. And because depositors could trust the FDIC, they would not queue up at banks at the slightest financial wobble.

In a way, it worked brilliantly. Banks quickly started advertising the fact that they were FDIC insured, and customers came to see deposits as risk-free. For 70 years, bank runs became a thing of the past. Banks were able to reduce costly liquidity and equity buffers, which fell year on year. An inefficient system of self-insurance fell away, replaced by low-cost risk-sharing, with central banks and deposit insurance as the backstop.

Yet this was not at all what Hamilton had hoped for. He wanted a financial system that made government more stable, and banks and markets that supported public debt to allow infrastructure and military spending at low rates of interest. By 1934 the opposite system had been created: it was now the state's job to ensure that the financial system was stable, rather than vice versa. By loading risk onto the taxpayer, the evolution of finance had created a distorting subsidy at the heart of capitalism.

The recent fate of the largest banks in America and Britain shows the true cost of these subsidies. In 2008 Citigroup and RBS Group were enormous, with combined assets of nearly $6 trillion, greater than the combined GDP of the world's 150 smallest countries. Their capital buffers were tiny. When they ran out of capital, the bail-out ran to over $100 billion. The overall cost of the banking crisis is even greater – in the form of slower growth, higher debt and poorer employment prospects that may last decades in some countries.

But the bail-outs were not a mistake: letting banks of this size fail

FIG 2.8 **Playing it safe?**
US commercial banks

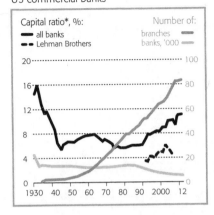

Capital ratio*, %:   Number of:
■ all banks   branches
■■ Lehman Brothers   banks, '000

*Equity as % of assets.
Sources: Federal Deposit Insurance Corporation;
Historical Statistics of the United States; Bloomberg

would have been even more costly. The problem is not what the state does, but that its hand is forced. Knowing that governments must bail out banks means parts of finance have become a one-way bet. Banks' debt is a prime example. The International Monetary Fund (IMF) estimated that the world's largest banks benefited from implicit government subsidies worth a total of $630 billion in the year 2011–12. This makes debt cheap, and promotes leverage. In America, meanwhile, there are proposals for the government to act as a backstop for the mortgage market, covering 90% of losses in a crisis. Again, this pins risk on the public purse. It is the same old pattern.

To solve this problem means putting risk back into the private sector. That will require tough choices. Removing the subsidies banks enjoy will make their debt more expensive, meaning equity holders will lose out on dividends and the cost of credit could rise. Cutting excessive deposit insurance means credulous investors who put their nest eggs into dodgy banks could see big losses.

As regulators implement a new round of reforms in the wake of the latest crisis, they have an opportunity to reverse the trend towards ever-greater entrenchment of the state's role in finance. But weaning the industry off government support will not be easy. As the stories of these crises show, hundreds of years of financial history have been pushing in the other direction.

April 2014

3 Lessons from the financial crisis

The origins of the crisis: crash course

The effects of the 2008 financial crisis are still being felt. What caused it?

THE COLLAPSE OF LEHMAN BROTHERS, a sprawling global bank, in September 2008 almost brought down the world's financial system. It took huge taxpayer-financed bail-outs to shore up the industry. Even so, the ensuing credit crunch turned what was already a nasty downturn into the worst recession in 80 years. Massive monetary and fiscal stimulus prevented a buddy-can-you-spare-a-dime depression, but the recovery remains feeble compared with previous post-war upturns. GDP is still below its pre-crisis peak in many rich countries, especially in Europe, where the financial crisis has evolved into the euro crisis. The effects of the crash are still rippling through the world economy: witness the wobbles in financial markets as America's Federal Reserve prepares to scale back its effort to pep up growth by buying bonds.

With half a decade's hindsight, it is clear the crisis had multiple causes. The most obvious is the financiers themselves – especially the irrationally exuberant Anglo-Saxon sort, who claimed to have found a way to banish risk when in fact they had simply lost track of it. Central bankers and other regulators also bear blame, for it was they who tolerated this folly. The macroeconomic backdrop was important, too. The "Great Moderation" – years of low inflation and stable growth – fostered complacency and risk-taking. A "savings glut" in Asia pushed down global interest rates. Some research also implicates European banks, which borrowed greedily in American money markets before the crisis and used the funds to buy dodgy securities. All these factors came together to foster a surge of debt in what seemed to have become a less risky world.

Start with the folly of the financiers. The years before the crisis saw a flood of irresponsible mortgage lending in America. Loans were doled out to "subprime" borrowers with poor credit histories who struggled to repay them. These risky mortgages were passed on to financial engineers at the big banks, who turned them into supposedly low-risk securities by putting large numbers of them together in pools. Pooling works when the risks of each loan are uncorrelated. The big banks argued that the property markets in different American cities would rise and fall independently of one another. But this proved wrong. Starting in 2006, America suffered a nationwide house-price slump.

The pooled mortgages were used to back securities known as collateralised debt obligations (CDOs), which were sliced into tranches by degree of exposure to default. Investors bought the safer tranches because they trusted the triple-A credit ratings assigned by agencies such as Moody's and Standard & Poor's. This was another mistake. The agencies were paid by, and so beholden to, the banks that created the CDOs. They were far too generous in their assessments of them.

Investors sought out these securitised products because they appeared to be relatively safe while providing higher returns in a world of low interest rates. Economists still disagree over whether these low rates were the result of central bankers' mistakes or broader shifts in the world economy. Some accuse the Fed of keeping short-term rates too low, pulling longer-term mortgage rates down with them. The Fed's defenders shift the blame to the savings glut – the surfeit of saving over investment in emerging economies, especially China. That capital flooded into safe American-government bonds, driving down interest rates.

Low interest rates created an incentive for banks, hedge funds and other investors to hunt for riskier assets that offered higher returns. They also made it profitable for such outfits to borrow and use the extra cash to amplify their investments, on the assumption that the returns would exceed the cost of borrowing. The low volatility of the

Great Moderation increased the temptation to "leverage" in this way. If short-term interest rates are low but unstable, investors will hesitate before leveraging their bets. But if rates appear stable, investors will take the risk of borrowing in the money markets to buy longer-dated, higher-yielding securities. That is indeed what happened.

From houses to money markets

When America's housing market turned, a chain reaction exposed fragilities in the financial system. Pooling and other clever financial engineering did not provide investors with the promised protection. Mortgage-backed securities slumped in value, if they could be valued at all. Supposedly safe CDOs turned out to be worthless, despite the ratings agencies' seal of approval. It became difficult to sell suspect assets at almost any price, or to use them as collateral for the short-term funding that so many banks relied on. Fire-sale prices, in turn, instantly dented banks' capital thanks to "mark-to-market" accounting rules, which required them to revalue their assets at current prices and thus acknowledge losses on paper that might never actually be incurred.

Trust, the ultimate glue of all financial systems, began to dissolve in 2007 – a year before Lehman's bankruptcy – as banks started questioning the viability of their counterparties. They and other sources of wholesale funding began to withhold short-term credit, causing those most reliant on it to founder. Northern Rock, a British mortgage lender, was an early casualty in the autumn of 2007.

Complex chains of debt between counterparties were vulnerable to just one link breaking. Financial instruments such as credit-default swaps (in which the seller agrees to compensate the buyer if a third party defaults

FIG 3.1 **Risk on**
Bank assets as % of GDP, selected countries

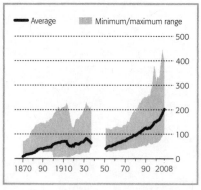

Source: Jorda, Schularick and Taylor, 2011

on a loan) that were meant to spread risk turned out to concentrate it. AIG, an American insurance giant, buckled within days of the Lehman bankruptcy under the weight of the expansive credit-risk protection it had sold. The whole system was revealed to have been built on flimsy foundations: banks had allowed their balance-sheets to bloat (see Figure 3.1), but set aside too little capital to absorb losses. In effect they had bet on themselves with borrowed money, a gamble that had paid off in good times but proved catastrophic in bad.

Regulators asleep at the wheel

Failures in finance were at the heart of the crash. But bankers were not the only people to blame. Central bankers and other regulators bear responsibility too, for mishandling the crisis, for failing to keep economic imbalances in check and for failing to exercise proper oversight of financial institutions.

The regulators' most dramatic error was to let Lehman Brothers go bankrupt. This multiplied the panic in markets. Suddenly, nobody trusted anybody, so nobody would lend. Non-financial companies, unable to rely on being able to borrow to pay suppliers or workers, froze spending in order to hoard cash, causing a seizure in the real economy. Ironically, the decision to stand back and allow Lehman to go bankrupt resulted in more government intervention, not less. To stem the consequent panic, regulators had to rescue scores of other companies.

But the regulators made mistakes long before the Lehman bankruptcy, most notably by tolerating global current-account imbalances and the housing bubbles that they helped to inflate. Central bankers had long expressed concerns about America's big deficit and the offsetting capital inflows from Asia's excess savings. Ben Bernanke highlighted the savings glut in early 2005, a year before he took over as chairman of the Fed from Alan Greenspan. But the focus on net capital flows from Asia left a blind spot for the much bigger gross capital flows from European banks. They bought lots of dodgy American securities, financing their purchases in large part by borrowing from American money-market funds.

In other words, although Europeans claimed to be innocent victims of Anglo-Saxon excess, their banks were actually in the thick of things. The creation of the euro prompted an extraordinary expansion of the financial sector both within the euro area and in nearby banking hubs such as London and Switzerland. Research published in 2012 by Hyun Song Shin, an economist at Princeton University, has focused on the European role in fomenting the crisis. The glut that caused America's loose credit conditions before the crisis, he argues, was in global banking rather than in world savings.

Moreover, Europe had its own internal imbalances that proved just as significant as those between America and China. Southern European economies racked up huge current-account deficits in the first decade of the euro while countries in northern Europe ran offsetting surpluses. The imbalances were financed by credit flows from the euro-zone core to the overheated housing markets of countries like Spain and Ireland. The euro crisis has in this respect been a continuation of the financial crisis by other means, as markets have agonised over the weaknesses of European banks loaded with bad debts following property busts.

Central banks could have done more to address all this. The Fed made no attempt to stem the housing bubble. The European Central Bank did nothing to restrain the credit surge on the periphery, believing (wrongly) that current-account imbalances did not matter in a monetary union. The Bank of England, having lost control over banking supervision when it was made independent in 1997, took a mistakenly narrow view of its responsibility to maintain financial stability.

Central bankers insist that it would have been difficult to temper the housing and credit boom through higher interest rates. Perhaps so, but they had other regulatory tools at their disposal, such as lowering maximum loan-to-value ratios for mortgages, or demanding that banks should set aside more capital.

Lax capital ratios proved the biggest shortcoming. Since 1988 a committee of central bankers and supervisors meeting in Basel has negotiated international rules for the minimum amount of capital banks must hold relative to their assets. But these rules did not define capital strictly enough, which let banks smuggle in forms of debt that did not have the same loss-absorbing capacity as equity.

Under pressure from shareholders to increase returns, banks

FIG 3.2 **Ill-founded optimism**
Weighted average for 17 global banks*

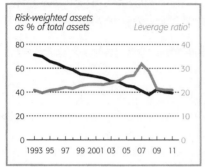

*Including: Deutsche Bank, BNP Paribas, Barclays, Citigroup,
UBS and BAML
†Total assets divided by Tier-1 capital
Source: *The Banker*, Bank of England

operated with minimal equity, leaving them vulnerable if things went wrong. And from the mid-1990s they were allowed more and more to use their own internal models to assess risk – in effect setting their own capital requirements. Predictably, they judged their assets to be ever safer, allowing balance-sheets to balloon without a commensurate rise in capital (see Figure 3.2).

The Basel committee also did not make any rules regarding the share of a bank's assets that should be liquid. And it failed to set up a mechanism to allow a big international bank to go bust without causing the rest of the system to seize up.

All in it together

The regulatory reforms that have since been pushed through at Basel read as an extended mea culpa by central bankers for getting things so grievously wrong before the financial crisis. But regulators and bankers were not alone in making misjudgments. When economies are doing well there are powerful political pressures not to rock the boat. With inflation at bay central bankers could not appeal to their usual rationale for spoiling the party. The long period of economic and price stability over which they presided encouraged risk-taking. And as so often in the history of financial crashes, humble consumers also joined in the collective delusion that lasting prosperity could be built on ever-bigger piles of debt.

September 2013

The dangers of debt: lending weight

How debt and deleveraging have magnified losses and pain in
the turmoil

IT WAS THE GROWING RATE of default on home mortgages in America
that precipitated the financial crisis in 2008. These delinquencies,
although not enormous in themselves, became impossible for some
investment banks to bear, thanks partly to their own heavy debts.
As the contagion spread throughout the financial sector in 2007-08,
nervous or cash-strapped banks and other creditors stopped lending,
thereby infecting the rest of the economy. Deep recessions and big
financial rescues then led to a surge in government debt. That, in
turn, raised fears about the solvency of various countries in the euro
area, culminating in Greece's default in 2012. Debt was, then, both a
cause and a consequence of the crisis, and remains a big reason for
its continuance.

Economists tend to see debt as a useful means to get money where
it is most needed, from creditors with an excess of it, to borrowers
who are short of it. The broadening and deepening of international
credit markets that preceded the financial crisis was considered a spur
to growth, since it gave ever more borrowers access to bigger loans
at lower rates of interest. When disaster struck, however, debt turned
from a ladder into a chute. Working out what went wrong, and when
debt turns dangerous, has become a preoccupation of economics in
recent years.

Debt is possibly the oldest financial instrument, older even than
money. Archaeologists have unearthed Babylonian tablets of sun-
dried clay recording obligations incurred in the third millennium
before Christ. But despite its venerability, debt is not much respected.
In German, the word for debt (*Schuld*) also means sin (a view that
many Germans still seem to hold). Those who run up debts are
assumed to be profligate and those who chase them down mercenary
and unfeeling. That is because debt is a peculiarly unforgiving
instrument: it must be paid in full and on time, come what may.

That distinguishes debt from some other financial liabilities, such as shares, which are more flexible, promising only a cut of the profits, whatever they may be.

Before 2008 most macroeconomic models made little room for debt (especially of the private, domestic sort), let alone default. At the level of the economy as a whole, after all, borrowers and lenders cancel each other out: every dollar owed by someone is also owed to someone. Thus the liabilities of all debtors and the assets of all creditors add up to zero. That makes debt seem trivial.

Clearly, debt is far from trivial, and its unwinding not always a zero-sum game. Yet including it in economic models requires macroeconomists to wrestle with awkward complications, such as "heterogeneity" (dividing the economy into debtors and creditors) and "discontinuity" (allowing for the abrupt breach of economic relations that default represents).

The alternative is to focus instead on empirical studies, poring over the historical record to find out when debt becomes dangerous. Those dangers, it turns out, differ depending on who owes the debt (governments, households, firms or financial intermediaries) and what kind of debt they owe (loans or bonds, short-term or long), as well as the currency in which they owe it.

Most empirical studies look at government debt. But the origins of the 2008 financial crisis lay instead in private-sector liabilities, especially mortgages, which account for a big part of household debt, and massive borrowing by the banks. The debts owed by non-financial firms played a big role in Japan's crisis in the early 1990s but not in the global crisis in 2008. Figure 3.3 shows the expansion of household and corporate debt in recent years for a variety of rich countries, expressed as a percentage

FIG 3.3 **What goes up**
Private-sector* debt as % of GDP

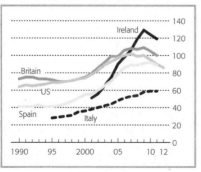

*Households and non-financial firms
Source: OECD

FIG 3.4 **Much obliged**
Debt as % of GDP, 2011

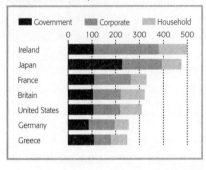

Source: OECD

of GDP; Figure 3.4 shows all three kinds of debt.

Much of what companies, households and governments owe, they owe to banks and other financial firms, which extend loans and also buy securities. These financial firms, in turn, owe a lot of money themselves: to their depositors, their bondholders and a variety of other "lenders to the lenders". Banks are in essence middlemen (or "financial intermediaries") that borrow in order to lend. They hold a lot of assets and a lot of liabilities at the same time.

Leveraging the lenders

In fact, the debts of financial companies often dwarf the debts of governments, households and non-financial firms. According to the OECD, Luxembourg's financial sector had debts worth over 4,900% of the country's GDP in 2011. The dinky duchy is an extreme case. But the figures are also striking in other countries with prominent financial sectors, such as Ireland (where financial-sector debt amounted to 1,434% of GDP) and Britain (837%). The scale of these debts can seem alarming, although in theory financial firms are also supposed to hold assets of comparable value.

When firms or households hold a lot of debt, however, even a small fall in the value of their assets can bring them to the brink of bankruptcy. If a family owns a $100,000 home and owes $90,000 to the bank, their net worth is $10,000. But if the value of their home drops by 5%, their net worth halves. The steep fall in asset prices during the crisis caused even more severe losses: many families found their homes were worth less than their mortgages, while financial institutions that had borrowed heavily to invest found that their losses exceeded their equity (the money the owners put into the business).

As well as being vulnerable to declines in asset prices, the highly indebted are also more exposed to fluctuations in their incomes. Their past borrowing leaves them less room for further borrowing to cushion financial blows. Thus highly indebted households find it harder to "smooth" their consumption and similarly burdened firms find it harder to invest when their revenues dip.

To assess the threat debt poses to economic stability, Douglas Sutherland and Peter Hoeller of the OECD have calculated trend rates of debt to GDP, smoothing out the cyclical ups and downs. They note that financial-sector debt tends to exceed its trend during big, long booms of the kind most rich countries enjoyed before the crisis.

But the build-up of this financial-sector debt makes it more likely that the boom will come to an end, Messrs Sutherland and Hoeller find. And the busts are often deeper, as has been the case this time. Much the same is true of household borrowing. They calculate that the odds of a recession are about one in ten when household debt is in line with its trend. But when it exceeds that trend by 10% of GDP, as it did in some of the worst afflicted countries before the crisis, the chances of a recession rise to about 40%.

Rather than looking at borrowing, other economists look at lending. They worry when credit from banks and other lenders to households and firms grows much faster than GDP, as it did before America's crisis in 2008, Japan's in 1991 and the Asian crisis of 1997. Economies can succumb to long "financial cycles", according to Claudio Borio and his colleagues at the Bank for International Settlements. Whereas a traditional business cycle manifests itself in the rise and fall of growth and consumer-price inflation, the financial cycle consists of longer, wider swings in credit and asset-price inflation.

Credit growth as a canary

Why does credit sometimes depart from its prior trend? It may depend on what it is spent on, argues Richard Werner of Southampton University. When a bank makes a loan, it credits the money to the borrower's deposit account. In so doing the loan adds to the money supply. If that money is spent on a new car, factory or other freshly produced good, it contributes to demand, helping the economy to make fuller use of its productive capacity. If the economy is already near full capacity, it will probably just raise prices instead. But either way, the bank lending will add both to debt and to nominal GDP, the money value of economic output, leaving the ratio of debt to GDP largely unchanged.

However, loans can also be spent differently. They can be used to buy existing assets, such as homes, office blocks or rival firms. Since the asset already exists, its purchase does not add directly to GDP, which measures only the production of new goods and services. As a consequence, debt increases, but GDP does not.

Furthermore, the purchase of an asset, such as a home, will help push up the market price of that asset. Other homeowners will then become more willing to take on debt (because they feel wealthier) and more able to do so (because their home's value as collateral has risen). In the years before the crisis, the net worth of American households continued to rise despite their accumulation of debt, because their home and other assets appreciated even faster. Borrowing to buy assets thus has a self-reinforcing effect: one person's purchase makes another's borrowing both more desirable and feasible.

Eventually the financial cycle peaks. Borrowers realise they do not have the income required to service further debt. At that point the cycle goes into reverse: as asset prices fall, collateral constraints tighten, squeezing borrowing, which results in further falls in prices. Unfortunately, one thing does not fall: the size of the debts that households and firms have incurred. The value of their liabilities remains obstinately fixed, as if written in sun-dried clay, even as the value of their assets plunges.

Households and firms will respond by "deleveraging", seeking to lighten their debt burdens. They can do this in three ways: by defaulting, by selling assets, or by spending less than they earn (and using the proceeds to repay debt).

Although deleveraging helps repair household and corporate finances, at the level of the economy as a whole it can make things worse. Since one person's outlay is another person's income, depressed spending will hurt incomes, resulting in what Richard Koo of the Nomura Research Institute has called a "balance-sheet recession". Even if incomes and prices do not actually decline, they will fall short of their previous trajectory, while the money value of debts remains unchanged. The economic weakness caused by debt can thus make debt even harder to bear, a trap that Irving Fisher, a Depression-era economist, called "debt deflation".

The deleveraging of the financial sector can be particularly deep, quick and nasty. Deep because banks hold a lot of debt relative to their equity (they are highly "leveraged"). Quick because those liabilities are typically of shorter maturity than their assets, giving banks little time to put their balance-sheets in order. Nasty because the process hurts their rivals and their customers alike. In 2007 and 2008 fire sales of securities by investment banks and other dealers depressed their prices, devaluing the portfolios of other banks with similar assets. Banks and other lenders also started calling in loans or at least withholding new ones, inflicting a credit crunch on the broader economy.

Is such a wrenching balance-sheet recession avoidable? In principle, as debtors spend less, savers could spend more, helping to sustain demand. To encourage this, the central bank can cut interest rates, easing debt-servicing costs for borrowers and discouraging saving by the thrifty. The Federal Reserve cut its policy rate from 5.25% in the summer of 2007 to 0-0.25% in December 2008 and the Bank of England followed suit.

In addition, the government can spend more than it collects in taxes, so that the private sector can earn more than it spends. In another paper Mr Sutherland and his co-authors show that run-ups in borrowing by firms (especially financial firms) tend to cause subsequent increases in public debt. That is precisely what happened in many rich countries in the aftermath of the crisis, when heavy government spending helped to compensate for severe cuts in corporate and household budgets – and sparked a fiery debate about the risks that entails.

September 2013

Monetary policy after the crash: controlling interest

How the financial crisis forced central bankers to adopt unconventional methods in order to stimulate growth

BEFORE THE FINANCIAL CRISIS life was simple for central bankers. They had a clear mission: temper booms and busts to maintain low and stable inflation. And they had a seemingly effective means to achieve that: nudge a key short-term interest rate up to discourage borrowing (and thus check inflation), or down to foster looser credit (and thus spur growth and employment). Deft use of this technique had kept the world humming along so smoothly in the decades before the crash that economists had declared a "Great Moderation" in the economic cycle. As it turned out, however, the moderation was transitory – and the crash that ended it undermined not only the central bankers' record but also the method they relied on to prop up growth. Monetary policy has been in a state of upheaval ever since.

The recession that accompanied the credit crunch in the autumn of 2008 delivered a massive blow to demand. In response central banks in the rich world slashed their benchmark interest rates. By early 2009 many were close to zero, approaching what economists call the "zero lower bound". Even so, growth remained elusive. Pushing rates below zero, though technically possible, would not have helped. Negative rates would merely have encouraged depositors to withdraw their money from banks and hold it as cash, on which the rate of return, at zero, would have been higher. Central banks in the developed economies faced a frightening collapse in output and soaring unemployment without recourse to the tool that had been the mainstay of monetary policymaking for a generation.

Central banks were not entirely unprepared for this challenge. In the 1990s the Japanese economy had slumped following an asset-price crash. Facing weak growth and deflation the Bank of Japan had slashed rates to near zero before embarking on a series of experiments

FIG 3.5 **As low as you can go**
Interest rates, %

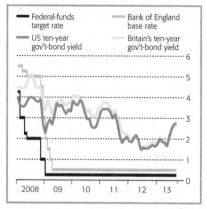

Source: Thomson Reuters

with unconventional monetary tools. Although the Bank of Japan's performance was widely considered disappointing, if not an outright failure, the rich world's central banks began by drawing upon its playbook.

Unconventional policy falls into two broad categories: asset purchases and "forward guidance". Asset purchases are a natural extension of central banks' more typical activities. America's Federal Reserve, for instance, has long bought Treasury bills and other bonds with short maturities to increase the money supply and reduce short-term interest rates. After its benchmark rate fell close to zero the Fed began buying longer-term securities, including ten-year Treasury bonds and mortgage-backed securities, to bring down long-run borrowing costs (see Figure 3.5).

Printing money to buy assets is known as "quantitative easing" (QE) because central banks often announce purchase plans in terms of a desired increase in the quantity of bank reserves. The Bank of Japan first attempted QE in 2001 when it promised to buy ¥400 billion-worth of government bonds a month in order to raise the level of reserves to ¥5 trillion. The central banks of America, Britain and Japan have all engaged in QE since

FIG 3.6 **Easing by printing**
Central-bank assets, $ trillion

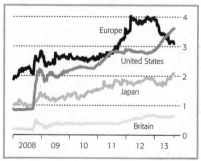

Sources: Bank of England; Bank of Japan; ECB; Federal Reserve; Thomson Reuters

the crisis struck, buying up a vast stock of financial assets (see Figure 3.6).

Economists reckon QE works in a few ways. Central bankers emphasise the "portfolio-balance effect". When central banks buy bonds from investors with newly created money, they use the proceeds to rebalance their portfolio by buying assets of different risk and maturity. In doing so they boost asset prices and depress interest rates (increased demand for bonds allows them to be sold at lower rates). Cheaper borrowing, in turn, prods businesses and households to invest.

QE can stimulate the economy via a fiscal effect, too: lower interest rates reduce government borrowing costs and so lower expected future taxation. And QE also helps shape expectations of inflation. A central bank announcing a new, higher inflation target might use QE to convince markets it will meet it, since, other things being equal, an increase in the amount of money in circulation leads to higher prices. If people think their money will be worth less in the future, they have an incentive to spend more of it now.

Talking prop

Forward guidance, the other main unconventional tool, is an attempt to boost the economy by signalling central banks' future policies more clearly. The Bank of Japan first attempted to talk the economy back to health in 1999, when it promised to keep its main interest rate near zero "until deflationary concerns subside". The Fed and the Bank of England have since mimicked this approach. In early 2009 the Fed said its interest rate was likely to remain low for "an extended period". In August 2011 it sought to improve this formulation by adding a date, specifying that low rates would stick around until at least mid-2013.

In December 2012 the Fed adjusted its communications again. It announced that rates would stay low until the unemployment rate had fallen to at most 6.5%, as long as short-run expectations of inflation were no more than 2.5%. In August 2013 the Bank of England followed suit, stating that it would not raise rates until unemployment had fallen to 7%, provided financial markets behaved themselves and inflation remained subdued.

Like QE, forward guidance works in several ways. A promise to tolerate higher inflation in the future, if believed, can stimulate economic activity in the present, just as the threat of higher prices due to an expanded money supply does. By the same token, a promise to hold short-term rates low for a long time should reduce long-term rates too, since long-term rates are typically compounded short-term rates along with a premium to allow for rising inflation and other risks.

In addition, investors respond to the "real" or inflation-adjusted interest rate, which equals the "nominal" or advertised interest rate minus expected inflation. When inflation is expected to be negative, meaning that prices are falling, the real interest rate may actually rise. Deflation, by raising the value of a unit of money in terms of other goods, in effect increases the cost of borrowing. If a central bank credibly promises more future inflation, by contrast, the real interest rate can fall and even dip below zero. A negative real interest rate works where a negative nominal interest rate does not: holding cash does no good, since inflation reduces the purchasing power of hard currency as well as deposits. It is therefore in everyone's interest to save less, and to borrow and invest more.

Studies of quantitative easing generally find that it has indeed reduced long-term interest rates. One rule of thumb has it that $600 billion in purchases brings down long-run rates by 0.15–0.2 percentage points, equivalent in impact to a cut of 0.75 percentage points in the Fed's benchmark short-term interest rate. Lower rates are estimated to have raised real output in Britain and America 2–3% higher than it would have been without QE, even though borrowing costs remained stubbornly high for British banks.

Research by John Williams of the Fed also suggests that QE plays a strong role in reinforcing a central bank's forward guidance. The Fed's signalling, for example, seems to be responsible for much of the movement in the prices even of assets it is not buying itself. And market bets on future interest rates reveal that investors find central banks' promises to keep rates low more credible when accompanied by QE purchases.

Whether forward guidance is effective at boosting output is harder to say. There is some agreement that communication about future policy reduces long-term interest rates. But it is unclear why rates fall. They could drop because markets believe the central bank's promise to keep short-term rates low, which should encourage more investment and growth. But they could drop because markets read the central bank's guidance as a signal that the economy is weaker than expected, implying less demand for loans. That could actually prove counterproductive if it discouraged new investment.

Some recent Fed research suggests the first effect – the credibility of the promise – is more important. Other work indicates that guidance may be more powerful when it clearly represents a "commitment" to a particular policy rather than a "forecast" of future economic conditions and the policy that is likely to flow from them.

What is certain is that for all the experimentation, the rich world's big economies are still struggling. Output in Britain remains below its pre-crisis peak. Some 10 million fewer Americans are now working than might reasonably have been expected in 2007. The euro area is only just escaping the second trough of a double-dip recession, and its unemployment rate remains in double digits. Unconventional monetary policy, in short, does not seem to be working as well as the conventional sort used to – but there is no agreement why.

Some economists maintain that monetary policy, conventional or otherwise, loses much of its power at the zero lower bound. Simon Wren-Lewis of Oxford University argues that monetary policy cannot stabilise the economy without fiscal easing, meaning more government spending or lower taxes, to transmit newly created money and low rates into the real economy. Others, such as Richard Koo of the Nomura Research Institute, reckon that highly indebted firms and households are simply unable to respond to lower long-term interest rates by borrowing more.

Some believe that unconventional policy would work better if central banks only pursued it more vigorously. Soon after Japan ran into its own zero lower bound, Ben Bernanke, who was then an economist at Princeton University and later chairman of the Fed, argued that the Bank of Japan needed to set a higher inflation target, buy more assets and devalue the yen by purchasing foreign currencies. Robert Hall of Stanford University suspects that pushing the real federal-funds rate down to –4% would be sufficient to get the

American economy moving faster. As long as the Fed keeps inflation around 2%, however, the real interest rate can go no lower than −2% (a zero federal-funds rate minus the 2% rate of inflation).

Christina Romer of the University of California, Berkeley, is one of the many economists who see a need for a psychological jolt to rouse the economy. She argues for "regime change", meaning not just a change in leadership, but also a dramatic shift in policy. She wants central banks to stop targeting inflation and to focus instead on total spending in the economy, or nominal GDP. Although in most circumstances the two approaches would deliver similar results, a nominal-GDP target gives a central bank more leeway to fight unemployment during steep downturns. Just as important, in her view, the policy change would signal to markets that the Fed meant to restore rapid growth once and for all.

Yet for every critic who believes that central banks have done too little, there is one who fears they have done far too much. By propping up asset prices artificially, some complain, central bankers are stoking inequality, rewarding financial firms despite their past misdeeds and sowing the seeds of the next crisis. Many, especially on the right in America, give warning that the massive increase in the money supply QE entails can lead only to a debasement of the currency and hyperinflation. Others gripe that low interest rates in the rich world have sent a flood of hot money towards emerging markets, generating financial instability.

It is likely to take years to discern which of these criticisms are warranted. Not until 1963 did Milton Friedman and Anna Schwartz publish *A Monetary History of the United States*, definitively establishing that misguided monetary policy had helped entrench the Great Depression. Unfortunately for the many countries still enduring sub-par growth, a similarly decisive resolution to today's monetary-policy debates is still far off.

September 2013

Stimulus v austerity: sovereign doubts

The financial crisis caused a surge in public debt and a heated debate about how quickly governments should cut it back

ECONOMISTS ARE an argumentative bunch. Yet before the crisis most found common ground in the notion that fiscal stimulus was an obsolete relic. Monetary policy seemed wholly capable of taming the business cycle. Government efforts to increase spending or cut taxes to battle unemployment would only muck things up. When crisis struck in 2008, however, that consensus evaporated.

The frightening speed of the economic collapse spurred governments to action, in spite of economists' doctrinal misgivings. In 2009 many countries rolled out big packages of tax cuts and extra spending in the hope of buoying growth. This stimulus amounted to 2% of GDP on average among the members of the G20 club of big economies. Among Barack Obama's first steps as president in 2009 was to sign the American Recovery and Reinvestment Act, a stimulus plan worth $831 billion, or almost 6% of that year's GDP, most of it to be spent over the next three years.

Keynes to the rescue

Supporters of stimulus looked to the ideas of John Maynard Keynes, a British economist. Depression, his acolytes reasoned, occurs when there is too much saving. When too many people want to save and too few to invest, then resources (including workers) fall idle. Firms and families might save too much because of financial uncertainty or because they are rushing to "deleverage" – to reduce the ratio of their debts to their assets.

In normal times central banks would try to spur growth by adjusting interest rates to discourage saving and encourage borrowing. Yet by early 2009 most central banks had reduced their main interest rates almost to zero, without the desired result. Overindebtedness, some surmised, might have been preventing people from borrowing as much as they would like, whatever the interest rate. Governments,

FIG 3.7 **Borrowed climb**
General government debt, % of GDP

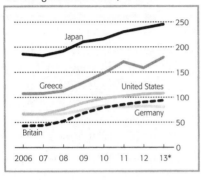

*Forecast
Source: IMF

Keynesians reckoned, needed to make up for hamstrung firms and families by borrowing and spending more (or taxing less) to put excess savings to work.

When there is slack in the economy, fiscal stimulus can be particularly powerful thanks to a "multiplier" effect. A dollar spent building a railway, for example, might go to the wages of a construction worker. He then spends the extra income on groceries, enriching a shopkeeper, who in turn goes shopping himself and so on. Every dollar of stimulus could thus result in two dollars of output – a multiplier of two. (Multipliers also apply to government cuts, amplifying the reduction in GDP.) That allows governments to deliver a hefty economic bang at moderate fiscal cost.

Yet fiscal stimulus is needed most when governments already have extra costs to bear. From 2007 to 2010 rich countries saw the ratio of their gross sovereign debt to GDP spike from 74% to 101% on average. British public debt jumped from just 44% of GDP to 79%, while America's leapt from 66% of GDP to 98%. Greece's soared by 40 percentage points, to 148% of GDP (see Figure 3.7). Greece's deficit was so high that when the government revealed it, the admission set off a crisis of confidence in public finances in southern Europe, and thus in the viability of the euro itself.

Stimulus was not the main reason debt piled up: the biggest drag on public finances came from lower tax receipts, thanks to weak profits and high unemployment. Financial bail-outs added to the fiscal toll, as did "automatic stabilisers" – measures like unemployment benefits that automatically raise spending and support demand when recession strikes. The IMF estimates that almost 60% of the rise in government debt since 2008 stems from collapsing revenues, more than twice the cost of stimulus and bail-outs combined.

FIG 3.8 **Extended gap year**
Government budget balances, % of GDP

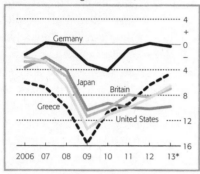

*Forecast
Source: IMF

As growth returned in 2010 some leaders argued that it was time to trim public spending. Others worried that the recovery was too fragile to permit any hint of austerity. There was no question that "fiscal consolidation" would eventually be necessary, but much dispute about when it should start.

Britain moved quickly towards sobriety, ending its stimulus in 2010 and planning future cuts. From 2010 to 2011 the government pared its "structural" budget deficit (ie, adjusted to account for cyclical costs such as automatic stabilisers) by two percentage points, with further drops of a percentage point in 2012 and 2013. Several southern European countries had to make even deeper cuts as the crisis spread. But America kept spending, adding new tax breaks to the previous stimulus. As a result, its structural deficit declined more slowly (see Figure 3.8).

The debate about these policies hinged on two crucial uncertainties. One was the size of the multiplier. Sceptics reckoned that it would be low, and that neither stimulus nor austerity would have much effect on output or jobs. Stimulus simply absorbs resources that would otherwise have been used by private firms, they argued. Moreover, firms and households would probably save their share of the proceeds, rather than bolster the economy by spending them, since they would assume that the government's largesse was only temporary and that tax bills would soon be going back up.

Those of a Keynesian bent downplayed these concerns. With unemployment high and private demand for loans low, there was little risk that the government would "crowd out" private activity. Indeed, in a "balance-sheet recession", with indebted households forced by falling asset prices to pay off loans quickly, a boost to incomes from a fiscal stimulus would speed the financial adjustment, and thus generate a faster recovery.

The other question was how much debt rich governments could take on without harming the economy. Typically, lenders will demand ever-higher rates of interest from spendthrift governments as public debts grow. That leads to higher rates for everyone else, crimping economic growth. But supporters of stimulus argued that a slumping economy with rock-bottom interest rates had no reason to fear the vigilantes of the bond market.

The academic evidence, inevitably, was also disputed. Carmen Reinhart and Kenneth Rogoff of Harvard University published a much-cited paper claiming that economic growth rates slow sharply when government debt tops 90% of GDP. Follow-on studies also turned up a negative relationship between growth and debt, although not always at the same threshold. Research by Alberto Alesina of Harvard and Silvia Ardagna of Goldman Sachs, an investment bank, showed that fiscal rectitude – especially in the form of spending cuts rather than tax rises – could actually boost growth.

Keynesians questioned Mrs Reinhart's and Mr Rogoff's conclusions, noting that slow growth might be a cause of high debt rather than a symptom of it. They also thought Mr Alesina's "expansionary austerity" was a pipe dream. In the past, they observed, it had occurred only under quite different conditions. Had government borrowing been gobbling up scarce credit, pushing interest rates for private firms upwards, then lower deficits could reduce rates and trigger an investment boom. But in most of the rich world interest rates were already low; excessive saving was the problem.

What is more, the Keynesians asserted, multipliers are much higher during nasty downturns than at other times. Research by Lawrence Christiano, Martin Eichenbaum and Sergio Rebelo of Northwestern University suggests that when interest rates are near zero the multiplier could be higher than two, since people have a greater incentive than usual to spend rather than save. A financial crisis also elevates multipliers, other studies found. Work by Larry Summers, the architect of Mr Obama's stimulus, and Brad DeLong of the University of California, Berkeley, argues that given the cost of prolonged unemployment, stimulus during a long recession might pay for itself.

Time has begun rendering verdicts. In 2012 a McKinsey study noted that financial deleveraging in America proceeded more quickly than in Britain and Europe. In the same year the IMF published an analysis of its economic forecasts which found that austerity crimped growth much more than it had expected. The larger the cuts a government planned, the IMF concluded, the farther below its forecast growth fell. The multiplier on spending cuts was perhaps twice what researchers had originally assumed. Spanish austerity reduced the government's structural deficit by more than two percentage points from 2011 to 2012. But cuts helped push the economy into recession. Net government borrowing actually rose.

In April 2013 research from the University of Massachusetts undermined the Reinhart-Rogoff finding that growth slows sharply when debt tops 90% of GDP. An analytical error and questionable data choices, it turns out, had underpinned the result. There is no consensus among economists as to what level of debt harms growth, or whether it is even possible to establish such a rule of thumb.

That does not mean that ballooning public debt is nothing to worry about, however. New research suggests that less-indebted governments are much more likely to resort to stimulus to foster economic growth, presumably because they feel they can afford to do so. It may be a long time coming (Japan's government debt now totals 245% of GDP), but at some point too much red ink will yield a debt crisis. Worries about a country's solvency will lead creditors to demand higher interest rates, which will then compound its fiscal woes.

Just when the bond market will turn depends on a number of factors. Economies seen as havens, such as America and Switzerland, have more latitude: economic upheaval tends to reduce their borrowing costs rather than raise them. It helps if most creditors are locals, too, as in Japan, since payments to them help boost the domestic economy.

Panic is more likely when debt is owed in a currency the government does not control, since the central bank cannot then act as a lender of last resort. Uncertainty over whether the European Central Bank would play this role fanned the euro-zone crisis, for example. Carried to extremes government-bond purchases may fuel worries about inflation. That in turn can lead to higher borrowing costs as creditors demand an inflation-risk premium. Yet during the crisis economies were so weak that central banks' purchases of government bonds proved reassuring to investors rather than worrisome, partly due to the reduced risk of panic and default.

The day of reckoning may nonetheless be closer than it appears. Failing banks can swiftly transform debt loads from moderate to crushing. Before the crisis the assets of Ireland's commercial banks swelled to over 600% of GDP. Ireland's debts duly exploded from 25% of GDP in 2007 to 117% in 2012, thanks mostly to the government's assumption of the banks' debts after the crisis struck.

Every cut has its day

Austerity, in short, still has its place. But what sort? Whereas some economists recommend spending cuts, other research indicates that higher taxes can also work. Both approaches have costs. Taxing pay can distort labour markets; consumption taxes can lead to inflation, prompting contractionary monetary policy. Yet cutting spending is more unpopular and can exacerbate inequality.

The experience of the past few years has left little debate about timing, however. The moment to turn to austerity, ideally, is when the economy can bear it. Not all governments have that luxury, of course: Greece's, for one, could not delay fierce cuts since it could no longer borrow enough to finance its deficits. Those with more breathing space should aim to stabilise their debts in the long run, the IMF suggests, by laying out plans to reduce their deficits. The more credible their plans, the more leeway they will have to depart from them should conditions warrant it. As Keynes insisted, the time for austerity is the boom not the bust.

September 2013

Making banks safe: calling to accounts

Is there a way to make banks safer without killing lending?

BANKS ARE a perplexing mix. The special institutions at the heart of capitalism, they provide an easy link between savers and borrowers: granting loans to those with the ideas and ambition to use them while at the same time providing peace of mind to squirrels who want to lock their cash away safely. Yet banks have a dark side too: they exist to manage risk, but often simply stockpile it. When they go bad they scythe away wealth and strangle economies. There is little argument that it was the banks that started the crisis in 2008. There is huge disagreement about how to put things right.

To see why banks are so vital, start with the finances of a typical household or firm. Their debts – mainly mortgages on homes, offices or factories – have fixed terms; they often have fixed interest rates too. In what is owed there is a lot of certainty. But firms' and families' financial assets are not bound by such rigid terms: deposits can be withdrawn with little notice; bonds and equity can be sold quickly if cash is needed or if investment tastes change. This combination of fixed-term debts and flexible assets is a comfortable set-up.

But one party's asset is another's liability. This means that corporate and personal finances have a mirror image in the balance-sheets of banks, where assets (the loans a bank has made) cannot be adjusted but where debts (its customers' deposits) can be called in overnight. That mix is risky: a rush of depositors demanding their money back can force cut-price asset sales. If debts are called in more quickly than assets can be sold, insolvency looms. Managing that risk is what banks do: by holding a risky balance-sheet they allow households and firms to have safe ones.

Since the maturities of their assets and liabilities do not match up, banks tend to give themselves some margin for error. They build resilience into their finances in two ways. Liquid assets – things like cash and government bonds that can be sold quickly and at relatively certain prices – are a safety valve. If investors suddenly shun a bank's bonds or depositors withdraw large sums, it can sell them. That allows the bank's balance-sheet to shrink safely, in line with creditors' demands.

But balance-sheets can shrink for other reasons too. The value of a bank's riskier assets – mortgages, bonds, loans to companies – can drop sharply if the prospects of the borrowers sour. The danger is that the value of the bank's assets could fall below its liabilities: with more owing than is owned, the bank would be bust. To forestall such failures banks maintain equity. This represents the money a bank's owners have invested in it. Equity takes the first hit when asset values drop. Since the bank's owners absorb the loss, its creditors – bondholders and depositors – can rest assured that they will not have to.

But a bank is not a charity, and the two shock absorbers are costly. Some rough rules of thumb show why: the return on cash is zero, with liquid assets like government bonds yielding a measly 2–3%. In contrast, mortgages might generate 5% and unsecured lending closer to 10%. Picking safe assets lowers returns. In addition, equity investors expect a return (via dividends or capital gains on their shareholding) of around 12%, compared with the 4% or so demanded by bondholders.

This sets up a tension between stability and profitability which banks' bosses must manage. Their failure to do so lies at the heart of the crisis. One simple equation explains their dire performance:

$$\text{Return on equity (RoE)} = \text{return on assets (RoA)} \times \text{leverage}$$

The idea is straightforward. A bank's equity-holders gain when the return on its assets rises. Maximising RoE means holding fewer safe assets, like cash or government bonds, since these provide low returns. When returns on all asset classes fall, as in the early 2000s, banks have another way to boost RoE: leverage (the ratio of their assets to their equity). Banks can increase their leverage by borrowing more from depositors or debt markets and lending or investing the proceeds. That gives them more income-generating holdings relative to the same pool of equity. In the short run, shareholders gain.

FIG 3.9 **Hitting the buffers**
British banks' liquidity and equity

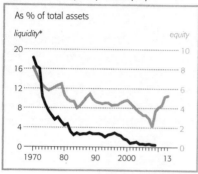

*Cash + Bank of England balances +
money at call + eligible bills + UK gilts
Source: Bank of England

Risk on

Of course, skimping on safety mechanisms makes banks more risky. Yet the RoE formula is hard-wired into banking, familiar to every chief executive and shareholder. A 2011 report by the Bank of England showed that Britain's biggest banks all rewarded their senior staff based on RoE targets. Bosses duly maximised short-term profits, allowing liquid assets and equity to fall to historic lows (see Figure 3.9).

By the mid-2000s leverage was out of control. Consider RBS and Citi, respectively the biggest banks in Britain and America in 2007 (RBS was also the biggest in the world). Official reports show that these lenders had leverage ratios of around 50 when the crisis hit: they could absorb only $2 in losses on each $100 of assets. That helps explain why the American subprime market, although only a small fraction of global finance, could cause such trouble. Top-heavy, with brittle accounts, the banks were riding for a fall.

The main regulatory response has been a revision of international banking regulations first agreed in Basel in 1989. Basel III, as the latest version is known, is more stringent than its predecessors on four basic measures of safety: it requires banks to hold more equity and liquid assets, to leverage themselves less (the maximum ratio is now 33) and to rely less on short-term funding. In countries where bank bailouts during the crisis caused outrage, however, or where the financial sector's liabilities are much bigger than the economy (making bailouts ruinous), regulators are determined to go further.

The most radical option is to carve up lenders deemed "too big to fail". Splitting them into smaller and simpler banks would make oversight easier, and prevent a bankruptcy from upending the local economy or the government's finances. But unravelling and reapportioning assets and liabilities might be impossibly tricky.

An alternative is to ban banks from the riskiest activities. In America, a rule proposed by Paul Volcker, a former head of the Federal Reserve, will prevent deposit-taking banks from engaging in "proprietary trading" (in essence, investing in stocks, bonds and derivatives using its customers' money). In theory, the "Volcker rule" will shield deposits from traders' losses. In practice, it is difficult to distinguish between trading conducted with a view to serving customers and that done solely for the bank's benefit.

Regulators in Europe are taking a different tack. In both Britain and the euro zone, they have proposed "ring-fences" that will separate customer deposits from banks' other liabilities. Against them, banks would only be allowed to hold assets like cash, government bonds and loans to individuals and firms. Activities deemed riskier, such as trading in shares and derivatives and underwriting companies' bond issuance, would sit outside the ring-fence, backed by a separate stash of capital.

But even once the new ring-fences are in place, banks will still grant mortgages. That is a risky business. Take British commercial-property lending (loans on offices and shopping centres). It is a large part of the mortgage market, over 20% of GDP at its peak. It is also volatile: commercial-property prices fell by almost 45% between 2007 and 2009. In America the share of even the best "prime" mortgages in arrears topped 7% in early 2010. None of this risk would be outside the ring-fence, or blocked by the Volcker rule.

That is one reason some argue that banks should hold significantly more equity than the new rules require. In their 2013 book *The Bankers' New Clothes*, Anat Admati of Stanford University and Martin Hellwig of the Max Planck Institute maintain that the cost of holding extra equity is overstated. For one thing, bigger buffers make banks safer, so the cost of other forms of funding (like bonds) should fall. In a related paper, David Miles, a member of the committee at the Bank of England that sets interest rates, estimates both the costs and benefits of increasing equity. The two are equal, he concludes, when equity is about 16–20% of banks' risk-adjusted assets – even higher than the Basel III rules require.

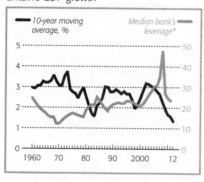

FIG 3.10 **No lever required**
Britain's GDP growth

*Ratio of total assets to shareholders' claims
Sources: *Optimal Bank Capital* by D. Miles *et al.*, 2012;
Bank of England

Bank bosses (most notably Jamie Dimon of JPMorgan Chase) regard that as far too high. Their concern is that banks are being forced to hold redundant equity. That would have two effects. First, it might reduce lending, since existing buffers would only be enough to cover a smaller stock of loans. Second, higher equity means lower leverage, which could reduce RoE below investors' expectations. That would make it hard to raise the equity regulators are demanding and – if sustained – prompt a gradual wind-up of the banks as investors opt to put their money elsewhere. The only alternative would be to raise RoA by charging borrowers much higher interest.

There is some truth on both sides. The academics are right to say that higher equity need not kill off lending. After all, equity is a source of funds, not a use for them. Historically, much lower leverage ratios have been associated with strong growth in lending and GDP (see Figure 3.10). Yet it is also true that without leverage to boost returns, banks might need to squeeze more from their assets: the cost of credit could rise.

There may be a third way. Some researchers think a better balance between equity and debt can be struck by using funding that has some of the attributes of both. They want banks to sell more "contingent capital" to investors. These IOUs act like bonds in normal times, paying a return and requiring full payback when they mature. But in bad times they change from debt into loss-absorbing equity.

Such ideas are attractive not just because they provide a clever solution to the debt v equity puzzle. Regulators are also pushing them for a related reason: they should encourage a bank's creditors to provide more oversight. Knowing that their bonds could be converted into risky equity, the theory runs, big investors like insurers and pension funds would go through banks' books with a fine-tooth comb, spotting any leverage-pumping activities on the part of profit-hungry CEOs. How cheap contingent capital will prove is uncertain: investors will presumably demand a higher return than for debt, particularly from risky-looking banks.

That might actually be a good thing: ideally markets as well as regulators would encourage banks to act prudently. In a 2010 paper Andrew Haldane of the Bank of England argued that banks' borrowing costs are distorted. Since investors assume the biggest ones will be bailed out in times of crisis, they accept relatively low rates of interest on the bonds they issue. That, in turn, distorts the banks' decisions: since such funding is cheap it is hardly surprising that profit-maximising bank bosses gorge on it.

Rigging and milking

All this turns banks from champions of capitalism into affronts to it, reliant on rigged markets and taxpayer subsidies. Regulators are working to change that. In a 2012 joint paper the Bank of England and the FDIC, the agency that insures bank deposits in America, set out their approach. When the next bank big enough to threaten the entire financial system fails, regulators plan to use "living wills" that explain how to unwind its holdings. They will take control, replacing a bank's managers and doling out losses to bondholders as well as equity investors.

The message is clear: regulators are not trying to prevent failures, but to prepare for them. They hope this will make managers react by holding enough capital and liquid assets to keep banks out of trouble. Yet some banks remain too sprawling and opaque to liquidate in an orderly manner and too big to let fail. Their state support, implicit or explicit, seems likely to remain. Newly cautious by obligation but not by choice, the world's biggest banks remain a perplexing mix of freewheeling capitalism, subsidies and regulation.

4   Building competitiveness

Taxi markets: a fare fight

Taxi markets are a perfect test of Europe's willingness to change

MANY A JOURNEY starts in a taxi. So it is with the road to deregulation in the euro zone's economies. Mario Monti, Italy's prime minister, has prioritised liberalisation of taxi licences; Italy's cabbies are striking as a result. Greek taxi-drivers have blockaded streets several times in protest against deregulation. Why have taxis become emblematic of the battle to free hidebound economies?

The superficial answer is that taxis are iconic: think of the badges, the bold colours and the recognisable models. The complex answer is that these features are themselves the result of regulation, and not just in the euro zone. From the turning-circle of a London taxi to the medallions on the hood of a New York cab, this industry picks up rules as easily as fares.

Taxi markets should be simple. Costs of entry are low. There are rarely large incumbent firms. On paper, competition should flourish. But low barriers to entry create a risk of having too many taxis on the roads. The number of taxi drivers in New York and Washington, DC, shot up between 1930 and 1932, as the unemployed sought work during the Depression. Such surges lead to rules to reduce congestion. America started to set up new regulatory authorities in the early 1930s; Britain established binding numerical limits on horse-drawn coaches way back in 1635.

Cab fares can be problematic, too. Unregulated competition means that fares fall to little more than a driver's expenses. These expenses are influenced by distance (fuel costs), duration (the cost of time) and destination. The end-point for a trip is vital: some destinations (airports, say) will pretty much guarantee a return fare; others will not. This means journeys of a similar distance can have very different costs, so working out a fair price is tricky. In an unregulated market passengers would have to search out a competitive price, a time-consuming process of hailing or calling a number of cabs. That allows taxi operators to run an opaque pricing structure.

The response to this problem in many jurisdictions has been regulation to establish a uniform price, giving customers certainty over what they will pay. But as a result journeys that are the same distance end up varying hugely in value for drivers. Short trips around tourist destinations are lucrative; trips to more remote areas, or on congested commuter routes, are much less profitable. Since full-time cabbies cannot raise prices, they may refuse to operate at less popular times or to carry passengers who live at the wrong end of town.

The answer has been to layer on yet more regulation aimed at enforcing uniform pricing, geographic coverage and quality standards. Rome and Mumbai operate hard geographic barriers to entry: those who live outside the cities cannot operate inside them. A better idea is imposing an entry cost for a permit that a driver loses if found to be violating the rules. This creates a commitment to the industry and an incentive to play fair. The New York medallion system works this way: a driver caught violating rules is banned and the medallion suspended, so both the driver and medallion-owner lose out.

But even well-thought-out regulations end up not working. Drivers of London's black cabs must learn the city's streets by heart but these tests can now take four years to complete (in 1960 it took up to a year), which acts as a bottleneck to new supply. That a New York medallion sells for over $1 million suggests well-intended commitment devices can simply become a barrier to entry.

Hackneyed protest

Incumbent drivers argue that more taxis might help travellers but would dent profits, putting low-value trips at threat and reducing cab quality. But the idea that markets are a zero-sum game is a bad one. Loosening quantity restrictions might benefit both drivers and passengers. More cabs mean lower waiting times and can increase the number of travellers who choose to use taxis. The market grows. This could boost utilisation rates and profits.

There is supporting evidence. In 1998 Dublin suffered from a distorted licensing system. Demand had doubled in the previous 20 years but the number of licences had not kept up. Waiting times were over an hour. Deregulation in 2000 reduced entry costs (the cost of a car and a licence) by 74%. The result was more than three times as many cabs on the roads, lower waiting times, maintained cab quality and higher passenger satisfaction – all in two years.

In Tehran taxi supply is flexible, rising and falling with demand. A shared-taxi system operates, allowing any private car to pick up passengers. Because travellers can hop on and hop off as they please, a driver can carry passengers travelling to different destinations at the same time. This boosts utilisation, just as a bus route does. The system also means the quantity of taxis is truly fluid, rising during rush hour as commuters pick up a few passengers on their way home. It would be hard to design regulation that worked this well.

The Swedish experience suggests one downside to deregulation. Following the country's banking crisis in 1990 lots of industries were deregulated. For taxis price controls, restricted operating times and regulated zones were all swept away. The year after deregulation the number of taxis per inhabitant had risen by 28%. But fares to rural areas (low-value one-way trips) rose, in line with theory. One solution would be to subsidise taxi fares to some rural areas where buses do not operate.

The regulatory straitjacket that characterises the taxi industry may have been fitted for valid reasons. But barriers to entry make markets smaller. Dismantling layers of regulation to increase market size and efficiency is the rationale behind structural-reform efforts in the euro zone. If these economies are to change, the taxi is as good a way as any to start the trip.

February 2012

Labour markets: insider aiding

Europe's labour markets have favoured older workers at the expense of younger ones

OF ALL THE EURO ZONE'S many problems, youth unemployment is perhaps the most distressing. Joblessness among young workers is around 30% in Portugal and nearly 50% in Spain. Above-average unemployment is the norm for young people, even in more liberal markets like America's. But Spain's youth unemployment rate jumped by nearly 20 percentage points between 2007 and 2009, compared with a rise of seven points in America. Labour-market regulations take much of the blame: while hard-to-fire older workers luxuriate on permanent contracts, the young are typically hired temporarily and are easier to sack.

Such "dual" labour markets are themselves products of reform. Although American unemployment quickly dropped following the troubles of the 1970s and early 1980s, European joblessness remained stuck at high levels. Leaders recognised the need to inject more flexibility into the labour market but powerful trade unions headed off a full-frontal assault on workers' rights. The answer was to create a less-protected class of employees.

The pain in Spain

Spain's experience is instructive. As the unemployment rate approached 20% in the mid-1980s, the government introduced fixed-term contracts of between six months and three years, which were subject to lower dismissal costs than those for workers on open-ended contracts. At the end of a three-year contract firms could either convert a worker to permanent employment or send him packing. The reforms got results. Unemployment fell from nearly 18% when they began in 1984 to around 14% six years later.

But the reforms had unintended consequences too. Temporary contracts surged, soon accounting for close to a third of Spanish employment. Workers churned from job to job: just 6% of temporary contracts were converted to permanent employment during the mid-2000s. When the economy turned down employees were shed in larger numbers and the unemployment rate rose faster than before. Those more likely to be employed on temporary contracts, such as the young, bore the brunt of the pain. The euro zone's long expansion from the mid-1990s until the crisis of 2008 disguised many of these problems. A construction boom helped Spanish unemployment back below 10%, even as immigration soared. But the crisis has exposed old weaknesses again.

Volatility is but one cost of dual labour markets. Frequent job turnover makes households' finances less certain, making it harder, for example, to save regularly for old age. More importantly, temporary employment discourages firms from investing in their workers. The cost to an employer of converting an expiring temporary contract into a permanent one is quite high because of a discontinuous jump in the cost of sacking the worker. So there is an incentive to get rid of him when his contract ends and to invest little in training him.

This systematic underinvestment drags productivity inexorably downwards. A 2011 study by Juan Dolado of Universidad Carlos III de Madrid, Salvador Ortigueira of the European University Institute and Rodolfo Stucchi of the Inter-American Development Bank pins 20% of the productivity slowdown in Spanish manufacturing between 1992 and 2005 on temporary work. The young are especially harmed. Between 2005 and 2007 roughly 80% of Spanish workers aged 16 to 19 were on temporary contracts, compared with 32% of 30-year-olds and 24% of 40-year-olds. A lack of training may weigh on them throughout their working lives.

A single, open-ended labour contract, in which severance pay rises continuously with tenure, should increase the incentive for firms to retain more employees for longer and to invest more in the human capital of new workers. Incremental protections should also moderate swings in employment. A study of French and Spanish labour markets found that the recent rise in Spain's unemployment rate might have been cut by a third had Spain followed the French example of a shallower gradient between labour-market tiers.

At this point, supporters of the model might well point to

Germany, where the youth unemployment rate is a mere 7.8% and overall joblessness is at its lowest level for decades. In many respects Germany's labour market mirrors that of its peers. It, too, responded to eurosclerosis with flexible, second-tier contracts. Permanent positions protected by strong employment rules still dominate its labour market.

But Germany also sought greater flexibility in other areas. Part-time work became increasingly common: Germany's *Kurzarbeit* programme, in which firms reacted to recession by cutting hours rather than employees, is just the latest example of this approach. Germany's better performance also relied on ever-stingier unemployment benefits, which increased labour supply and reduced upward wage pressure. Clauses in collective-bargaining agreements allowed individual firms to stray from wage deals when competitive pressures demanded it.

Dual purpose

Germany may have pursued wage restraint, but that is no easy route to prosperity. Indeed, dual labour markets are more likely to have the opposite effect. Permanent workers fearlessly seek higher wages, confident that job losses will fall first on temporary workers. Soaring Spanish unemployment has produced little wage moderation. During 2009 the pay of permanent workers rose by 4% in real terms.

And attractive as the German model is now, across decades American jobless rates are tough to match. The Anglo-Saxon preference for little or no employment protection may be the most effective at herding workers from declining industries to growing ones, driving job creation and innovation. Dyspeptic bond markets are now pushing Spain and others towards reforms that make it easier and cheaper to lay off workers again. Not before time.

February 2012

Efficient infrastructure: ports in the storm

Portugal needs to privatise its ports to reap the full benefits of its location

LISBON'S HARBOUR mixes pleasure with business. Bars and restaurants sit alongside industrial machinery and colossal container ships. The combination works: shiny cranes gleam in the sunset as tourists and locals eat and drink at the water's edge. But Portuguese ports are a less happy blend of private and public control. The government is set to take a fresh look at ports as part of a wider programme of IMF-mandated structural reforms. What should it do?

Passing through seaports can be expensive, accounting for a big chunk of goods' wholesale costs. Price-sensitive shippers will seek out prime ports, looking for value, speed and reliability. Port efficiency is in turn linked to ownership structure.

In general, private-sector involvement improves things. Typical benefits include shorter queuing times, cheaper container unloading, longer opening hours and higher capacity utilisation. Until 1984, Portugal's ports sat at the state-controlled end of the ownership spectrum (much of the country's aviation infrastructure still does). Since then, they have gradually moved to an intermediate public-private "landlord" model. This can work well: the government owns the land and water access, while private firms finance, build and operate tugboats, cranes and warehouses.

This liberalisation process has made Portuguese ports better – investment has increased capacity and productivity has improved. But further improvements are needed, according to Rui Marquez and Carlos Cruz of the Technical University of Lisbon, if Portugal is to compete effectively for container-ship business.

These ships keep on getting bigger. The bulkiest vessels can carry 14,000 twenty-foot containers – a cargo that would require a train 85km (53 miles) long if transported by rail. The result is huge economies of scale: the cost per container on an Asia-to-Europe trip has fallen from around $1,000 to below $300, according to one study.

FIG 4.1 **Portugal's opportunity**
Major maritime trade routes TEUs*, 2009, million

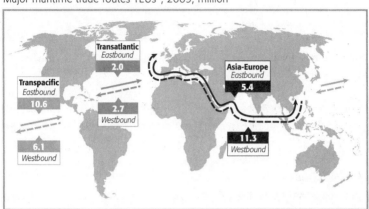

*Twenty-foot equivalent units
Source: UNCTAD

Big ships will stop at only four or five destinations in Europe, raising the stakes for ports trying to win their custom, according to Neil Davidson of Drewry Shipping Consultants. To lure them, ports need deeper harbours and bigger cranes to unload the cargo. They also need to offer an attractive onward route to final customers. This can be overland using trucks, or by sea if the port offers connections with lots of smaller ships. For Portugal, this means competing to serve the cities of Seville and Malaga by lorry or train, or acting as a shipping hub by battling with rival ports in Spain and Morocco.

Portugal should be well placed to compete. Its coast is right on the enormously busy Asia-Europe shipping route (see Figure 4.1). Its highest-capacity container port – Terminal XXI at the Port of Sines – can handle the biggest ships. It is well within reach of southern Spain, with onward rail and road connections that have been made much better in recent years. But despite improvements between 2009 and 2010, the port is still a minnow by European standards. To make further gains, especially in the ultra price-sensitive transshipment market, Portugal needs to steer past two obstructions: powerful service providers and unionised workers.

Getting private firms to compete at ports is tricky. Setting up an unloading business requires significant investment – a single crane can cost €8 million ($11 million) – meaning that expected returns have to be decent. To attract operators, port authorities typically grant long contracts – 20 to 30 years – often to just one or two firms. The competition safeguard is that these contracts are won as part of a transparent tendering process.

The problem is that incumbents are hard to budge. They can use the need to invest in new equipment to bargain for a contract extension. As a result, current players get deals extended without the tendering process being rerun. There is little switching at the end of contracts. The consequent dulling of competition is a feature of the Portuguese system.

A second drag is the absence of a competitive labour market. Port workers are highly unionised and have huge bargaining power because of their ability to block imports and exports. In 2005 port workers successfully foiled European Commission plans to liberalise labour at ports. In January 2012, 600 dockers across Portugal went on strike for five days in response to plans to close a company operating at Aveiro, a second-tier port.

Charting a new course

Other countries' experience suggests three ways to bolster Portugal's seaport performance. First, more competition is needed at the ports: contracts should be extended only after transparent retendering, with new competitors invited to bid. This can reap real benefits: in the Netherlands service costs dropped by a quarter after a new tugboat operator entered. Second, the unions must be tackled. Encouraging more firms to provide services would again improve things: in Hong Kong seven companies provide loading services and six offer ship repairs.

Finally, Portugal should reconsider its role as a port landlord. Selling up has worked in Britain, Australia and New Zealand. Private owners would be better at taking on vested interests. A sale could raise around €1 billion for the cash-strapped exchequer. And since efficient ports often lead to a strong export sector, according to the United Nations, it could have wider benefits, too.

March 2012

Job market frictions: mobile moans

It should be easier for unemployed Europeans to move in search of work

NEARLY A QUARTER of Spain's workforce – and roughly half of Spain's young people – have no jobs. Unemployment rates in Austria, Germany and the Netherlands, by contrast, are dramatically lower. When Americans are faced with depressed labour markets, many saddle up in search of work. But Europeans are far less likely to uproot, both within borders and, especially, across them (see Figure 4.2).

There is an obvious reason for that: Europe's linguistic diversity. Language matters. In Canada, for example, mobility is much higher across the country as a whole than it is between French-speaking Quebec and the English-speaking provinces and territories. An analysis of European language borders, by Nicola Fuchs-Schündeln of Goethe University Frankfurt and Kevin Bartz of Harvard University, concludes that language hurdles are better predictors of low mobility than national borders. Europe's demography also counts. Migration does less good to older workers, who have fewer working years ahead of them in which to benefit from moving.

FIG 4.2 **Repelling borders**
Cross-border mobility, % of total population, 2010 or latest

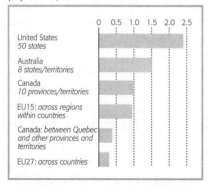

Source: OECD

Such built-in barriers make the need to clear away other obstacles all the more important. In principle, migration across European Union borders, except Bulgaria's and Romania's, is as easy as migration within member states. In practice, residents face a pile of disincentives.

Tax and benefit policies that compress Europe's wage distribution are one of these.

Income differentials gave east Europeans a very good reason to move to western Europe after the 2004 enlargement. But income gaps are much smaller within the euro zone. Generous severance packages and unemployment benefits also reduce the incentives to migrate. Peripheral governments are under pressure to rein in such benefits – Spain and Italy are trying to chip away at lavish severance pay, for instance – but opposition is fierce.

The housing market is another source of friction. Transaction fees and taxes for home-buyers are much higher in Europe than America, according to the OECD. Transaction costs are 10–15% of the price of a house in Greece, Italy and Spain, compared with roughly 5% in America. Renters are discouraged from moving by generous rent-control policies and public-housing programmes.

Research by Peter Rupert of the University of California at Santa Barbara and Etienne Wasmer of Sciences Po in Paris suggests that housing-market frictions may account for about half of the difference in mobility rates between Europe and America. The push for austerity across the euro zone may yield thinner public-housing subsidies: Spain cut housing benefits as part of its post-crash austerity plan, for example. But budget problems may actually increase governments' reliance on property taxes, making it less likely they will be cut.

However persistent the European Commission's demands for uniform labour-market treatment of all EU citizens, the red tape between national labour markets remains frustratingly thick. For those who are employed, changing countries often endangers national pension-scheme rights. Workers may lose part of the value of earned pension benefits or the right to continue accumulating generous benefits in their native country. And inconsistent application of laws on pension taxation means that residents run the risk of double taxation if they move. The commission routinely argues for greater pension portability. In April 2012 it also called for exportability of national unemployment benefits. It may seem curious to ask indebted governments to pay citizens to live on the dole in another country, yet increased employment should eventually result, as those who move find work.

Professional qualifications act as a further barrier to movement across borders. EU law states that qualifications from one member state should be valid in another, but in practice recognition often requires negotiating a tangle of local rules. The OECD notes that just seven out of more than 800 professions identified by the commission qualified for automatic recognition of qualifications across borders. In 2011 the commission proposed simplifications to recognition procedures, including a European "professional card" that would summarise relevant professional information. Progress has been slow.

Hurdles are highest for workers within the public sector. Such jobs are still occasionally reserved solely for nationals, even outside "sensitive" sectors. In 2005 2.5% of British teachers were non-nationals. That compared with 0.7% in Portugal, 0.4% in Greece and too few to count in Italy.

Raising these numbers is not easy, of course, despite a reported jump in demand for German-language tuition in peripheral economies. Job-seeking Europeans will never be as footloose as their American counterparts. But the gap can be narrowed. The periphery may now be the main target of structural reform, but streamlining relevant rules in the core economies would do as much to help euro-zone citizens.

April 2012

PART 2

Firms, jobs and pay

How the world works now

The gyrations of markets and woes of banks are far from the only global economic worries. Far more pressing for most people are their job prospects. Labour-market puzzles abound. Companies are changing in ways that have knock-on effects for both the economy and their employees. The hordes of unemployed need both continued growth and a labour market that can match them with jobs, but are unclear they will get it. Cash-strapped workers wonder when the days of decent pay rises might return.

This section starts with firms. Businesses themselves are an economic puzzle: Chapter 5 starts by summarising the work of Ronald Coase, an economist, who explained why managers set them up in the first place. Firms are changing shape: historical waves of mergers, which often follow slumps, explain why some have become so large. Although these new megafirms often seem strong, their rise is troublesome. Many are so large they are inefficient. Some are so big their failure can rupture an entire economy.

Healthy firms are crucial because of workers' biggest problem: unemployment. With the International Labour Organisation predicting that over 200 million adults will be unemployed by 2019, Chapter 6 looks at their prospects. It laments the number of unemployed young people in both America and the euro zone, and suggests that by encouraging the free flow of workers within countries joblessness could fall.

In an ideal world a good job brings plentiful pay and a decent amount of leisure time, too. Chapter 7 asks why that ideal is so far off. Not only have pay rises been scant, with the share of labour in total income falling, but workers in rich countries are taking less time off. Evidence shows that a simple response – a higher minimum wage – can lift pay without creating unemployment as long as the shifts are moderate. But the future of pay is likely to be more nuanced, with managers designing "performance wages" to reward good work, and the best deals paying not just cash but shares as well, turning workers into capitalists.

Miserable pay rises are made even more aggravating because those at the top of the distribution are doing so well, as Chapter 8, which studies inequality, shows. A study tracking surnames and income reveals just how little intergenerational mobility there is. And new research shows that inequality can have surprising causes, such as the rise of megafirms, and unexpected effects, such as more frequent financial crashes. The chapter concludes with an argument that policies to redistribute income can both pinch inequality and spur growth.

The global economy will need all the help it can get if the terrifying theory – secular stagnation – explained in Chapter 9 turns out to be true. The first article explains why the idea that the world might get stuck in a rut of low growth, low inflation and low investment was first posed in the 1930s, and why it is in fashion again. As well as rising inequality, demographic shifts and the problem of ageing societies are potential causes of economic stagnation. The final article is less gloomy: a long-run perspective of history suggests that stagnation might be short-lived.

5   Changing firms

Ronald Coase: one of the giants

Meet Ronald Coase, the economist who explained why firms exist

"I HAVE MADE NO INNOVATIONS in high theory," was how Ronald Coase modestly summed up his life's work. "My contribution to economics has been to urge the inclusion ... of features of the economic system so obvious that ... they have tended to be overlooked." Attention to the overlooked helped Mr Coase transform both law and economics.

Born in the London suburb of Willesden in 1910 to working-class parents, Mr Coase had an academic temperament and an interest in science but lacked a taste for mathematics, a flaw that might have kept him out of economics in later decades. He studied "commerce" at the London School of Economics (LSE), a course tailored to those destined for middle management ("a choice of occupation for which I was singularly ill-suited").

The degree included instruction in economics, and he quickly fell for the dismal science. A one-year travelling scholarship gave him the chance to apply what he had learned. He chose to tour America's industrial cities in the hope of answering a question that troubled him: why did companies exist?

Economists of the time were enthralled by the special magic of the price mechanism. In a free market, prices should adjust to allocate resources where they are most valued. A certain price for wool, for example, encourages farmers to raise sheep and bring wool to market to meet consumer demand. As more is produced and demand is sated the price falls, discouraging farmers from wasting time and resources producing unwanted goods. Yet whereas some parts of the economy rely on prices to guide materials and labour to their best uses, others do not. Within firms tasks are doled out by fiat and strategies are set by the politburo of the corporate board. Mr Coase wanted to know why.

As he watched American car plants in action, he realised that the existence of the firm compensated for a critical flaw in the price-setting mechanism. In the real world it is often costly for buyer and seller to arrive at a final price. "Transaction costs", like the need to negotiate or draw up contracts, prevent the price mechanism from working smoothly. Firms would exist, he reckoned, when it was cheaper and easier to co-ordinate activity within a centrally planned organisation than to spell out contract details for every step in the production process. Mr Coase first presented his proposition in a lecture in Dundee in 1932, at the tender age of 21. In 1937 he published "The Nature of the Firm", an article based on the Dundee lecture.

An entire field of research would eventually be built on this paper, but it garnered scant attention at first. Mr Coase bounced around British academia in the 1930s and 1940s, from Dundee to Liverpool and back to the LSE, researching the workings of public utilities as he went. In 1951 he migrated to America and proved similarly itinerant, until an article on radio-spectrum property rights caught the eye of scholars at the University of Chicago.

In 1959 he was invited to Chicago to air his views. His audience included future Nobel prizewinners like George Stigler and Milton Friedman: confident, room-commanding men sceptical of Mr Coase's conclusions. Over the course of a two-hour discussion the measured Mr Coase won them around. He was asked to write up his arguments and in 1961 produced "The Problem of Social Cost", another landmark text. By 1964 Mr Coase was on the University of Chicago's faculty.

His debates with the Chicago academics centred on market "externalities": economic choices that impose social costs or benefits on others. Factory pollution may disturb or poison nearby residents, for example. Earlier generations of economists diagnosed a market failure that governments could set to rights. The polluting factory does not face any costs from spouting black smoke over a town: the costs are "external" from its perspective. A tax on pollution would internalise the cost, however. The price mechanism would work once more, as the tax encouraged the factory's managers to reduce pollution to socially optimal levels.

Coase was clear

Mr Coase's work suggested another answer. In the world of theory, without transaction costs, no government intervention would be needed to address externalities. The factory owners and the residents could work out side-payments on their own. Residents might pay the factory to emit less or the factory might pay the town for leeway to pollute more. Either way an efficient outcome should result without government help. This Panglossian view became known as the Coase Theorem. (Post-Soviet "shock therapists" who supported rapid privatisation in the belief that markets would reallocate resources handed to oligarchs were sometimes accused of "vulgar Coase-ism".)

Yet Mr Coase himself recognised life is more complex than theory. Neither private bargaining nor a pollution tax can make a market perfectly efficient given transaction costs like the expense of monitoring a factory's emissions. Mr Coase reckoned the law had a critical economic responsibility: to minimise the disruptive effect of these costs on markets. A system of clear and easily transferable property rights (in this case, the right to pollute) can play a role like that of the firm, allowing useful economic activity to take place that might otherwise be gummed up by the hassle of negotiating and enforcing contracts. His insight revolutionised policy. Tradable emissions permits, which helped eliminate acid rain as an environmental problem in America, are a direct application of his work.

Almost 70 years after that first Dundee lecture Mr Coase won the Nobel prize in economics. "A scholar must be content with the knowledge that what is false in what he says will soon be exposed," he noted in his speech. "As for what is true, he can count on ultimately seeing it accepted, if only he lives long enough."

September 2013

Surf's up: merger waves

Merger waves mean that markets can consolidate rapidly

IN 1900 AMERICA had around 500 carmakers; by 1908 it had 200. In 1960 Britain had 16 banks; ten years later it had just six. In both cases, this rapid consolidation came about because of a flurry of mergers. From soft drinks to steelworks, plenty of other industries have seen similar patterns. Mergers happen in waves, so the number of firms collapses suddenly rather than dwindling over time. And the next one may soon crest.

The first merger wave in America peaked in 1899. During that wave, which lasted for five years, 700 mining and milling companies disappeared, along with 500 food retailers. The next four waves in America occurred in the 1920s and 1960s and again in the late 1980s and 1990s (see Figure 5.1, left side). Other countries have experienced the same phenomenon.

Research suggests that shocks start merger waves. Some firms are quicker than others to respond to the disruption, or suffer less damage. This divergence allows the strong to mop up the weak. As far back as 1937 Ronald Coase, an economist, proposed that technological shifts like the telephone and the telegraph would lead to fewer, larger firms. In the late 1990s, waves of mergers in computer manufacturing and business services, markets which were disrupted by the internet, are cases in point.

Other types of shock are important, too. A slump in demand can leave factories and stores idle, so there is spare capacity in an industry. In a 2004 paper Gregor Andrade, now of AQR Capital Management, and Erik Stafford of Harvard Business School examined data for 1970–94. They found that merger waves were most likely when an industry shock had resulted in spare capacity, prompting efficient firms to take over weaker ones. In another paper Mr Andrade and Mr Stafford showed that regulatory shocks are important, too; the shock of deregulation triggered many deals in the late 1990s.

Once one merger occurs, copycat transactions in the same

FIG 5.1 **Cresting**

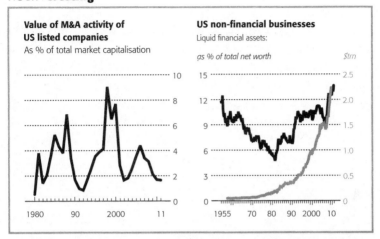

Value of M&A activity of US listed companies
As % of total market capitalisation

US non-financial businesses
Liquid financial assets:
as % of total net worth   *$trn*

Sources: Federal Reserve; Jay Ritter, University of Florida

industry become more likely. The first deal removes a competitor, potentially raising the profitability of all firms and making other targets look attractive to acquisitive bosses. More pessimistic firms observe the creation of a bigger rival, able to exploit economies of scale, and seek defensive unions. The sensible strategic response to one deal may therefore be another. A wave starts to form. Managers' personal incentives also play their part. Bosses attempt to time their acquisitions well, buying firms with lower price-earnings ratios than their own when the targets' prices are depressed. That mechanically increases the acquirer's earnings per share, boosting bosses' bonuses. Since competing managers use similar valuation models, they may decide the time is right to splash out just as their rivals do.

Shocks and strategies explain how merger waves start within an industry, but not why different industries' waves occur at the same time. A paper by Jarrad Harford of the University of Washington Business School provides an answer. Mr Harford looks at 35 merger waves in 28 industries between 1981 and 2000, and finds that financial conditions are important, too. Even if a shock has occurred, managers still need to raise money for a merger. That might be debt but it could also be hard cash. Mr Harford finds firms that built up large piles of cash on their balance-sheets were more active acquirers.

These findings suggest conditions are now aligning for a perfect merger wave. A global shock has hit most industries, and there is plenty of spare capacity. Many businesses, particularly in Europe, face deregulation as lagging economies seek to boost competitiveness through structural reform. The merger impulse is there. Many firms are already sitting atop piles of cash (see Figure 5.1, right side). Industries that are fragmented, have firms with dispersed levels of performance and have been hit hardest by shocks are most likely to see mergers. Gold mining could be one candidate: the ten biggest gold-mining companies have just 40% of the market, and efficiency varies greatly. Banking and construction also tick the same boxes.

The macroeconomic implications of another great merger wave are likely to be positive overall. From a firm's perspective a merger is a form of investment: buying a rival provides instant capacity. And although mergers do not increase aggregate capacity, they move it to more efficient players. This can lower prices and raise output. As for firms operating in industries that have already consolidated or that have exhausted economies of scale, they may seek to apply their skills in new industries, seeking economies of scope instead. The evidence on the benefits of these "conglomerate mergers" is more mixed, but would still be better than excessive corporate saving.

Deal or no deal

What about the concern that a burst of mergers will crimp competition? Even very concentrated industries can be brutally fought over. Just three big rivals can be enough for a price war, as American car companies showed in 2005. And profitable firms can be slow to spot changes in technology and tastes, allowing new entrants a foothold. The American coffee market is a good example. In 1987 General Foods, Procter & Gamble and Nestlé supplied about 90% of the market. Then Starbucks arrived, shifting tastes and toppling incumbents. As long as barriers to entry are low, the threat of newcomers should keep large firms' pricing keen and standards high. If not, antitrust regulators can step in.

There is another worry, though, brought home by the financial crisis. The biggest companies have state-like characteristics. They employ millions and manage vast pension pots. Between 2008 and 2009 the American government was forced to invest $80 billion in General Motors and Chrysler. When the waters from the next merger wave recede, the "too big to fail" problem might stretch far beyond banking.

May 2012

Megafirms: land of the corporate giants

Economies of scale run out at a certain point. The largest firms in America may be beyond it

SOME THINGS ONLY get bigger. From boats and planes to skyscrapers and shopping malls, size records are routinely broken. Companies are operating at record scale, too. But if the trend towards growing ever larger is clear, the economics of bigness are far murkier. In some cases, like boats, greater size still promises greater efficiency, as fixed costs are spread over higher output. In others, like buildings, the gains from scale may be running out. Where do firms lie on this spectrum?

Container ships provide a good example of economies of scale in action. Introduced in the late 1950s, the first ships could carry 480 twenty-foot equivalent (TEU) containers. By 2006 the biggest could shift 15,000 TEUs. Cost factors explain the rise: transport adds nothing to the final value of a good so cost minimisation is all-important. Since the shipping cost per container keeps on falling as ship size rises, container ships are set to keep growing. A new range of 18,000 TEU ships was launched by Maersk in 2013. Per container they are the most efficient yet.

But it is possible to exhaust the savings that come with size. Between 1931 and 2007 the record for the world's tallest building rose from 381 to 828 metres. At first, as buildings get taller, the fixed cost of land per square metre of office space falls. But other height-related changes offset this saving. The wind force on a building rises exponentially with height, meaning design becomes more complex and costly. A 2010 study by Steve Watts and Neal Kalita of Davis Langdon, a consultancy, shows that construction costs per square metre rise as a building gets taller. In addition, the useable space per extra floor starts to fall as the central "core" of the building gets bigger. Most very tall buildings are at an inefficient scale, propelled skyward for reasons of prestige rather than efficiency. If developers were focused on cost alone, they would opt for clusters of mid-rise buildings.

FIG 5.2 **Firming up**

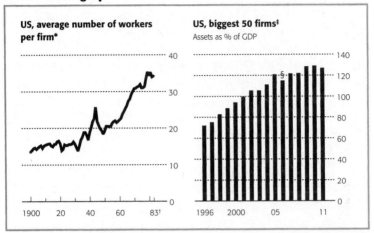

US, average number of workers per firm*

US, biggest 50 firms‡
Assets as % of GDP

*Non-farm   †Series ends
‡By assets, based on biggest 500 firms by revenue, excluding government-sponsored enterprises
§New series
Sources: Historical Statistics of the United States; *Fortune*; Bloomberg; IMF; *The Economist*

Businesses have also been getting bigger. A snapshot of the American economy shows huge dispersion in firm size: around a third of American workers are employed by one of the 6 million small firms with fewer than 100 workers, and another third are employed by one of the 980 large firms that have over 10,000 workers. But the long-run trend seems to be towards bigger companies. In a 1978 paper Robert Lucas of the University of Chicago documented how average firm size in America had increased over a 70-year period (see Figure 5.2, left side).

And at the very top end of the scale, the world's biggest firms keep on getting bigger. This can happen gradually, as firms outdo their rivals, or suddenly as firms merge. Indeed, mergers are particularly important in explaining gigantism. In the 15 years to 2012 the assets of the top 50 American companies have risen from around 70% of American GDP to around 130% (see Figure 5.2, right side). All of the top ten American firms were involved in at least one large merger or acquisition between 1987 and 2012.

So are businesses like boats or buildings: are they seeking out economies of scale, or are they too big to be efficient? One way to answer this question is to estimate how output levels influence the costs of production in a competitive industry. This relationship – known as a "cost function" – can be tricky to establish because firms often have multiple inputs and outputs. Take farming. Estimating a cost function requires complex information on how each farm's outputs (milk, meat and crops) and inputs (labour, energy, feed and capital) interact.

But once the cost function has been pinned down, it can be used to identify scale economies. If average costs fall as a firm of a given size grows bigger, this suggests economies of scale exist for firms of that size. Results vary by industry. American dairy farms, for example, have been getting bigger but a 2009 paper shows there are still economies of scale to exploit, especially at those many farms with fewer than 200 cattle. By contrast, rail-industry studies show dwindling economies of scale over time as companies have grown. Overall, estimated cost functions suggest the limits of scale may have been reached for some very large firms.

Merger studies support this. The "winner's curse" describes the phenomenon of mergers destroying value for the shareholders of an acquiring firm. Research by McKinsey, a consultancy, provides one explanation: close to two-thirds of managers overestimate the economies of scale a merger will deliver, often overegging the benefits by more than 25%. Size can even drive costs up, if firms get too big to manage efficiently.

Top dogs and fat cats

If size does not keep driving down costs, why do big firms keep expanding? One possibility is that they are seeking to boost profits not by driving down costs but by raising prices. Buying up rivals softens competition and enables firms to charge more. American antitrust regulators looked back at past health-care mergers and found that prices rose significantly after some deals. Another view is that mergers are driven by something other than profit. The "empire-building" theory holds that managers are out to increase the scale of their business whatever the cost in terms of creeping inefficiencies.

State safety nets can distort incentives, too. America's leading three car manufacturers have all grown through mergers: each of them employs over 50,000 workers, and the government balked at letting them fail during the crisis. Some firms may be growing not to lower costs but to receive the comfort of implicit state support. A 2011 paper by Federal Reserve staff supports this conclusion, suggesting banks pay a premium to merge if the tie-up gives them "too-big-to-fail" status. None of these reasons for operating at a vast size is benign. All suggest that antitrust authorities should be much more sceptical about mergers that claim to be justified because of economies of scale.

November 2012

The goliaths: big firms and volatility

The fate of large firms helps explain economic volatility

IN DECEMBER 2004 Microsoft paid a massive $33 billion dividend to its shareholders. The largest payment of its kind, it made up 6% of the increase in Americans' personal income that year. Examples of how big firms can have a big impact do not come much starker. These kinds of firm-specific shocks are typically excluded from economists' models, which assume that individual businesses' ups and downs tend to cancel each other out. Yet to understand how things like trade and GDP evolve, tracking the biggest companies is essential.

At first sight, the numbers seem to justify taking a top-down view. The business world is huge: America has around 27 million firms, Britain 4.8 million. Each country trades with hundreds of other countries across hundreds of industries, producing thousands of country–industry trade links. The global network runs to the millions. Because economies are built of millions of firms and trading relationships, each seems like a speck of dust: individual companies and export channels should not matter. This suggests that only common shocks can explain aggregate fluctuations: a workers' strike at one firm is not enough, but a general strike is.

Yet aggregate shocks do not explain volatility very well. A 2007 Bank of Spain paper studies OECD countries' trade balances. Common shocks (to whole countries or global industries) explain only 45% of the variations. Hunting for the cause of the other 55% of trade fluctuations, the authors used finer data on 8,260 country–industry "flows" (59 industries and 140 trading partners) for each OECD member. The data show that the picture of trade as millions of links is inaccurate; in fact, flows are extremely concentrated. Most links are unimportant. For America 99% of trade flows accounted for just 25% of trade. But a few are vital: for the average OECD country the 25 main country–industry flows explain two-thirds of trade, and the 100 largest 85%.

Even such detailed data mix lots of firms. The flow of cars between

America and Japan includes GM, Ford and Chrysler with Toyota, Nissan and Honda. So the researchers dug down another level to study individual companies. In a case study for Japan they found yet more concentration: the top five Japanese firms accounted for 20% of exports. That suggests that trade volatility, an aggregate statistic, could stem from just one firm's behaviour.

Some companies are certainly big enough to have that sort of effect. In America the 2008 census showed that 981 firms with 10,000 or more staff account for a quarter of all jobs. Of Italy's 4.6 million firms, 96% are "micro" SMEs (small and medium-sized enterprises) with fewer than ten people; a giant like Fiat, a carmaker, sits at the other end of the scale. Samsung alone notched up 17% of South Korea's exports in 2011. Finland is perhaps the most extreme example, with Nokia, a telecoms titan, contributing 20% of exports and 25% of GDP growth on its own between 1998 and 2007.

This is a problem for the top-down view of the economy. A 2011 paper by Xavier Gabaix of New York University explains how diversification works when firms are independent and their sizes follow a regular "bell-shaped" distribution. Imagine an economy where one firm produces everything: its volatility of earnings determines volatility in GDP. But as the number of firms grows GDP volatility shrinks, because firms' shocks cancel out. With 100 firms, volatility falls to a tenth of the level in a one-firm economy; with 1 million firms, it falls to a thousandth. Since there are more firms than this, company-specific shocks disappear.

That's the theory, at any rate. When the distribution of firms has "fat tails" (ie, there are more very small firms and very big ones) the theoretical relationship breaks down. An economy now needs 22,000 firms for volatility to fall to a tenth of the level in a one-firm economy (there would never be enough firms for it to fall to a thousandth). The logic of diversification fails when companies are sufficiently large. Firm-specific shocks do matter.

Mr Gabaix tests this new "granular" theory against data for the largest 100 American firms between 1951 and 2008. Stylised facts support his hypothesis. There is a fat tail of very big firms: the 100 largest had sales equivalent to 35% of GDP in 2009, up from 30% in the mid-1980s. Their performance is volatile: sales fluctuate by an average of 12% a year. And the correlations between firms are low, suggesting shocks are firm-specific rather than economywide. Next Mr Gabaix examines how well shocks involving these big firms explain changes in GDP. Very well, it turns out. Up to 48% of the volatility of American GDP can be traced to the performance of individual big firms.

On the rocks

The importance of the goliaths extends to trade. A widely held view is that trade lowers volatility: exporting to more markets means greater diversification. But in a 2012 paper Julian di Giovanni of the IMF and Andrei Levchenko of the University of Michigan find that more foreign trade exposes economies more to the fortunes of large firms, since they trade disproportionately.

Central bankers should take note. Mr Gabaix shows that taking account of firm-specific shocks can help improve economic forecasts. The models that determine economywide decisions might be improved by looking at how big firms are doing. There is also something to chew on for governments. The granular approach shows that what is good for GM really is good for America. But the converse also applies: when big firms do badly, everyone suffers. Ford, GM and Chrysler employ close to 0.6 million people. When markets tanked in late 2008, they successfully tapped the taxpayer for billions in bailout money. The problems of being "too big to fail" stretch far beyond banking.

June 2013

Big firms and competition: corporate sardines

How incumbent firms pack markets to deter entry

THE MODERN HIGH STREET can give an overwhelming sense of déjà vu. Fans trundling to the football stadium of Tottenham Hotspur, a team from north London, pass six William Hill bookmakers on the main approach. Tourists traipsing along a half-mile stretch of 23rd Street in New York pass five Starbucks outlets. In Tokyo, 7-Eleven boasts 15 stores within a similar distance of Shinjuku station. The crush of chain stores frustrates those who like one-off boutiques. Economists fret for another reason: firms may be cramming markets in order to keep rivals out.

One of the first studies of the way firms compete for space was published in 1929 by Harold Hotelling, then of Stanford University. He showed that firms face trade-offs: locate too near a rival and ferocious competition hits profits; edge too far away and too large a chunk of the market is lost. Since the trade-off will vary by market, Hotelling's theory explained why firms in some industries cluster, while others scatter.

When firms own multiple outlets new tactics are possible and new trade-offs arise. If a franchise adds a new outlet it will "cannibalise" the profits of existing ones, pinching its own customers as well as rivals'. But there are upsides: more outlets soak up demand, so that outsiders' gains from entering fall. When there are big costs to setting up shop, "pre-emption" can keep rivals out.

This helps explain not just the physical proximity of some firms' outlets, but also the similarity of products sold by a single company. Breakfast cereals are an example: in 1950 America's six big producers offered around 25 types of cereal; by 1972 it was around 80. Trust-busters suspected that the proliferation was not just a response to shoppers' varied tastes. Rather, the market was being crammed with options in order to reduce the "space" for new entrants.

If anything, worries about proliferation are greater today, as waves of mergers have left fewer, larger firms. Ubiquitous chains like 7-Eleven and Starbucks face protests when new stores open. To establish exactly how firms choose a location, a 2013 paper by Mitsuru Igami and Nathan Yang of Yale University tests a simple market: burgers. First, the authors trawled through archived telephone directories to track the number and location of burger joints in Canada between 1970 and 2005. In the 256 local markets they identified, the average number of outlets rose over that period from 1 to 2.5 as five big chains, including Burger King, McDonald's and Wendy's, expanded.

The researchers' statistical tests confirm the theory: if a rival burger joint is already in place, the return falls; own-brand cannibalisation hurts too. The impact of location on profits was particularly strong between 1970 and 1988 (when markets were first filling up) and in Vancouver (where there are few burger joints), suggesting a fiercer race when there is space to play for.

Despite cannibalisation, opening multiple outlets might be profitable for a chain as a whole if that keeps rivals at bay. To test this theory, the researchers modelled the number of stores in each market that would have yielded the highest profits for McDonald's, had it and its competitors reacted only to variables like income and population, and ignored one another's presence. They concluded it would never have opened a new joint in a market where it already had two outlets. Yet about half of openings by McDonald's between 1970 and 2005 fit that description, suggesting they can be pinned on pre-emption.

Different products lend themselves to different forms of competition for space, as a paper published in 2011 by Nathan Wilson, an economist at America's Federal Trade Commission, shows. Mr Wilson collects financial data on hotels in Texas, supplemented by data on quality, location and brand. Plotting them on a map allows him to identify 94 separate markets. Looking across the Lone Star state as a whole suggests concentration, with six firms accounting for 91% of the branded hotels in the sample.

Yet there is little geographic clumping. A new hotel in a Texan city is much more likely to be an outlet of a brand not already present, rather than a twin. Mr Wilson's analysis explains why. Customers tend to favour particular brands. This makes pre-emptive investment to fill the market less worthwhile: since an incumbent has its own natural customer base, a rival's entry dents profits by only 5%. For the same reason, opening a twin is painful: cannibalisation means a 10–12% profit drain.

Instead, hotel chains seem to "fill" the market another way. Rather than opening lots of the same joint, they open differentiated lodgings, with the six largest hotel groups operating 32 brands. Though some of these vary in quality, many compete head-to-head: Courtyard and Fairfield, both owned by Marriott, cater to similar budgets, as do Comfort Inn, Econo Lodge and Quality Inn, all part of Choice Hotels. Mr Wilson finds that this approach softens cannibalisation, and can make pre-emption a more profitable strategy.

Blame the shoppers, not the shops

Although this number crunching gives a good picture of how location strategies can dissuade entry, it is not clear that regulators should fret. Clearly, the underlying motive – to keep rivals out – is the sort of thing antitrust watchdogs are supposed to worry about. Yet to achieve that aim, the big chains use means that their punters value. In markets where customers value proximity over brand, outlets mushroom; when shoppers like more options, differentiated brands proliferate. Those that would like a rustic high street packed with artisans should blame their fellow shoppers. To keep rivals out, a firm has to mop up demand. That means giving customers what they want.

May 2014

Youth unemployment: generation jobless

Around the world almost 300 million 15- to 24-year-olds are not working. What has caused this epidemic of joblessness? And what can abate it?

HELDER PEREIRA is a young man with no work and few prospects: a 21-year-old who failed to graduate from high school and lost his job on a building site. With his savings about to run out, he went to his local employment centre in the Paris suburb of Sevran to sign on for benefits and to get help finding something to do. He'll get the cash. Work is another matter. Youth unemployment in Sevran is over 40%.

A continent away in Athlone, a gritty Cape Town suburb, Nokhona, a young South African mother of two, lacks a "matric" or high-school qualification, and has been out of work since her contract as a cleaner in a coffee shop expired. She hopes for a job as a maid, and has sought help from DreamWorker, a charity that tries to place young jobseekers in work. A counsellor helps Nokhona brush up her interview skills. But the jobless rate among young black South Africans is probably around 55%.

Official figures assembled by the International Labour Organisation say that 76 million young people are unemployed, or 6% of all 15- to 24-year-olds. But going by youth inactivity, which includes all those who are neither in work nor in education, things look even worse. The OECD counts 26 million young people in the rich world as "NEETs": not in employment, education or training. A World Bank database compiled from households shows more than 260 million

FIG 6.1 **Idle hands**
Youth unemployment and inactivity*

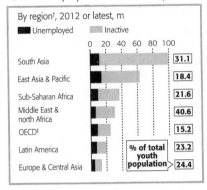

By region†, 2012 or latest, m
■ Unemployed   ▨ Inactive

South Asia	31.1
East Asia & Pacific	18.4
Sub-Saharan Africa	21.6
Middle East & north Africa	40.6
OECD‡	15.2
Latin America	23.2
Europe & Central Asia	24.4

% of total youth population

*15–24 year olds not in education
†Regions exclude OECD countries
‡Not in education or training
Sources: OECD; World Bank; *The Economist*

young people in developing economies are similarly "inactive". *The Economist* calculates that, all told, almost 290 million are neither working nor studying: almost a quarter of the planet's youth (see Figure 6.1).

If the figures did not include young women in countries where they are rarely part of the workforce, the rate would be lower; South Asian women account for over a quarter of the world's inactive youth, though in much of the rich world young women are doing better in the labour force than men.

On the other hand, many of the "employed" young have only informal and intermittent jobs. In rich countries more than a third, on average, are on temporary contracts which make it hard to gain skills. In poorer ones, according to the World Bank, a fifth are unpaid family labourers or work in the informal economy. All in all, nearly half of the world's young people are either outside the formal economy or contributing less productively than they could.

Young people have long had a raw deal in the labour market. Two things make the problem more pressing now. The financial crisis and its aftermath had an unusually big effect on them. Many employers sack the newest hires first, so a recession raises youth joblessness disproportionately. In Greece and Spain over a sixth of the young population are without a job (see Figure 6.2). In 2013 the number of young people out of work in the OECD was almost a third higher than in 2007.

Second, the emerging economies that have the largest and fastest-growing populations of young people also have the worst-run labour markets. Almost half of the world's young people live in South Asia, the Middle East and Africa. They also have the highest share of young

FIG 6.2 **Turning grey**

Youth unemployment, including those in education and training, as % of population aged 15–24 years

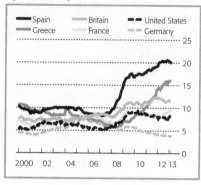

Sources: Eurostat; *The Economist*

people out of work or in the informal sector. The population of 15- to 24-year-olds in Africa is expected to rise by more than a third, to 276 million, by 2025.

In rich countries with generous welfare states this imposes a heavy burden on taxpayers. One estimate suggests that, in 2011, the economic loss from disengaged young people in Europe amounted to $153 billion, or more than 1% of GDP. And failure to employ the young not only lowers growth today. It also threatens it tomorrow.

A clutch of academic papers, based mainly on American statistics, shows that people who begin their careers without work are likely to have lower wages and greater odds of future joblessness than those who don't. A wage penalty of up to 20%, lasting for around 20 years, is common. The scarring seems to worsen fast with the length of joblessness and is handed down to the next generation, too.

The overall ageing of the population might blunt this effect by increasing demand for labour. But Japan's youth joblessness, which surged after its financial crisis in the early 1990s, has stayed high despite a fast fall in the overall workforce. A large class of *hikikomori* live with their parents, rarely leaving home and withdrawn from the workforce.

Economists know much less about "scarring" in poor countries. A big study by Richard Freeman of Harvard University and Wei Chi and Hongbin Li of Tsinghua University suggested any impact of joblessness on young Chinese earnings disappears after three years. But studies elsewhere have reported more troubling results. An analysis of the labour market a decade after Indonesia's financial crisis in 1997 suggested that young people who lost their jobs then were less likely to be in the workforce, and if they were, to have only informal jobs. A study of Argentina and Brazil found that young people who joined the labour force during a recession fared systematically worse as adults.

The damage may be less in dynamic economies and greatest in stagnant ones where unemployment comes in long bouts – as in the swathe of countries around the Mediterranean. Spain, France, Italy and Greece have some of the highest youth joblessness in the rich world. Morocco, Egypt and other north African and Middle Eastern countries have among the worst rates in the emerging world. Though they are at different stages of development, these countries all suffer disproportionately from employment's main curses: low growth, clogged labour markets and a mismatch between education and work.

Low growth is the most obvious of the three. Joblessness in southern Europe has surged as economies have shrunk. South Africa's high jobless rate is stoked by the fact that it is now one of Africa's slowest-growing economies. But rigid labour markets probably matter even more. Countries that let business cartels curb competition, with high taxes on labour and high minimum wages, and where regulations make it hard to fire people, are bad places for the young jobless. In India big factories and firms face around 200 state and federal laws governing work and pay. South Africa has notably strict laws on firing. Despite a few recent reforms, it is hard to fire older workers in southern European countries (young jobless, often living with parents whose livelihoods would be threatened, are wary of reform). North Africa and the Middle East suffer from a bloated and over-regulated public sector, heavy taxes on labour and high minimum wages.

Where are the skilled ones?

Economists are now emphasising a third problem: the mismatch between the skills that young people offer and the ones that employees need. Employers are awash with applications – but complain that they cannot find candidates with the right abilities. McKinsey, a consultancy, reports that only 43% of the employers in the nine countries that it has studied in depth (America, Brazil, Britain,

Germany, India, Mexico, Morocco, Saudi Arabia and Turkey) think that they can find enough skilled entry-level workers. Middle-sized firms (between 50 and 500 workers) have an average of 13 entry-level jobs empty.

The most obvious reason for the mismatch is poor basic education. In most advanced economies (whether growing or shrinking) the jobless rate for people with less than a secondary-school education is twice as high as for those with university degrees. But two more subtle reasons deserve attention, too.

Countries with the lowest youth jobless rates have a close relationship between education and work. Germany has a long tradition of high-quality vocational education and apprenticeships, which in recent years have helped it reduce youth unemployment despite only modest growth. Countries with high youth unemployment are short of such links. In France few high-school leavers have any real experience of work. In north Africa universities focus on preparing their students to fill civil-service jobs even as companies complain about the shortage of technical skills. The unemployment rate in Morocco is five times as high for graduates as it is for people with only a primary education. The legacy of apartheid means that young black South Africans often live and go to school many miles from where there are jobs.

Companies used to try to bridge that gap themselves by investing in training; today they do so less. Peter Capelli of Wharton business school argues that companies regard filling a job merely like buying a spare part: you expect it to fit. In 1979, he notes, young workers in large American firms received an average of two and half weeks of training a year. In 1991 only 17% reported receiving any training during the previous year. By 2011 only 21% reported gaining any during the past five. Accenture, a consultancy, says that only 21% of the 1,000 American workers they surveyed gained new skills from company-provided training between 2008 and 2013.

Mismatch and training gaps may explain why over the same period youth unemployment in flexible economies like America and Britain has risen more than in previous recessions and stayed high. Britain, which has one of the world's most flexible labour markets, has around 1 million NEETs. More than twice as many young

FIG 6.3 **A blighted generation**

Youths not in employment, education or training (NEETs), % of population aged 15–24 years

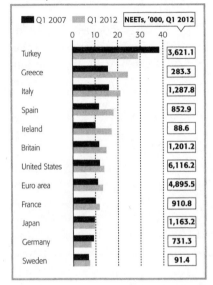

	NEETs, '000, Q1 2012
Turkey	3,621.1
Greece	283.3
Italy	1,287.8
Spain	852.9
Ireland	88.6
Britain	1,201.2
United States	6,116.2
Euro area	4,895.5
France	910.8
Japan	1,163.2
Germany	731.3
Sweden	91.4

Sources: OECD; *The Economist*

Britons (11.5% of the labour force) are unemployed as young Germans (3.9%) (see Figure 6.3). Some blame the minimum wage, but Britain also has a long-standing prejudice against practical education. In 2009 only about 8% of English employers trained apprentices compared with up to four times that number in the best continental European countries; 29% of British employers say work experience is "critical", but the share of British children who get a shot at it fell in the 15 years to 2013. Only 7% of pupils say they had any mentoring from a local employer and only 19% had visited one.

A more entrepreneurial British economy may have worsened the problem. The share of private-sector employees at big firms (with 250 or more workers) fell from 50% to 40% in 1998–2000. The share at micro-businesses (4 and fewer) rose from 11% to 22%. Small firms are less likely to provide apprenticeships or work experience.

Many countries are now trying to bridge the gap between education and work by upgrading vocational schools, encouraging standard schools to form closer relations with local companies, and embracing apprenticeships. In 2010 South Korea created a network of vocational "meister" schools – from the German for "master craftsman" – to reduce the country's shortage of machine operators and plumbers. The government pays the students' room and board as well as their tuition. It also refers to them as "young meisters" in order to counteract the country's obsession with academic laurels. In Britain some further-education colleges are embracing the principle that the best way to learn is to do: North Hertfordshire College has launched a business venture with Fit41ess, a low-cost gym. Bluegrass College in Kentucky and Toyota have created a replica of a car factory, where workers and students go to classes together.

But it is not enough simply to embrace the German model of training and apprenticeships: you need to update it. Some policymakers want to transform unemployment systems from safety nets into springboards, providing retraining and job placement. The Nordic countries have been to the fore in this, introducing "youth guarantees" – personalised plans to provide every young person with training or a job. When Germany liberalised its labour market in 2003–05 it also created new ways of getting people back into jobs. For example, to make someone who has been out of work for a long stretch more employable, the state will pay a big chunk of his wages for the first two years of a new job.

Practicality constrains poorer countries' ability to implement such active labour-market policies. The well-to-do Nordic countries found that they could hardly cope with the surge in unemployment after the crisis, despite spending up to 2% of GDP on training. Countries like Spain and Italy, with millions of unemployed people, could not hope to follow suit in a time of boom let alone one of austerity. Culture matters, too. Britain's Labour government raised the number of apprenticeships but diluted their quality in order to keep unemployment figures down. The coalition government tried to improve quality – but some firms merely relabelled existing training programmes in order to obtain taxpayers' money.

A deeper worry is that business is going through a particularly dramatic period of creative destruction. New technology is unleashing a storm of "disruptive innovation" which is forcing firms to rethink their operations from the ground up. Companies are constantly redesigning work – for example, they are separating routine tasks (which can be automated or contracted out) from skilled jobs. They are also constantly redesigning themselves by "upsizing", "downsizing" and "contracting out". The life expectancy of companies is declining, as is the job tenure of chief executives. Policymakers are finding it more difficult to adapt their labour-market institutions quickly enough.

However, some firms are taking more interest. IBM has sponsored a school in New York. McDonald's has an ambitious new training scheme. India's IT giant, Infosys, plans to train 45,000 new employees a year, including 14,000 at a time at its main campus in Mysore. Americana Group, a regional food and restaurant company with headquarters in Kuwait, allows trainees to spend up to half their time at work and the rest in college.

In addition, technology is providing solutions as well as exacerbating problems. It is greatly reducing the historically high cost of vocational education. "Serious games" can provide young people with a chance to gain "virtual" experience at minimum cost: McDonald's uses competitive video games to teach people how to use the till and interact with customers, for example. Mozilla, the creator of the Firefox web browser, has created an "open badges" initiative that allows people to gain recognition for programming skills. Technology is also making it easier to take work to people who live in work-deprived areas or who are shut out of the market by cartels. Amazon's Mechanical Turk, an internet marketplace, enables companies to hire workers to perform simple tasks such as identifying people in photographs. They can take part from anywhere.

It is hard to be optimistic about a problem that is blighting the lives of so many people. But it is perhaps time to be a bit less pessimistic. Policymakers know what to do to diminish the problem – ignite growth, break down cartels and build bridges between education and work. New technology gives them powerful tools too. Countries that make the investments and choices needed to grapple with their unemployed youth could see some dramatic improvement ahead.

April 2013

Boosting employment: go for the churn

The number of job-to-job moves by American workers tells a bleak story

FIGURES ON EMPLOYMENT tend to encourage a black-or-white view of an economy. Either conditions are worsening and firms are shedding workers, as they did by the hundreds of thousands in 2008 and 2009, or times are improving and businesses are creating new jobs. Spirits leapt on February 3rd 2012 on news that America's private businesses boosted their payrolls by 257,000 jobs in January, capping the country's best 12-month employment performance in the private sector for over five years. But the headline figures represent just the tip of a large labour-market iceberg. Data provided by the relatively new Jobs Openings and Labour Turnover Survey (JOLTS) illuminate these depths.

Even in the darkest of days, labour markets remain busy. Growing firms hire to expand and even shrinking businesses seek out workers to fill important vacant positions. In December 2008, for instance, overall American employment dropped by nearly 700,000 jobs. Yet in that month more workers – over 4.1 million in total – were hired into new positions than in December of the previous year, when net payrolls grew by 203,000. During a relatively placid economic period like the mid-2000s, about 65% of all hiring is associated with what economists have dubbed "churn" – the job-to-job movement of workers through the labour force, which neither adds to nor subtracts from total employment. Of the 12 million or so hires that occurred in a typical pre-recession quarter, some 8 million came from firms luring workers away from other firms.

Churn is a mechanism by which labour markets reallocate workers towards more efficient ends. In the typical job-to-job move (that is, without any intervening stint of unemployment) an American worker can expect a rise in wages of over 8%. This gain represents, at least in part, an improvement in productivity. As workers obtain skills and find better job matches, their output and earnings rise. And as

FIG 6.4 **A slow convalescence**
US labour market

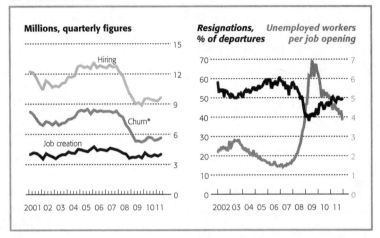

*Job-to-job employee moves
Sources: "Hiring, Churn and the Business Cycle" by Edward Lazear and James Spletzer,
NBER Working Paper, 2011; Bureau of Labour Statistics

firms obtain ever more suitable labour, they can afford to pay higher wages. In this way, the churning of the labour market contributes to growth in the potential output of the economy.

Although this ebb and flow is always happening, its strength is subject to the forces of the business cycle. When hard times hit, workers are less likely to make the leap from one firm to another. And when employees do move, firms are often reluctant to fill the freshly vacated positions. In an analysis Edward Lazear of Stanford University and James Spletzer from the Bureau of Labour Statistics examine how the recent recession affected these job-to-job moves. Just 9 million workers were hired in the second quarter of 2009 – the last of the recession – down from 12.8 million in the fourth quarter of 2007, a fall of about 30%. About 80% of this decline in hiring was attributable to a fall in churn rather than a decline in job creation (see Figure 6.4, left side). The number of workers voluntarily leaving a job fell by nearly 40%, for instance. The pace of job creation in the economy slowed sharply, it is true, but most of the hiring chill can be attributed to a decline in churn.

A freeze of this sort matters. Based on the typical wage gain from job-to-job moves, Mr Lazear and Mr Spletzer estimate the efficiency cost of reduced labour-market churn during the crisis at about 0.4% of GDP a year between the onset of recession in December 2007 and the middle of 2011. That is the equivalent of $208 billion of lost output – a small hit compared with the impact of the recession itself but a meaningful and underappreciated economic cost of prolonged labour-market weakness.

This cost falls disproportionately on the young. Individuals who graduate from college and enter the labour force during a typical recession can expect an initial earnings loss of about 9% (compared with what they might expect in normal circumstances). This decline can be mitigated and eventually eliminated by leaps from firm to firm, through which young workers obtain new skills and find ever better ways to use their talents. That process is frustrated by a general slowing of labour-market churn.

A pickup in hiring alone is not enough to grant the labour market a clean bill of health, according to this analysis. Just as important is whether workers feel comfortable leaving the security of an old job for the prospect of higher returns in a new one. If a falling unemployment rate does not translate into more risk-taking among workers in jobs, then the labour market may be further from normality than is appreciated.

Quit to get ahead

America is doing better than it was. The number of unemployed workers per job opening – a measure of labour-market tightness – has fallen from a peak of around seven workers to below four. That is contributing to greater job-to-job movement. The share of resignations in total job departures, which sank from nearly 60% to under 40% during the recession, is back at 50% (see Figure 6.4, right side). Yet there is still a long way to go. As of the second quarter of 2011, churn was just 8% higher than it was at its trough.

Firms' hiring behaviour remains subdued. When there are plenty of jobless workers to go around it becomes much easier for firms to find qualified individuals for open positions, and less important for them to lure employees from other businesses. But as markets tighten companies raise what economists call "recruiting intensity". Work by Steven Davis of the University of Chicago, Jason Faberman of the Federal Reserve Bank of Chicago and John Haltiwanger of the University of Maryland suggests that firms' recruiting efforts – as represented by advertising spending, hiring standards and compensation packages – explain about a third of the variation in the pace at which vacancies are filled. Recruiting intensity dropped by nearly 22% during the recession, they reckon, and has since rebounded by less than 6%.

New employment growth is most welcome, of course. But until employment churn returns to pre-crisis levels, the costs of America's recession will continue to mount.

February 2012

Inflation and jobs: the price of getting back to work

Inflation may help determine how fast labour markets recover from recession

IT IS SOMETHING OF A MYSTERY, and not as happy a one as it sounds. In both America and Britain, the unemployment rate fell far faster during 2013 than the tepid recoveries in both countries seem to justify. The pace of the decline caused difficulties for Mark Carney, the governor of the Bank of England, and Janet Yellen, head of America's Federal Reserve. Both central banks gave "forward guidance" about when they might consider raising interest rates tied to levels of unemployment that will now be reached much sooner than either expected. Understanding the surprisingly quick fall and responding to it appropriately may be the pivotal task of the two central bankers' tenure.

On the face of things, Britain's drop looks the more meaningful: it is down to rapid employment growth, whereas America's owes a great deal to frustrated workers leaving the labour force. The British and American economies have diverged markedly in recent years. Output in both economies tumbled sharply in 2008-09. Yet America's GDP bounced back relatively quickly, reaching a new high by early 2011. Employment in America, by contrast, suffered a more dramatic decline and a weaker recovery. In Britain the trends were reversed. Output suffered a brutal decline and a feeble rebound, prompting fear of a looming employment disaster. Yet the downturn in employment was unexpectedly mild (see Figure 6.5, left side).

This divergence is commonly explained with nods to Britain's "productivity puzzle". America, the thinking goes, suffered a "normal" recession. Its low rate of inflation is symptomatic of weak demand, which can account for its output loss and much of the shortfall in jobs. In Britain, in contrast, tumbling demand has been matched by a strange decline in workers' productivity. Falling productivity

FIG 6.5 **A tale of two recoveries**

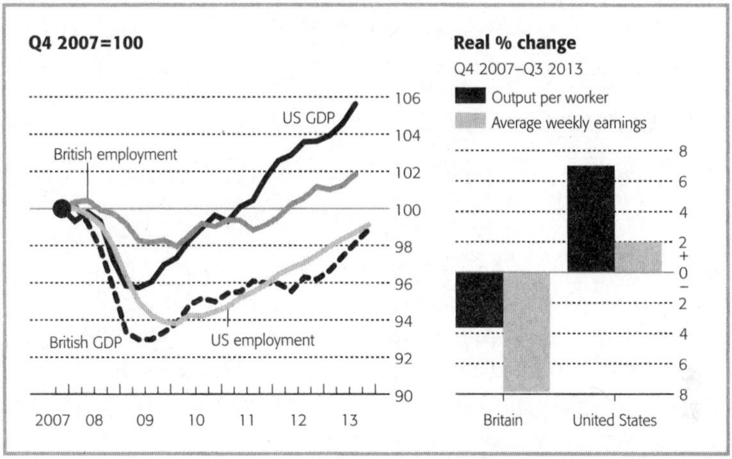

Sources: BEA; BLS; ONS; *The Economist*

cushioned the economy against large job losses, since more workers were needed to do the same amount of work. But it also reflected a loss of productive capacity, the evidence for which was stubbornly high inflation. Between 2007 and 2013 annual inflation in Britain was almost twice as high as in America, at 3.1% to 1.8%.

This explanation just deepens the mystery, however, for why should a nation of workers suddenly become worse at producing things? Bill Martin and Robert Rowthorn of the University of Cambridge argue that those puzzling over Britain's productivity may have causation the wrong way round: wages did not fall in response to declining productivity; declining productivity was instead a consequence of falling real wages.

The change in the real wage is simply the change in the nominal wage – the one listed in the contract or on the payslip – adjusted for inflation. Since the end of 2007, nominal wages in Britain have risen by about 1.6% a year on average. But annual inflation of more than 3% over that period generated a cumulative decline in real wages of 7.8%. British workers became cheaper relative to the prices of goods and services (see Figure 6.5, right side).

Moderately high British inflation may therefore have been the difference between a jobless recovery and a job-filled one. Studies suggest that nominal wages are generally "sticky": it is hard to make existing workers take a pay cut in hard times, due to contract requirements, issues of worker morale and other complications. Moderate inflation rates can restore wage flexibility by eroding the real purchasing power of a given wage rate. Messrs Martin and Rowthorn reckon that lower real wages encouraged firms to use more labour and less capital in production. That caused productivity to fall but propped up employment.

America's nominal wage growth has been similar to Britain's, but inflation has been far milder. As a result, America's real wages have actually gone up since late 2007, by about 2%. That, in turn, may have discouraged hiring and encouraged firms to squeeze higher levels of productivity from existing workers.

Wages v jobs

A working paper from the National Bureau of Economic Research by Mark Bils and Yongsung Chang of the University of Rochester and Sun-Bin Kim of Yonsei University in South Korea supports that view. The authors find evidence that in industries with inflexible wages firms respond to weak demand by pushing workers to produce more. Productivity in such industries rises in recessions, reducing the real cost of employing a given worker. But because firms can then use fewer employees to meet reduced demand, they have little incentive to hire.

The authors suggest that when sticky wages are a constraint, a given shock to demand should produce a large drop in employment. In America low inflation impeded wage adjustment, leading to rising productivity and weak employment growth. In Britain higher inflation kept wages in check, encouraging firms to hire despite weak demand.

Uncovering why reduced wages should be necessary to put people to work is a trickier matter. In a 2012 paper Guillermo Calvo and Pablo Ottonello of Columbia University and Fabrizio Coricelli of the Paris School of Economics blame financial havoc. After crises chastened banks are willing to lend only to firms with tangible capital – like buildings and equipment – that can be seized after a default. Firms that rely more on machines than labour therefore perform better in the recovery, pushing down demand for workers. Without a big drop in wages, weak demand for labour yields a jobless recovery. The economists examine data on financial crises since the second world war and find that post-crisis recoveries are jobless when inflation is low, but merely "wageless" when inflation is relatively high. Low inflation may help consumers in good times, but higher inflation is a useful shock absorber when recession strikes.

February 2014

7 Pay

Pay and economic growth: a shrinking slice

Labour's share of national income has fallen. The right remedy is to help workers, not punish firms

IMAGINE THE PROCEEDS of economic output as a pie, crudely divided between the wages earned by workers and the returns accrued to the owners of capital, whether as profits, rents or interest income. Until the early 1980s the relative sizes of those slices were so stable that their constancy became an economic rule of thumb. Much of modern macroeconomics simply assumes the shares remain the same. That stability provides the link between productivity and prosperity. If workers always get the same slice of the economic pie, then an improvement in their average productivity – which boosts growth – should translate into higher average earnings.

More recently, however, economics textbooks have been almost the only places where labour's share of national income remains constant. Over the past 30 years, the workers' take from the pie has shrunk across the globe. In America, their wages used to make up almost 70% of GDP; now the figure is 64%, according to the OECD. Some of the biggest declines have been in egalitarian societies such as Norway (where labour's share has fallen from 64% in 1980 to 55% in 2013) and Sweden (down from 74% in 1980 to 65% in 2013). A drop has also occurred in many emerging markets, particularly in Asia.

The scale and breadth of this squeeze are striking. And the consequences are ugly. Since capital tends to be owned by richer households, a rising share of national income going to capital worsens inequality. In countries where the gap in wages between high earners and the rest has also increased, the two effects compound each other. In America, the share of national income going to the bottom 99% of workers has fallen from 60% before the 1980s to 50%. When growth is sluggish, as it is now, these shifts mean that most workers are getting a smaller morsel of a smaller slice of a slow-growing pie.

Politically, that is dangerous, and it is producing a lot of predictably polarised debate. The left blames fat-cat firms and the weakness of unions for workers' declining share. Those on the right, if they acknowledge a problem at all, argue that the fault lies with big government and high taxes.

These explanations are hard to square with the fact that the shrinkage in labour's share of the pie has occurred in so many countries, with widely differing levels of unionisation and sizes of government. Indeed, studies comparing the trends in different countries' labour markets suggest that the sorts of things politicians argue about, from corporate-governance rules to trade-union laws, are not what really count here. Bigger global forces seem to be at work. Innovation, especially in information technology, has dramatically increased the wages of workers with the skills to harness it, while hitting others. It has also squeezed labour's overall share of the pie, as firms substitute ever-cheaper machines for less-skilled workers. Some economists also emphasise the role of globalisation, especially trade with China, in adding to the pinch.

All this points to the sorts of things policymakers can do to help. They should focus on improving the prospects of the low-paid and low-skilled. And they should aim to spread capital's gains more widely.

The goal should be to strengthen workers without hamstringing firms. Growth, rather than employment protection, is the priority. More work means a stronger labour market, which would bid up employees' slice, as it did in America in the 1990s when unemployment was at record lows. But even in a growing economy a worker competing with a machine can lose out. So education and training need a reboot too: a greater emphasis on technical subjects, from maths to mechanics, would help ensure that more workers are not replaced by machines but design and operate them.

The charms of popular capitalism

Other sensible reforms may seem counterintuitive. A cut in corporate tax rates is one: combined with a narrowing of the difference between tax rates on individuals' income from capital and from labour (which is often more heavily taxed), the result would be a more efficient system that promoted economic growth, and thus jobs. Policymakers could also think more creatively about broadening capital ownership, whether through pension reform or more privatisation. Paradoxical as it may sound, a good antidote to labour's falling share of national income would be to boost ordinary workers' share of capital.

November 2013

Pay and leisure time: nice work if you can get out

Why the rich now have less leisure than the poor

FOR MOST OF HUMAN HISTORY rich people had the most leisure. In *Downton Abbey*, a drama about the British upper classes of the early 20th century, one aloof aristocrat has never heard of the term "weekend": for her, every day is filled with leisure. On the flip side, the poor have typically slogged. Hans-Joachim Voth, an economic historian at the University of Zurich, shows that in 1800 the average English worker laboured for 64 hours a week. "In the 19th century you could tell how poor somebody was by how long they worked," says Mr Voth.

In today's advanced economies things are different. Overall working hours have fallen over the past century. But the rich have begun to work longer hours than the poor. In 1965 men with a college degree, who tend to be richer, had a bit more leisure time than men who had only completed high school. But by 2005 the college-educated had eight hours less of it a week than the high-school grads. Figures from the American Time Use Survey, released in 2013, show that Americans with a bachelor's degree or above work two hours more each day than those without a high-school diploma. Other research shows that the share of college-educated American men regularly working more than 50 hours a week rose from 24% in 1979 to 28% in 2006, but fell for high-school dropouts. The rich, it seems, are no longer the class of leisure.

There are a number of explanations. One has to do with what economists call the "substitution effect". Higher wages make leisure more expensive: if people take time off they give up more money. Since the 1980s the salaries of those at the top have risen strongly, while those below the median have stagnated or fallen. Thus rising inequality encourages the rich to work more and the poor to work less.

The "winner-takes-all" nature of modern economies may amplify the substitution effect. The scale of the global market means businesses that innovate tend to reap huge gains (think of YouTube, Apple and Goldman Sachs). The returns for beating your competitors can be enormous. Research from Peter Kuhn of the University of California, Santa Barbara, and Fernando Lozano of Pomona College shows that the same is true for highly skilled workers. Although they do not immediately get overtime pay for "extra" hours, the most successful workers, often the ones putting in the most hours, may reap gains from winner-takes-all markets. Whereas in the early 1980s a man working 55 hours a week earned 11% more than a man putting in 40 hours in the same type of occupation, that gap had increased to 25% by the turn of the millennium.

Economists tend to assume that the substitution effect must at some stage be countered by an "income effect": as higher wages allow people to satisfy more of their material needs, they forgo extra work and instead choose more leisure. A billionaire who can afford his own island has little incentive to work that extra hour. But new social mores may have flipped the income effect on its head.

The status of work and leisure in the rich world has changed since the days of *Downton Abbey*. Back in 1899 Thorstein Veblen, an American economist who dabbled in sociology, offered his take on things. He argued that leisure was a "badge of honour". Rich people could get others to do the dirty, repetitive work – what Veblen called "industry". Yet Veblen's leisure class was not idle. Rather they engaged in "exploit": challenging and creative activities such as writing, philanthropy and debating.

Veblen's theory needs updating, according to a 2014 paper from researchers at Oxford University. Work in advanced economies has become more knowledge-intensive and intellectual. There are fewer really dull jobs, like lift-operating, and more glamorous ones, like fashion design. That means more people than ever can enjoy "exploit" at the office. Work has come to offer the sort of pleasures that rich people used to seek in their time off. On the flip side, leisure is no longer a sign of social power. Instead it symbolises uselessness and unemployment.

The evidence backs up the sociological theory. The occupations in which people are least happy are manual and service jobs requiring little skill. Job satisfaction tends to increase with the prestige of the occupation. Research by Arlie Russell Hochschild of the University of California, Berkeley, suggests that as work becomes more intellectually stimulating, people start to enjoy it more than home life. "I come to work to relax," one interviewee tells Ms Hochschild. And wealthy people often feel that lingering at home is a waste of time. A study in 2006 revealed that Americans with a household income of more than $100,000 indulged in 40% less "passive leisure" (such as watching TV) than those earning less than $20,000.

Condemned to relax

What about less educated workers? Increasing leisure time probably reflects a deterioration in their employment prospects as low-skill and manual jobs have withered. Since the 1980s, high-school dropouts have fared badly in the labour market. In 1965 the unemployment rate of American high-school graduates was 2.9 percentage points higher than for those with a bachelor's degree or more. Today it is 8.4 points higher. "Less educated people are not necessarily buying their way into leisure," explains Erik Hurst of the University of Chicago. "Some of that time off work may be involuntary." There may also be change in the income effect for those on low wages. Information technology, by opening a vast world of high-quality and cheap home entertainment, means that low-earners do not need to work as long to enjoy a reasonably satisfying leisure.

April 2014

Minimum wages: the argument in the floor

Evidence is mounting that moderate minimum wages can do more good than harm

MINIMUM-WAGE LAWS have a long history and enduring political appeal. New Zealand pioneered the first national pay floor in 1894. America's federal minimum wage dates from 1938. Most countries now have a statutory pay floor – and the ranks are still swelling. Even Germany, one of the few big countries without, may at last introduce a national one. And in an era of budget austerity and widening inequality, the political temptation to prop up wages at the bottom by fiat may well grow.

Economists have tended to oppose minimum wages on the grounds that they reduce employment, hurting many of those they are supposed to help. Milton Friedman called them a form of discrimination against low-skilled workers. In standard models of competitive markets, anything that artificially raises the price of labour will curb demand for it, and the first to lose their jobs will be the least-skilled workers.

Yet economic theory allows for the possibility that wage floors can boost both employment and pay. If employers have monopsony power as buyers of labour and are able to set wages, for instance, they can keep pay below its competitive rate. Academic supporters of wage floors, mainly economists on the left, appealed to this logic. But most of their colleagues disagreed; and until about 1990, most empirical studies found that higher minimum wages cost jobs, particularly among young workers.

Then a pioneering case study by two noted labour economists, David Card and Alan Krueger, examined the response of fast-food restaurants to a rise in New Jersey's state minimum wage. It found that this had actually increased employment. The paper spawned a flood of similar "case-study" research, a flurry of revisionist thinking and a heated academic debate. The most prominent critics of the new research were David Neumark of the University of California at Irvine and William Wascher of the Federal Reserve. They disputed Messrs Card and Krueger's findings for New Jersey and argued that a comparison of different states over time showed that higher minimum wages hurt jobs.

Almost two decades later, the minimum-wage debate has matured, not least because policy changes have brought heaps of new evidence to analyse. Britain introduced a national minimum wage in 1999. America's states saw numerous adjustments in their minimum wages, and the federal floor was raised by 40% between 2007 and 2009.

America's academics still do not agree on the employment effects. But both sides have honed their methods and, in some ways, the gap between them has shrunk. Messrs Card and Krueger moved on to other work, but Arindrajit Dube at the University of Massachusetts-Amherst and Michael Reich of the University of California, Berkeley, have generalised the case-study approach, comparing restaurant employment across all contiguous counties with different minimum-wage levels between 1990 and 2006. They found no adverse effects on employment from a higher minimum wage. They also argue that if research showed such effects, these mostly reflected other differences between American states and had nothing to do with the minimum wage.

Messrs Neumark and Wascher still demur. They have published stacks of studies (and a book) purporting to show that minimum wages hit jobs. In a 2013 paper they defend their methods and argue that the evidence still favours their view. But even they are no longer blanket opponents. In a 2011 paper they pointed out that a higher minimum wage along with the Earned Income Tax Credit (which tops up income for poor workers in America) boosted both employment and earnings for single women with children (though it cost less-skilled, minority men jobs).

Britain's experience offers another set of insights. The country's national minimum wage was introduced at 46% of the median wage, slightly higher than America's. A lower floor applied to young people. Both are adjusted annually on the advice of the Low Pay Commission. Before the law took effect, worries about potential damage to employment were widespread. Yet today the consensus is that Britain's minimum wage has done little or no harm.

The most striking impact of Britain's minimum wage has been on the spread of wages. Not only has it pushed up pay for the bottom 5% of workers, but it also seems to have boosted earnings further up the income scale – and thus reduced wage inequality. Wage gaps in the bottom half of Britain's pay scale have shrunk sharply since the late 1990s. A new study by a trio of British labour-market economists (including one at the Low Pay Commission) attributes much of that contraction to the minimum wage. Wage inequality fell more for women (a higher proportion of whom are on the minimum wage) than for men and the effect was most pronounced in low-wage parts of Britain.

The British way versus the American way

This new evidence leaves economists with lots of unanswered questions. What exactly is going on in labour markets if minimum wages do not hurt employment but reduce wage gaps? Are firms cutting costs by squeezing wages elsewhere? Are they improving the productivity of the lowest-wage workers? Some of the newest studies suggest firms employ a variety of strategies to deal with a higher minimum wage, from modestly raising prices to saving money from lower turnover.

Policymakers face practical issues. Bastions of orthodoxy, such as the OECD and the IMF, now assert that a moderate minimum wage probably does not do much harm and may do some good. Their definition of moderate is 30–40% of the median wage. Britain's experience suggests it might even be a bit higher. The success of the Low Pay Commission points to the importance of technocrats rather than politicians setting wage floors. Britain's small, regular changes may be easier for firms to absorb than America's infrequent but hefty minimum-wage increases. Whatever their flaws, minimum wages are here to stay.

Wages and performance: making pay work

Why bosses should be careful when using performance-related pay

OF ALL A FIRM'S INPUTS, its workers' effort is perhaps the oddest. It is as vital as land, factories or machines, but much harder to control. It is often impossible even to measure. A manager can gauge the firm's output, but not the effort people put in, beyond crude gauges such as the time they spend on the job. Employees have the informational edge, knowing their own effort, output and skill level. This asymmetry makes it hard for managers to distinguish, for instance, between the low-skilled but diligent and the skilled but lazy. Monitoring schemes to reward hard-working employees and punish slackers can boost effort, but they can backfire badly, too.

What should firms do? A good place to start is with the worst kind of behaviour: crime. In a paper published in 1968, Gary Becker of the University of Chicago set out the factors which policymakers should consider when deciding on what resources they should devote to detection. In his model criminals calculate the risks and benefits of bad behaviour, taking into account the possible monetary reward, the probability of being caught and the subsequent punishment. To cut crime authorities must increase the probability of being caught, the severity of the punishment, or both. This approach can also be applied to less extreme forms of bad behaviour, such as slow or sloppy work: firms may have to monitor individual workers, and then reward the good and punish the bad.

But a system like this comes with costs. People do not work hard for money alone. They also have other motives, such as doing a good job. In a 1971 paper, Edward Deci of Rochester University tested the effect that external rewards – cash bonuses or fines – have on such "intrinsic" motivation. Two groups were given a 3D puzzle and asked to create a variety of shapes. Because the puzzle was fun and mentally taxing, intrinsic motivation was high. One group, left to proceed at its own pace, worked hard. A second group was monitored, and given a $1 reward for each shape that was successfully replicated. This payment was later withdrawn, with the result that the second group now put in less effort than the first. Its members switched off, turning instead to *Playboy* or the *New Yorker*. Monetary rewards, Mr Deci reasoned, had killed their intrinsic motivation.

Watching workers closely can have other drawbacks. Setting up an incentive scheme for a particular task costs time and money. And it reveals something about the task: that it is important for a firm's success and considered difficult. In a 2003 study, Roland Bénabou of Princeton University and Jean Tirole of Toulouse University showed how this can lead employees to work more slowly. Efforts might simply shift from speed to accuracy.

The effects of monitoring may be even worse if "reciprocity" is taken into account. Matthew Rabin of the University of California, Berkeley, explored this concept in a paper in 1993. People with a strong sense of fairness like to help those whom they perceive as helpful. But the flip side is that they will punish those they see as being unhelpful. So a monopolist charging rip-off prices may be shunned, even if the shopper really wants the product. Similarly, an unfair boss may be punished with bad work, even if this hurts the worker too.

If monitoring has both benefits and costs, what is the right level? Michèle Belot of Edinburgh University and Marina Schröder of Magdeburg University have devised a test. They gave volunteers boxes containing 780 euro coins of different values and asked them to separate these into different types. The job is trickier than it sounds, because the euro zone has 160 different types of coin: eight values, from one cent to €2, in 20 designs, one for each of the zone's 17 members plus Monaco, San Marino and the Vatican. The task, for which volunteers were paid €20, has some clever properties. First, it can be completed perfectly with effort but not much skill (time pressure was minimal and volunteers were allowed to take the boxes home). Second, bad work can be measured and comes in several forms. The coins could be badly sorted. The box could be returned late. And the coins might be stolen: the boxes contained Vatican coins which are worth more to collectors than their face value. By replacing a 50-cent piece from the Vatican (worth around €3 in online auctions) with a regular 50-cent coin, the volunteer could net €2.50.

High bar or no bar

The researchers tested different configurations of monitoring and rewards. A control group was not supervised at all and paid immediately regardless of performance. Two other groups were watched, and rewarded according to their performance. The first scheme was pretty lax: workers lost just €1 for every ten mistakes. The second was much harsher: the payment was cut by €15 if more than two coins were wrongly identified.

The results suggest that lax monitoring is a bad option: 30% of volunteers made more than ten mistakes – worse than the group with no supervision. On top of this, late returns increased. This means that the resources devoted to monitoring were wasted. The stricter regime, however, did offer some benefits. Accuracy improved, with only 16% of volunteers making more than ten mistakes. But some also shifted their effort, working more slowly and handing the coins in late. Neither system had any effect on theft: in all three groups one in ten volunteers stole coins.

In economics opting for the middle ground is usually best. But in this case the extremes seem to be a better choice: monitor hard, or do not monitor at all. A little bit of monitoring only annoys the good workers, causing them to slacken off. And sometimes the wisest thing is just to let people get on with the job.

May 2013

Share as pay: turning workers into capitalists

. **Employee share ownership has merit. But that does not justify further government incentives**

IN AN EFFORT TO REBUILD New England's cod industry after the war of independence, George Washington signed a law in 1792 giving shipowners "allowances" (ie, subsidies) to offset the tariffs they had to pay on their inputs. Two conditions were attached to the support: shipowners had to sign a profit-sharing agreement with their crew, with whom they also had to split the allowance. Thus one of America's first tax breaks was designed to encourage owners to share profits with their workers.

This was no accident, according to *The Citizen's Share*, a book by Joseph Blasi and Douglas Kruse of Rutgers University and Richard Freeman of Harvard University. The authors argue that America's founders put priority on shared rewards and the broad ownership of capital, and were not afraid to use the federal government to advance them. This mindset, the authors explain, has periodically motivated American business and politics ever since, from the 19th-century Homestead Acts (which distributed land free to those willing to till it) to the 1974 legislation creating employee stock-ownership plans (ESOPs), tax-advantaged trusts that borrow money to buy shares for workers.

As a result, surprisingly large numbers of American workers share in some way in their employers' success. Based on a series of national surveys, the authors reckon that some 47% of full-time workers have one or more forms of capital stake in the firm for which they work, whether from profit-sharing schemes (40%), stock ownership (21%) or stock options (10%). About a tenth of *Fortune* 500 companies, from Procter & Gamble to Goldman Sachs, have employee shareholdings of 5% or more. Almost a fifth of America's biggest private firms, including behemoths like Cargill and Mars, have profit-sharing or share-ownership schemes. Some 10 million people work for companies with ESOPs.

In most cases the stakes are fairly small: the median employee shareholding is worth $10,000. The scale of workers' equity has not increased enough to counter two bigger trends that have dramatically increased inequality of incomes in America over the past 30 years: the widening gap in pay between the top 1% and the rest, and the overall squeeze in the share of national income going to wages. To counter this concentration of wealth, and live up to the ideals of the country's founders, Messrs Blasi, Freeman and Kruse argue that America needs another dose of Washington's medicine: more incentives for employees to build ownership stakes in the firms they work for.

These academics – two economists and a sociologist – are on the centre-left. The same logic, however, is motivating policy in the Conservative-led government of America's former colonial master. Britain also has a tradition of employee share ownership. John Lewis, a big retailer that is owned by a trust on behalf of its employees, is one example. To boost what is often dubbed the "John Lewis economy", the government has made it easier to set up employee share schemes, and created some £50 million ($81 million) of tax incentives to encourage ownership by employees. In the privatisation of the Royal Mail, one-tenth of the shares were distributed to the firm's workers.

The political appeal of employee share ownership is not in doubt. Broader stock ownership appeals to the right. Helping squeezed workers appeals to the left. Economically, however, the merits of using government incentives to encourage the phenomenon are less clear.

Most academic analyses of employee ownership have focused on the gains to firms. Worker participation plainly does not guarantee success: Lehman Brothers was 30% employee-owned. A flagship firm in Mondragon, a huge Spanish co-operative, filed for bankruptcy in 2013. But a host of studies show that firms in which employees have a significant stake tend to be more productive and innovative, to retain staff better and to fire them less readily. These findings come with a proviso, however. The effects often depend on whether the employees' ownership stake also brings a greater say in how the firm is run.

Would larger stakes benefit employees? There, too, the answer is not clear. If share ownership comes at the expense of wages, workers may simply be shifting from a stable and liquid form of compensation to a riskier one. Messrs Blasi, Freeman and Kruse argue that share ownership should be, and usually is, additional compensation. Surveys suggest that over 70% of workers who benefit from a profit-sharing or other share-ownership scheme say their wages are at or above prevailing market rates – presumably thanks to their firms' superior performance.

Reward and risk

Even if the compensation is genuinely additional, employee share-ownership can have disadvantages. It may lead workers to hold too much of their wealth in their own company's stock. The authors acknowledge this risk and recommend that workers should diversify their portfolios. But since most Americans have very few savings, that caveat sharply limits the potential expansion of employee share schemes, especially for poorer people.

All this casts doubt on the merits of bigger government incentives to promote employee share ownership, especially in the light of the cost and distortions inherent in any tax break. Growing inequality and concentration of share ownership are troubling, but there are better ways to address them. Capital-gains taxes could be made more progressive: today richer workers benefit disproportionately from the lower tax rate on capital gains. Tax breaks that encourage the concentration of capital, such as the carried-interest loophole, which dramatically lowers private-equity partners' bills, should be eliminated. America's founding ethos of broad-based capitalism is admirable. But it is best promoted by getting rid of special incentives, not by creating new ones.

November 2013

8   Inequality

Long-run inequality: all men are created unequal

Revisiting an old argument about the impact of capitalism

INEQUALITY IS ONE of the most controversial attributes of capitalism. Early in the industrial revolution stagnant wages and concentrated wealth led David Ricardo and Karl Marx to question capitalism's sustainability. Twentieth-century economists lost interest in distributional issues amid the "Great Compression" that followed the second world war. But a modern surge in inequality has new economists wondering, as Marx and Ricardo did, which forces may be stopping the fruits of capitalism from being more widely distributed.

Capital in the Twenty-First Century by Thomas Piketty, an economist at the Paris School of Economics, is an authoritative guide to the question. Mr Piketty's book, which was published in 2013 in French and in English in 2014, self-consciously builds on the work of 19th-century thinkers; his title is an allusion to Marx's magnum opus. But he possesses an advantage they lacked: two centuries' worth of hard data.

The book suggests that some 20th-century conventional wisdom was badly wrong. Inequality does not appear to ebb as economies mature, as Simon Kuznets, a Nobel-winning economist, argued in the 1950s. Neither should we expect the share of income flowing to capital to stay roughly constant over time: what another economist, Nicholas Kaldor, labelled a key fact of economic growth. Mr Piketty

FIG 8.1 **Capital crimes?**

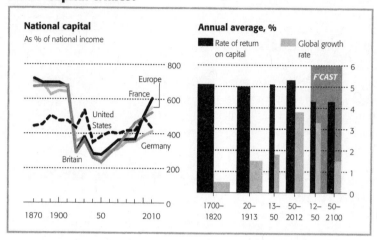

Source: *Capital in the Twenty-First Century* by Thomas Piketty

argues there is no reason to think that capitalism will "naturally" reverse rising inequality.

The centrepiece of Mr Piketty's analysis is the ratio of an economy's capital (or equivalently, its wealth) to its annual output. From 1700 until the first world war, the stock of wealth in western Europe hovered at around 700% of national income. Over time the composition of wealth changed; agricultural land declined in importance while industrial capital – factories, machinery and intellectual property – gained prominence. Yet wealth held steady at a high level (see Figure 8.1, left side).

Pre-1914 economies were very unequal. In 1910 the top 10% of European households controlled almost 90% of all wealth. The flow of rents and dividends from capital contributed to high inequality of income; the top 10% captured more than 45% of all income. Mr Piketty's work suggests there was little sign of any natural decline in inequality on the outbreak of the first world war.

The wars and depressions between 1914 and 1950 dragged the wealthy back to earth. Wars brought physical destruction of capital, nationalisation, taxation and inflation, while the Great Depression destroyed fortunes through capital losses and bankruptcy. Yet capital has been rebuilt, and the owners of capital have prospered once more. From the 1970s the ratio of wealth to income has grown along with income inequality, and levels of wealth concentration are approaching those of the pre-war era.

Mr Piketty describes these trends through what he calls two "fundamental laws of capitalism". The first explains variations in capital's share of income (as opposed to the share going to wages). It is a simple accounting identity: at all times, capital's share is equal to the rate of return on capital multiplied by the total stock of wealth as a share of GDP. The rate of return is the sum of all income flowing to capital – rents, dividends and profits – as a percentage of the value of all capital.

The second law is more a rough rule of thumb: over long periods and under the right circumstances the stock of capital, as a percentage of national income, should approach the ratio of the national-savings rate to the economic growth rate. With a savings rate of 8% (roughly that of the American economy) and GDP growth of 2%, wealth should rise to 400% of annual output, for example, while a drop in long-run growth to 1% would push up expected wealth to 800% of GDP. Whether this is a "law" or not, the important point is that a lower growth rate is conducive to higher concentrations of wealth.

In Mr Piketty's narrative, rapid growth – from large productivity gains or a growing population – is a force for economic convergence. Prior wealth casts less of an economic and political shadow over the new income generated each year. And population growth is a critical component of economic growth, accounting for about half of average global GDP growth between 1700 and 2012. America's breakneck population and GDP growth in the 19th century eroded the power of old fortunes while throwing up a steady supply of new ones.

Victorian values

Tumbling rates of population growth are pushing wealth concentrations back towards Victorian levels, in Mr Piketty's estimation. The ratio of wealth to income is highest among demographically challenged economies such as Italy and Japan (although both countries have managed to mitigate inequality through redistributive taxes and transfers). Interestingly, Mr Piketty reckons this world, in which the return to capital is persistently higher than growth, is the more "normal" state. In that case, wealth piles up faster than growth in output or incomes. The mid-20th century, when wealth compression combined with extraordinary growth to generate an egalitarian interregnum, was the exception.

Sustained rates of return above the rate of growth may sound unrealistic. The more capital there is, the lower the return should be: the millionth industrial robot adds less to production than the hundredth. Yet somewhat surprisingly, the rate of return on capital is remarkably constant over long periods (see Figure 8.1, right side). Technology is partly responsible. Innovation, and growth in output per person, creates investment opportunities even when shrinking populations reduce GDP growth to near zero.

New technology can also make it easier to substitute machines for human workers. That allows capital to gobble up a larger share of national income, raising its return. Amid a new burst of automation, wealth concentrations and inequality could reach unprecedented heights, putting a modern twist on a very 19th-century problem.

January 2014

Redistribution: inequality v growth

Up to a point, redistributing income to fight inequality can lift growth

ON THE CAMPAIGN TRAIL in 2008 Barack Obama stumbled into a memorable encounter with Joe "the Plumber" Wurzelbacher. Explaining the logic of a proposal to raise taxes on the rich, Mr Obama mused that "when you spread the wealth around, it's good for everybody". The soundbite, soon an attack-ad mainstay, failed to derail the Obama campaign. But the disagreement between Joe the Plumber and Barack the Senator still trips up governments around the world: is there a trade-off between economic growth and redistribution?

Some inequality is needed to propel growth, economists reckon. Without the carrot of large financial rewards, risky entrepreneurship and innovation would grind to a halt. In 1975 Arthur Okun, an American economist, argued that societies cannot have both perfect equality and perfect efficiency and must choose how much of one to sacrifice for the other.

While most economists continue to hold that view, the recent rise in inequality has prompted a new look at its economic costs. Inequality could impair growth if those with low incomes suffer poor health and low productivity as a result. It could threaten public confidence in growth-boosting policies like free trade, reckons Dani Rodrik of the Institute for Advanced Study in Princeton. Or it could sow the seeds of crisis. In a 2010 book Raghuram Rajan, now governor of the Reserve Bank of India, argued that governments often respond to inequality by easing the flow of credit to poorer households. When the borrowing binge ends everyone suffers.

Pinning down the precise relationship between growth and inequality is a challenge. Some studies reckon inequality is mildly bad for growth. Others suggest the relationship changes as poor countries grow rich, while still others reckon it is the trend in inequality rather than its level that matters.

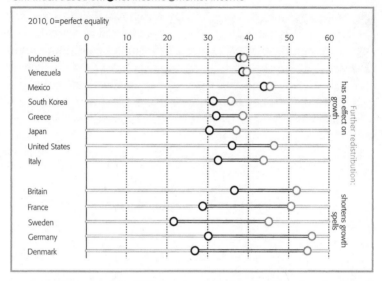

FIG 8.2 **A little off the top**
Gini index based on: ● net income ○ market income

Sources: Standardised World Income Inequality Database; "Redistribution, inequality, and growth" by J. Ostry *et al.*, IMF Staff Discussion Note, 2014

Research by economists at the IMF aims to add clarity to the debate. In a 2011 paper Andrew Berg and Jonathan Ostry argued that it is the duration of spells of growth that is most important for long-run economic performance: getting an economy growing in the first place is much easier than keeping the growth spell rolling. They reckon that when growth falters, inequality is often a culprit. Latin America's Gini index is about 50, well above that in emerging Asia, which has a Gini of about 40. (A Gini index is a measure of income concentration that ranges from 0, representing perfect equality, to 100, where all income flows to a single person.) Were Latin America to close half of that gap in inequality, its typical growth spurt might last twice as long, on average.

Others reckon that it may not be inequality itself that harms growth but rather governments that tax and spend to try to reduce it. In a 2014 paper Messrs Berg and Ostry and Charalambos Tsangarides tease out the separate effects of inequality and redistribution. They turn to a data set put together by Frederick Solt, a political scientist at the University of Iowa, containing Gini indices for 173 economies spanning a period of five decades. Mr Solt provides Ginis for both market income and net income (after taxes and transfers). The difference between the two gives the authors a measure of redistribution (see Figure 8.2). In America, which does relatively little of it, redistribution trims the Gini index by roughly ten points. In Sweden, in contrast, it cuts the Gini by 23 points – more than half. Using these figures, the economists can separate out the different effects of redistribution and inequality on growth.

Redistributing prejudice

The authors find that governments in more unequal countries redistribute more, and rich economies do more than poor ones. As a result, differences in inequality across rich countries are mostly down to the generosity of redistribution; Germany is more unequal than Britain before redistribution but much less so after.

Up to a point, spreading the wealth around carries no growth penalty: growth in income per person is not meaningfully lower in countries with more redistribution. But economies that redistribute a lot may enjoy shorter growth spells, the authors reckon. When the gap between the market and net Ginis is 13 points or more (as in much of western Europe) further redistribution shrinks the typical expansion. The authors caution against drawing hasty conclusions. Details surely matter; nationalising firms and doling out profits would presumably be worse for growth than taxing property to fund education.

Inequality is more closely correlated with low growth. A high Gini for net income, after redistribution, corresponds to slower growth in income per person. A rise of 5 Gini points (moving from the level in America to that in Gabon, for instance) knocks half a percentage point off average annual growth. And holding redistribution constant, a one-point rise in the Gini raises the risk that an expansion ends in a given year by six percentage points. Redistribution that reduces inequality might therefore boost growth.

If redistribution is benign, that could be because it substitutes for shaky borrowing. In their 2011 paper Messrs Berg and Ostry note that more unequal societies do poorly on social indicators such as educational attainment, even after controlling for income levels. This suggests that households with lower incomes struggle to finance investments in education. In a 2014 paper Barry Cynamon of the Federal Reserve Bank of St Louis and Steven Fazzari of Washington University in St Louis reckon most Americans borrowed heavily before 2008 to prop up their consumption. That kept the economy growing – until crisis struck. Sensible redistribution could mean the difference between a healthy growth rate and one that is decidedly subprime.

March 2014

Surnames and social mobility: nomencracy

Surnames offer depressing clues to the lack of social mobility over generations

THE "GREAT GATSBY CURVE" is the name Alan Krueger, an economic adviser to Barack Obama, gave to the relationship between income inequality and social mobility across the generations. Mr Krueger used the phrase in a 2012 speech to describe the work of Miles Corak of the University of Ottawa, who has shown that more unequal economies tend to have less fluid societies. Mr Corak reckons that in some places, like America and Britain, around 50% of income differences in one generation are attributable to differences in the previous generation (in more egalitarian Scandinavia, the number is less than 30%).

Even that may paint too rosy a picture. Mr Corak's work draws on studies that compare income levels between just two generations: fathers and sons. That is out of necessity; good data covering three or more generations are scarce. But reliance on limited data could lead to overestimates of social mobility.

Gregory Clark, an economist at the University of California, Davis, notes that across a single generation some children of rich parents are bound to suffer random episodes of bad luck. Others will choose low-pay jobs for idiosyncratic reasons, like a wish to do charitable work. Such statistical noise makes society look more changeable than it is. Extrapolating the resulting mobility rates across many generations gives a misleadingly sunny view of long-term equality of opportunity. Mr Clark suggests that family history has large effects that persist for much greater spans of time. Fathers matter, but so do grandfathers and great-grandfathers. Indeed, it may take as long as 300–500 years for high- and low-status families to produce descendants with equal chances of being in various parts of the income spectrum.

Mr Clark confronts the lack of good data by gleaning information from rare surnames. You can tease mobility trends from surnames in two ways. One method relies on past links between certain names and high economic status. In a 2012 paper, for instance, Mr Clark examines prosperous Swedes. The unusual surnames of 17th-century aristocrats and the Latinised surnames (such as Linnaeus) adopted by highly educated 18th-century Swedes are both rare in the Swedish population as a whole. By tracking the overrepresentation of those names in elite positions, he is able to work out long-run mobility rates.

As late as 2011 aristocratic surnames appear among the ranks of lawyers, considered for this purpose a high-status position, at a frequency almost six times that of their occurrence in the population as a whole. Mr Clark reckons that even in famously mobile Sweden, some 70–80% of a family's social status is transmitted from generation to generation across a span of centuries. Other economists use similar techniques to reveal comparable immobility in societies from 19th-century Spain to post-Qing-dynasty China. Inherited advantage is detectable for a very long time.

A second method relies on the chance overrepresentation of rare surnames in high- or low-status groups at some point in the past. If very few Britons are called Micklethwait, for example, and people with that name were disproportionately wealthy in 1800, then you can gauge long-run mobility by studying how long it takes the Micklethwait name to lose its wealth-predicting power. In a paper written by Mr Clark and Neil Cummins of Queens College, City University of New York, the authors use data from probate records of 19th-century estates to classify rare surnames into different wealth categories. They then use similar data to see how common each surname is in these categories in subsequent years. Again, some 70–80% of economic advantage seems to be transmitted from generation to generation.

Mr Clark's conclusion is that the underlying rate of social mobility is both low and surprisingly constant across countries and eras: the introduction of universal secondary education scarcely affects intergenerational mobility rates in Britain, for example. This consistency, he suggests, shows that low mobility may be down to differences in underlying "social competence". Such competence is potentially heritable and is reinforced by the human tendency to mate with partners of similar traits and ability.

Bob's your uncle, unfortunately

This is a distressingly fatalistic view of opportunity. Studies using the few multigenerational data sets that exist offer a slightly more encouraging picture. A Swedish analysis of the city of Malmo, using data covering individual families over four generations, finds a meaningful relationship between a child's educational attainment and that of his great-grandparents, more evidence that a look at just one generation leads to overestimates of mobility. By subjecting the same data to a surname analysis, Mr Clark calculates that 60% of income differences in Malmo are attributable to economic advantages in previous ones – lower than his own rate but still higher than Mr Corak's single-generation estimates.

Painstaking work by Jason Long of Wheaton College and Joseph Ferrie of Northwestern University provides another perspective. They have spent the past decade poring over census returns from America and Britain, identifying families with children in one count, tracking down the same children as adults in another, and thereby building up a multigenerational data set. An analysis of three generations shows that in both America and Britain the effect of high (or low) incomes in one generation lasts for at least two more. Yet their study also suggests it is possible to break patterns of immobility. Although American and British mobility rates had converged by the middle of the 20th century, America's social order was considerably more fluid than Britain's in the 19th century. The past has a tight grip on the present. But in the right circumstances, it can apparently be loosened.

February 2013

Inequality and crashes: body of evidence

Is a concentration of wealth at the top to blame for financial crises

IN THE SEARCH for the villain behind the global financial crisis, some have pointed to inequality as a culprit. In his 2010 book *Fault Lines*, Raghuram Rajan of the University of Chicago [now governor of the Reserve Bank of India] argued that inequality was a cause of the crisis, and that the American government served as a willing accomplice. From the early 1980s the wages of working Americans with little or no university education fell ever farther behind those with university qualifications, he pointed out. Under pressure to respond to the problem of stagnating incomes, successive presidents and Congresses opened a flood of mortgage credit.

In 1992 the government reduced capital requirements at Fannie Mae and Freddie Mac, two huge sources of housing finance. In the 1990s the Federal Housing Administration expanded its loan guarantees to cover bigger mortgages with smaller down-payments. And in the 2000s Fannie and Freddie were encouraged to buy more subprime mortgage-backed securities. Inequality, Mr Rajan argued, prepared the ground for disaster.

Mr Rajan's story was intended as a narrative of the subprime crisis in America, not as a general theory of financial dislocation. But others have noted that inequality also soared in the years before the Depression of the 1930s. In 2007 23.5% of all American income flowed to the top 1% of earners – their highest share since 1929. In a 2010 paper Michael Kumhof and Romain Rancière, two economists at the IMF, built a model to show how inequality can systematically lead to crisis. An investor class may become better at capturing the returns to production, slowing wage growth and raising inequality. Workers then borrow to prop up their consumption. Leverage grows until crisis results. Their model absolves politicians of responsibility; inequality works its mischief without the help of government.

New research hints at other ways inequality could spur crisis.

In a 2012 paper Marianne Bertrand and Adair Morse, both of the University of Chicago, study patterns of spending across American states between 1980 and 2008. In particular, they focus on how changes in the behaviour of the richest 20% of households affect the spending choices of the bottom 80%. They find that a rise in the level of consumption of rich households leads to more spending by the non-rich. This "trickle-down consumption" appears to result from a desire to keep up with the Joneses. Non-rich households spend more on luxury goods and services supplied to their more affluent neighbours – domestic services, say, or health clubs. Had the incomes of America's top 20% of earners grown at the same, more leisurely pace as the median income, they reckon that the bottom 80% might have saved more over the past three decades – $500 per household per year for the entire period between 1980 and 2008, or $800 per year just before the crisis. In states where the highest earners were wealthiest, non-rich households were more likely to report "financial duress".

The paper also reveals how responsive government is to rising income inequality. The authors analyse votes on the credit-expansion measures cited in Mr Rajan's book. When support for a bill varies, the authors find that legislators representing more unequal districts were significantly more likely to back a loosening of mortgage rules.

Inequality may drive instability in other ways. Although sovereign borrowing was not a direct contributor to the crisis of 2008, it has since become the principal danger to the financial system. In another 2012 paper, Marina Azzimonti of the Federal Reserve Bank of Philadelphia, Eva de Francisco of Towson University and Vincenzo Quadrini of the University of Southern California argue that income inequality may have had a troubling effect in this area of finance, too.

The authors' models suggest that a less equitable distribution of wealth can boost demand for government borrowing to provide for the lagging average worker. In the recent past this demand would have coincided with a period of financial globalisation that allowed many governments to rack up debt cheaply. Across a sample of 22 OECD countries from 1973 to 2005, they find support for the notion that inequality, financial globalisation and rising government debt do indeed march together. The idea that inequality might create pressure for more redistribution through public borrowing also occurred to Mr Rajan, who acknowledges that stronger safety nets are a more common response to inequality than credit subsidies. Liberalised global finance and rising inequality may thus have led to surging public debts.

Reasonable doubt

Other economists wonder whether income inequality is not wrongly accused. Michael Bordo of Rutgers University and Christopher Meissner of the University of California at Davis studied 14 advanced countries from 1920 to 2008 to test the inequality-causes-busts hypothesis. They turn up a strong relationship between credit booms and financial crises – a result confirmed by many other economic studies. There is no consistent link between income concentration and credit booms, however.

Inequality occasionally rises with credit creation, as in America in the late 1920s and during the years before the 2008 crisis. This need not mean that the one causes the other, they note. In other cases, such as in Australia and Sweden in the 1980s, credit booms seem to drive inequality rather than the other way around. Elsewhere, as in 1990s Japan, rapid growth in the share of income going to the highest earners coincided with a slump in credit. Rising real incomes and low interest rates reliably lead to credit booms, they reckon, but inequality does not. Mr Rajan's story may work for America's 2008 crisis. It is not an iron law.

March 2012

Firm size and pay: the bigger, the less fair

The growing size of firms may help to explain rising inequality

SINCE ITS PUBLICATION in 2014, Thomas Piketty's *Capital in the Twenty-First Century* has ignited a furious debate about inequality in the rich world. He focuses on the increasingly unequal distribution of wealth, and pays less attention to the growing disparity in wages over the past three decades. Yet that disparity is ballooning, too: in America, for instance, the best-paid 1% of workers earned 191% more in real (ie, inflation-adjusted) terms in 2011 than they did in 1980, whereas the wages of the middle fifth fell by 5%. Similar trends can be observed all over the world, despite widely varying policies on tax, the minimum wage and corporate pay.

The standard explanation says that technology plays a big role: modern economies require more skilled workers, raising the pay premium they can demand. A 2015 paper by Holger Mueller, Elena Simintzi and Paige Ouimet adds a new and intriguing wrinkle to this: the rising size of the average firm. Economists have long recognised that economies of scale allow workers at bigger firms to be more productive than those at smaller ones. That, in turn, allows the bigger firms to pay higher wages. This should not, in theory, cause a rise in inequality. If the chief executive and cleaner at a larger firm are both paid 10% more than their counterparts at a small firm, the ratio between their wages – and thus the overall level of inequality – should remain the same.

But the paper shows that the benefits of scale are not shared equally among all workers. Using data on wages at British firms, they divide workers into nine groups according to how skilled they are. Over time, they find that the proportional difference in wages between the groups grows as firms get bigger. This trend is driven entirely by a rising gap between wages at the top compared with the middle and bottom of the distribution. As the authors note, this is very similar to the trend in income inequality in America and Britain

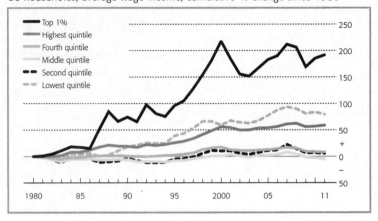

FIG 8.3 **The wages of scale**
US households, average wage income, cumulative % change since 1980

Sources: Congressional Budget Office; *The Economist*

as a whole since the 1990s, when pay for low and median earners began to stagnate (see Figure 8.3).

The authors suggest two possible explanations. First, larger firms should find it easier to automate tasks than smaller ones, and may therefore find it easier to resist demands for pay rises from relatively unskilled workers who could be replaced by machines. Second, entry-level workers in the middle of the income distribution may be willing to accept lower pay from big firms since in the long run the chances of winning a promotion are greater than at small firms.

Top hogs

The benefits of size are thus enjoyed only by the most senior workers at a firm, who can extract a bigger premium for their skills and experience. A cleaner at a single shop does the same sort of work as those at a large chain. But managing a multinational firm such as Walmart requires a different – and much rarer – set of skills than that required to run a corner store. Over time this pushes up the salaries of the top brass at Walmart compared with corner-shop managers.

The authors find that the relationship between the growth in the size of companies and the level of inequality holds across the rich world. They looked at data from 1981 to 2010 on wages and the size of largest firms for 15 countries in the OECD. The relationship between rising levels of income inequality and the size of firms was strong.

This effect is particularly noticeable in America and Britain, where firms have grown rapidly in recent decades. In America, for instance, the number of workers employed by the country's 100 biggest firms rose by 53% between 1986 and 2010; in Britain the equivalent figure is 43.5%. On the other hand, in places where the size of firms has not changed much, such as Sweden, or where it has shrunk, such as Denmark, wage inequality has grown much less. Part of what is perceived as a global trend towards greater disparity in wages may actually be the result of the biggest firms employing a greater share of workers.

A 2014 paper by Albert Bollard, Peter Klenow and Huiyu Li, which looks at manufacturing in America, China and India from 1982 to 2007, suggests that the trend towards bigger firms is only likely to accelerate. Big firms' higher productivity, it argues, raises the barriers to entry for new – and presumably smaller – competitors. Larger factories are more productive than smaller ones, so bigger firms can entrench their position over time. That will skew the income distribution even more. There is plenty of evidence across America and Europe that start-up rates for companies are falling, allowing the biggest firms to get bigger unhindered by competition. Since the financial crisis, higher barriers to entry in the form of limited access to capital have caused the number of new businesses to collapse.

Not all economists see this as a dreadful thing. After all, bigger firms have much higher investment rates than smaller ones, which helps to fuel growth throughout the economy. The preponderance of small firms in such places as Greece, Italy and Portugal seems to be one of the factors holding those economies back.

But if governments wish to reverse the inequality big firms foment, reforms to the labour market are unlikely to do the trick. Instead, they will have to spur competition by reducing barriers to entry for smaller firms, most notably by improving their access to credit. That should reduce income inequality and boost economic growth at the same time.

Voters dislike the growing inequality of incomes, and often

agitate for redistributive policies to reverse it. Yet too much crude redistribution can be counterproductive in that it tends to dampen economic growth. The link between firm size and inequality suggests a better option. By boosting competition, policymakers can please both populists and economists at the same time.

March 2015

Outlaw economics: shifting income from rich to poor

Policies to shift income from rich to poor may prove less effective than imagined

IN A WORLD OF INEQUALITY the egalitarian thief is an attractive character. From England's Robin Hood to America's Jesse James and Mexico's Pancho Villa many countries lionise brave outlaws who take from the rich and give to the poor. Economics, in its down-to-earth way, seems to support their cause: since the cash-laden tend to save more, diverting income to penniless people who will spend it immediately should boost consumption, and GDP. The electoral calculus of redistribution appears favourable, too. The best-off are small in number, so taxing their mansions seems likely to win more votes than it loses. But those who fancy taxing the wealthy should tread carefully. Designed badly, such policies could do more harm than good.

The idea that redistribution could help spur growth has long attracted adherents. In 1920 Arthur Cecil Pigou argued that an annual transfer of resources from the "relatively rich to the relatively poor" would increase national output. Pigou discussed three uses for income: consumption or investment by the rich, and consumption by the poor. Shifting purchasing power to the poor would do little to hurt rich folks' spending. The outcome of soaking the rich – decreased investment – would be outweighed by purchases of better food, clothing and education by the poor. Thus redistribution would boost output.

Pigou's argument rests on the idea that poor families would spend more if they had the means, and that the wealthy would be able to smooth consumption if they suddenly lost income. To investigate whether this assumption holds, Greg Kaplan and Justin Weidner of Princeton University and Giovanni Violante of New York University used huge microeconomic data sets to paint a picture of household income and wealth across eight advanced economies. For each household they totted up income from salaries, public handouts and private transfers such as alimony payments. They also measured liquid wealth: cash in bank accounts, along with bonds and stocks that are directly held and so could be quickly sold. The researchers were looking for families that lacked a buffer of liquid assets (or credit facilities) to offset short-term changes in income. This group, whose consumption has to adjust as income changes, are those that live "hand to mouth" and would be likely to spend most from a government windfall.

But the term "hand to mouth" is not as straightforward as it seems. The data show that the median American holds some liquid wealth in bank deposits, as well as illiquid wealth (retirement accounts and houses, net of mortgage debt), but hardly any shares or bonds. Surprisingly, although around 30% of households live from payslip to payslip, two-thirds of these cash-poor people have sizeable illiquid wealth. They do not fit neatly into the Robin Hood bifurcation between rich and poor: their cash barely covers outgoings but they sit on large illiquid assets.

Housing debt is one reason people end up short of cash. Focusing in on American homeowners, the researchers find that of those with small mortgages, only 20% live hand to mouth. But once total debt approaches the value of the house, a much higher number – close to 50% – are income-constrained. Age is also a factor. Although the likelihood of genuine poverty tends to fall with age as workers build up buffers, the chances of being wealthy but cash-strapped peak around the age of 40.

These findings matter because cash shortfalls affect behaviour. Using another data set that tracks 5,000 American households, the researchers measure the reaction to short-term income shocks between 1999 and 2011. The results confirm Pigou's hunch. Those with lots of liquid wealth spend just 13% of an unexpected windfall; those living hand to mouth spend 24%. The wealthy-but-income-constrained react most, spending 30% of any windfall, suggesting they are even more cash-strapped. That chimes with a study by James Cloyne of the Bank of England and Paolo Surico of London Business School, which found that Britons with large housing debts react sharply when taxes are raised or cut. In other words, taxing those with large but illiquid assets could cause more of a fall in spending than previously expected.

Growing old conservatively

If policymakers need to draw more nuanced distinctions between rich and poor, they also ought not to assume that hard-up citizens will support redistribution. In a working paper, Vivekinan Ashok and Ebonya Washington of Yale University and Ilyana Kuziemko of Princeton University explain that support for redistribution should, in theory, rise the more a worker's earnings fall short of a country's mean income. Yet American attitudes have shown the opposite pattern: support for redistribution has remained flat or fallen as inequality has risen.

Much of this is down to age. Those below 40 follow the expected template: support for redistribution rises in line with inequality. The over-65s are different, perhaps because there are fewer in the "cash-poor" category. In the 1970s, when surveys began, they were more supportive of redistribution than the rest of the population. By the mid-2000s they were much less in favour, doubtless fearing that help for the poor would cut health benefits.

Those twiddling the fiscal dials should mull on these findings. They suggest that the benefits of a fiscal stimulus package would be lower if targeted on the basis of income: short-term largesse should be used on the wealthy, too. It also means redistribution from rich to poor may not be a one-way bet: in particular taxes on the wealthiest should be phased in slowly so they can liquidate assets rather than cut spending. And politicians betting on their Robin Hood credentials should be wary of greying voters. They may be more inclined to back the Sheriff of Nottingham.

April 2015

9 Secular stagnation

The stagnation hypothesis: stagnant thinking

An old explanation for economic drift gains a new following

EVEN BEFORE THE FINANCIAL CRISIS, there was a lurking suspicion that bubbles were the only way listless rich economies could keep growth up and unemployment down. "Recession-plagued nation demands new bubble to invest in," joked the *Onion*, a satirical newspaper, in 2008. In a speech in November 2013 Larry Summers, an economist at Harvard University, gave the idea new credibility when he suggested that the rich world might be suffering from "secular stagnation". He joins a growing rank of economists worrying that advanced economies will keep inflating bubbles in a doomed attempt to resurrect growth.

Secular stagnation is not a new idea. It was first popularised by Alvin Hansen, an economist and disciple of John Maynard Keynes, in the stagnant 1930s. Hansen thought a slowing of both population growth and technological progress would reduce opportunities for investment. Savings would then pile up unused, he reasoned, and growth would slump unless governments borrowed and spent to prop up demand. Following the economic boom of the 1950s, interest in the hypothesis dwindled.

The theory is now popular again. Interest rates have been trending downwards for more than a decade (see Figure 9.1, left side), hinting that too much saving has too few places to go. Even as asset bubbles inflated before the financial crisis, growth in the rich world's

FIG 9.1 **Limp and laden**

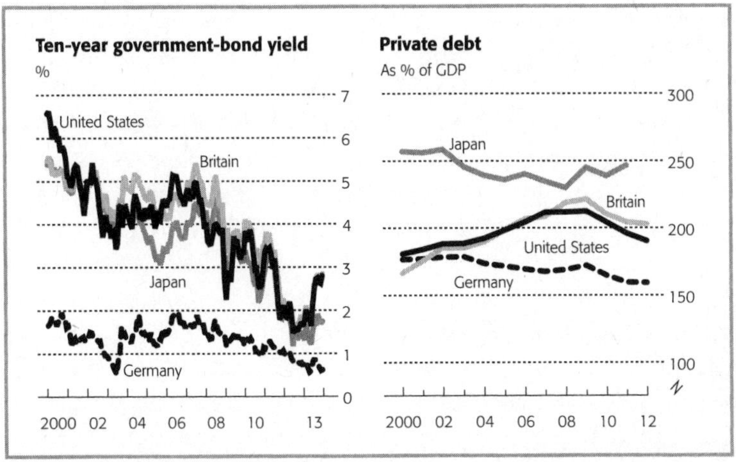
Ten-year government-bond yield
%
United States
Britain
Japan
Germany
7
6
5
4
3
2
1
0
2000 02 04 06 08 10 13
Private debt
As % of GDP
Japan
Britain
United States
Germany
300
250
200
150
100
2000 02 04 06 08 10 12

Sources: OECD; Thomson Reuters

economies was hardly breakneck, hinting at a lack of productive investment opportunities. This combination could be evidence of the secular stagnation Hansen warned of.

Structural defects

Look closely, however, and the argument is not all that convincing. In explaining how a country might fall prey to secular stagnation, Hansen focused on the investment side of the equation. Structural economic changes, like an ageing population or a slowdown in innovation, could permanently curb expectations of growth. Bearish firms might then sit on cash rather than splash out on job-generating equipment or factories.

In some parts of the rich world the ageing of the population may be bearing down on growth, but the rest of the story does not fit current conditions. In the midst of the information-technology revolution, a dearth of innovation does not seem a plausible source of stagnation. Housing aside, private investment in America has recovered reasonably well from the crisis, and tech-industry investments are positively booming. Markets do not appear to be sceptical of the potential returns from technology.

Yet optimism in Silicon Valley has not proved sufficient to free the economy from the doldrums. Some reckon other structural changes in the economy are deterring firms from undertaking more capital spending. Andrew Smithers of Smithers & Co, a consultant, argues that compensation for managers creates incentives to boost share prices in the short run. He suggests that this encourages managers to plough cash into share buy-backs, which raise stock prices, rather than into productive investments that might do more to boost growth.

Might a surge in saving rather than moribund investment be the prime cause of secular stagnation? Again, the timing is tricky. Before the financial crisis, excessive thrift in emerging economies may have played a role. In 2005 Ben Bernanke identified a "global saving glut" as the reason for low interest rates. Many emerging economies, particularly China, had rising current-account surpluses. They sent their surplus savings to the rich world, by building up large foreign-exchange reserves, mostly in the form of rich-world bonds. This drove up asset prices and fuelled housing bubbles. A 2013 working paper from the National Bureau of Economic Research reckons that foreign capital flows to America drove down interest rates and accounted for as much as a third of the increase in house prices in the 2000s.

But this explanation for economic stagnation in the rich world is difficult to square with today's data. Global growth in foreign-exchange reserves slowed dramatically in 2013. Yet rich economies are still struggling while asset prices continue to soar.

Another theory holds that high savings reflect a cramping of consumption due to rising inequality of incomes. The share of income earned by the top 1% began climbing in the early 1980s and now stands close to the record set in 1928. Rich households save more than poorer ones. A paper published in 2013 by Barry Cynamon of the St Louis Fed and Steven Fazzari of Washington University in St Louis estimates that prolific saving by the top 5% has been suppressing demand since the mid-1980s. That squeeze was mostly offset by increased borrowing by the bottom 95%, they find. America and Britain, unlike Germany and Japan, saw rapid growth in private debt in the 2000s (see Figure 9.1, right side). But when the crisis forced households to deleverage, the underlying inequality-driven stagnation may have reasserted itself.

Over to Occam

Yet deleveraging alone may be enough to explain the sluggish growth of recent years. In 2009 Carmen Reinhart of the University of Maryland and Kenneth Rogoff of Harvard University published a study of big post-war banking crises and concluded that they are typically followed by weak recoveries, whether or not they were preceded by a surge in income inequality.

Just as important, central banks have been at sea since reducing their benchmark policy rates to near zero in 2008–09, to battle recession. Many economists – including Mr Summers – reckon this "zero lower bound" has kept central banks from slashing interest rates enough to get investment going and economies back on track. America has been in similar straits before, in the 1930s, when Hansen was devising his theories. Secular stagnation may someday prove a problem. The rich world's current headaches, however, look more like a nasty hangover.

December 2013

Demography and stagnation: no country for young people

Demography may explain secular stagnation

IN THE LATE 1930S economists trying to explain how a depression could drag on for nearly a decade wondered if the problem was a shortage of people. "A change-over from an increasing to a declining population may be very disastrous," said John Maynard Keynes in 1937. The following year another prominent economist, Alvin Hansen, fretted that America was running out of people, territory and new ideas. The result, he said, was "secular stagnation – sick recoveries which die in their infancy and depressions which feed on themselves and leave a hard and seemingly immovable core of unemployment".

In 2013 Larry Summers of Harvard University revived the term "secular stagnation" to describe the rich world's prolonged malaise. Weak demand and excess savings were making it impossible to stimulate growth with the usual tool of low short-term interest rates, he argued. Demographics may play a central role in the ailment Mr Summers described – indeed, a more central one than in the 1930s.

An ageing population could hold down growth and interest rates through several channels. The most direct is through the supply of labour. An economy's potential output depends on the number of workers and their productivity. In both Germany and Japan, the working-age population has been shrinking for more than a decade, and the rate of decline will accelerate in coming years (see Figure 9.2). Britain's potential workforce will stop growing in coming decades; America's will grow at barely a third of the 0.9% rate that prevailed from 2000 to 2013.

All else being equal, a half percentage-point drop in the growth of the labour force will trim economic growth by a similar amount. Such an effect should be felt gradually. But the recession may have accelerated the process by encouraging many workers to take early retirement. In America the first baby boomers qualified for Social

FIG 9.2 **The vanishing worker**
Working-age population, % change on a year earlier

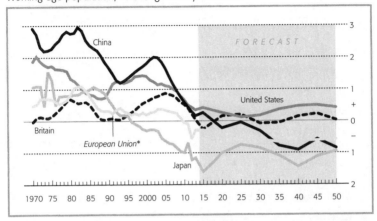

*Excluding Britain
Source: World Bank

Security, the public pension, in 2008, on turning 62. According to several studies, this can probably explain about half the drop since then in the share of the working-age population either working or looking for work, from 66% to below 63%. (This echoes the experience of Japan, which slid into stagnation and deflation in the 1990s around the same time as its working-age population began to shrink.)

The size and age of the population also influences how many customers and workers businesses can tap, and so how much they will invest. Keynes and Hansen worried that a falling population would need fewer of the products American factories made. Contemporary models of economic growth assume that firms need a given stock of capital per worker – equipment, buildings, land and intellectual property – to produce a unit of output. If there are fewer workers to hire, firms will also need less capital.

In a research note, Eugénio Pinto and Stacey Tevlin of the Federal Reserve note that net investment (gross investment minus depreciation) is close to its lowest as a share of the total capital stock since the second world war. This is partly cyclical, since the recession led businesses to curtail expansion plans. But it is also secular. Growth of the capital stock slowed from 3.1% a year in 1994–2003 to 1.6% in the subsequent decade. The economists attribute about a third of the deceleration to slower growth in the workforce, and the rest to less innovation. In other words, businesses are buying less machinery because they have fewer workers to operate it and fewer technological breakthroughs to exploit.

A borrower's world

The third means by which demography can influence growth and interest rates is through saving. Individuals typically borrow heavily in early adulthood to pay for education, a house and babies, save heavily from middle age onwards, and spend those savings in retirement. Coen Teulings of Cambridge University has calculated what various countries' collective savings should be given their demographics. Higher population growth and shorter retirements require less saving, older populations more.

For America, the required stock of savings equalled -228% of GDP in 1970: households should have been borrowers rather than savers since their relative youth and lower life expectancy meant they had ample future income to repay their debts and finance retirement. But as the population aged, its growth slowed and time in retirement lengthened thanks to increased lifespans, the required level of savings rose to 52% of GDP in 2010. For Japan, required savings went from -176% to 119% of GDP in the same period, Germany's from 189% to 325%, and China's from -40% to 86%.

The simultaneous effort by so many countries to save for retirement, combined with weak investment, slowing potential growth, fiscal retrenchment, corporate cash hoarding and inequality (which leaves more of the national income in the hands of the high-saving rich) is depressing the "equilibrium" interest rate that brings investment and saving into balance. There is, however, at least one obvious policy fix. "A higher retirement age reduces saving," Mr Teulings and Richard Baldwin of the Graduate Institute in Geneva write in a 2014 e-book. "There simply is a limit to the extent to which we can save today in exchange for leisure and high consumption tomorrow. Somebody has to do the work tomorrow; we cannot all be retired by that time."

Moreover, at some point, an ageing population starts to use

up the savings it has accumulated. Charles Goodhart and Philipp Erfurth of Morgan Stanley note that the ratio of workers to retirees is now plunging in most developed countries and soon will in many emerging markets. Japan is already liquidating the foreign assets its people acquired during their high-saving years; China and South Korea are starting to do so and Germany will soon. This, they predict, will drag real interest rates, which are now negative, back to the historical equilibrium of 2.5–3% by 2025.

November 2014

Escaping stagnation: still, not stagnant

Economic history suggests that talk of American secular stagnation may be overblown

IS AMERICA STUCK in a rut of low growth, feeble inflation and rock-bottom interest rates? Lots of economists believe in the idea of "secular stagnation", and they have plenty of evidence to point to. The population is ageing and long-run growth prospects look dim. Interest rates, which have been near zero for years, are still not low enough to get the American economy zipping along. A 2015 paper published by the University of Chicago's Booth School of Business, however, reckons that secular stagnation is not quite the right diagnosis for America's ills.

A country in the grip of secular stagnation cannot find enough good investments to soak up available savings. The drain on demand from these underused savings leads to weak growth. It also leaves central banks in a bind. If the real (ie, inflation adjusted) "equilibrium" interest rate (the one that gets an economy growing at a healthy clip) falls well below zero, then central bankers will struggle to push their policy rate low enough to drag the economy out of trouble, since it is hard to push nominal (ie, not adjusted for inflation) rates deep into negative territory. Worse, in the process of trying, they may end up inflating financial bubbles, which lead to unsustainable growth and grisly busts.

Stagnationists argue that this is not a bad description of America since the 1980s. Real interest rates have been falling for years, they note, a sign of a glut of savings. Recoveries from recent recessions have been weak and jobless. When growth has perked up, soaring asset prices and consumer borrowing appear to have done the heavy lifting.

The authors of the Chicago paper – James Hamilton, Ethan Harris, Jan Hatzius and Kenneth West – dispute this interpretation of events. Stagnationists are right, they note, that real interest rates have been falling, and have in fact been negative for much of the past 15 years.

But low real rates do not necessarily imply that future growth will be weak, as many economic models assume. The authors examine central-bank interest rates, inflation and growth in 20 countries over 40 years. They find at best a weak relationship between economic growth and the equilibrium rate. If there is a long-run link, they argue, it tends to be overshadowed by other factors.

After the second world war, for example, government controls on rates ("financial repression") prevented the market from having its say. In recent years short-run woes have dragged down the equilibrium rate, such as the "50-miles-per-hour headwinds" that Alan Greenspan, the chairman of the Federal Reserve, described in 1991, when bad loans pushed big American banks to the brink of insolvency. The authors note that such stormy periods are usually short-lived, and that when the headwinds abate the equilibrium rate tends to pop back up.

They also reckon the stagnationists are misinterpreting some of the evidence. Growth in the 1990s was not illusory, they argue. The stockmarket boom only really got going in 1998, after America's unemployment rate had already fallen below 5%.

The expansion of the 2000s looks like a better example of secular stagnation. Investment in housing, which rose from 4.9% of GDP in 2001 to 6.6% at the market's peak in 2006, helped sustain the boom. Rising house prices made Americans feel flush, propelling consumer spending. Expanding credit added about one percentage point to growth each year, says the paper.

Yet the behaviour of the economy in this period looks more like a product of distortion than stagnation. At the time China and oil-producing states were running enormous current-account surpluses with America and building up large foreign-exchange reserves, contributing to what Ben Bernanke, Mr Greenspan's successor as Fed chairman, labelled a "global saving glut". Expensive oil and rising Chinese imports placed a drag on growth that more or less offset the boost from housing. Take away the savings glut and the housing boom, and the American economy would not necessarily have grown any faster or slower, just more healthily.

FIG 9.3 **They'll come crawling back**
Real interest rates, %

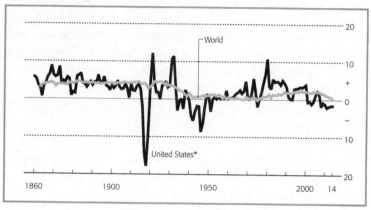

*Based on expectations of inflation
Source: "The Equilibrium Real Funds Rate: Past, Present and Future" by James Hamilton *et al.*,
US Monetary Policy Forum, University of Chicago Booth School of Business, 2015

Wallowing

What about the situation now? Some of the distorting forces of recent years are slowly fading. Household finances are certainly in better shape after a long period of deleveraging. That is helping to power a consumer-driven recovery in America that will eventually lead to higher interest rates.

On the other hand, stagnationists argue that the effects of demographic change are intensifying. Baby-boomers approaching retirement may be stashing more money away. Longer lifespans continue to spur saving. Axel Gottfries and Coen Teulings of Cambridge University have found that the increase in life expectancy over the past 40 years in rich and middle-income countries has raised the desired stock of savings by two times GDP.

Global conditions must also be taken into consideration. The authors of the Chicago paper calculate that over the long term, America's real interest rate tracks the one prevailing across the world as a whole (see Figure 9.3). Yet since about 2000 the real rate in America has generally been well below that of the world as a whole. The authors argue that thanks to the mobility of international capital that gap should soon close (albeit in part because global rates will probably fall). On their best estimates America's equilibrium rate has probably fallen a little, relative to the average from the 1960s until 2007 of about 2%. But, they argue, the decline is smaller than many stagnationists believe, and the rate is almost certainly positive. Nor is a lower rate now a sign that growth will permanently fall below past averages.

That is still no reason to breathe easy. A low equilibrium rate raises the risk that central-bank interest rates will sometimes become stuck at zero, leaving an economy in a prolonged slump. Even if the risk of secular stagnation is overdone, the authors reckon that the Fed has good reason not to raise rates too soon.

March 2015

PART 3

The future of economics

The elderly versus the robots

Under the shadow of rising debt and a world of work with pitiful pay, there is plenty of reason to be gloomy about the state of both economics and the world economy. The final part of this book looks forward to the exciting prospect of a new form of economy and a new brand of economics, and the challenges that both will bring.

Many people are trying to reinvent economics, yet Chapter 10 starts with an article about a Briton who has a good claim to be the discipline's founder: William Petty. Also an inventor and professor of anatomy, his careful data analysis created the first system of national accounts in the 1600s and set the course for economics as an empirical subject. Petty's concerns remain to this day, with economists trying to improve their favourite measure, GDP, by taking into account things like research and development spending. The urge to improve economics is a matter of theory and teaching too, and the chapter follows a band of economists stretching from Bloomsbury to Bangalore seeking to reform the discipline.

Those who suggest economics is overly academic and theoretical are missing a new movement. At the cutting edge of business there is much going on. For a decade or so, top-level academic economists have been quietly tinkering with firms such as Google and Microsoft. Now that trend is catching on, with a new breed of young Silicon

Valley economists helping to design firms. Sometimes the systems they set up are unpopular: for example, Uber's "surge pricing", which both attracts new drivers onto the road and can mean costly journeys. But these firms are using economists to make markets work better, meaning that the rise of the smartphone economy offers huge gains.

Armed with better knowledge about how humans behave, economists are coming up with striking new insights. Some are fun, such as how to avoid herd behaviour in choosing lottery numbers (which tends to cut your jackpot if you win), or how to stop pesky chatterboxes talking in a train's silent carriages. Others are much more heavyweight. Research shows that by appealing to economic incentives, crime could be deterred – but only if fines for criminal activity are much higher. And the use of behavioural economics can help policymakers prevent the worst outcomes for the users of doorstop lending.

Yet even the smartest policies might not be enough to overcome what could be the biggest challenge of the next 20 years. As the work of William Baumol, an economist, shows, a "cost disease" is driving up the cash required to fund health care, education and the arts. As the article on demographics in Chapter 13 shows, in an ageing world that could mean crippling bills. The best hope is that increases in productivity mean health-care savings can be found. But with research and development rates worryingly low in many rich countries, and big drug companies intent on renewing old patents rather than coming up with genuinely new drugs, those hopes could be dashed.

A final solution to rising costs could be robots, the subject of the final chapter. The advent of the "robocolleague" promises to make human workers far more productive. By helping teachers, nurses and doctors work more efficiently, this could help offset Baumol's cost disease. But the final question for the book, and one of the biggest in economics, is whether an economy fuelled by robots and machines will also drive up unemployment for the workers that compete with the automatons.

Reinventing economics

The man who invented economics: Petty impressive

Meet Sir William Petty, the man who invented economics

WILLIAM PETTY was an innovation machine. He designed an early form of catamaran, conceived of a mechanical grain planter, proposed attaching engines to boats and patented a "double-writing" instrument (it produced an extra copy of whatever a writer put down on paper). Petty, who died at Christmas in 1687, was also an innovator in the world of theories. By tinkering with data and simple models, this little-known Englishman came up with many of the ideas – how to measure GDP, why the money supply and banks matter, how lasting unemployment affects the economy – that form the bedrock of modern economics.

Born in 1623, the young Petty showed an early interest in clockmaking and joinery but did not enter either trade. His hometown, Romsey, is close to the sea and he left home on a ship, as a cabin boy, aged 14. That brought the first of two mishaps that changed the course of his life. After breaking his leg in a nautical accident he was put ashore for treatment in Normandy. As the injury healed he enrolled in a Jesuit college in Caen and developed an interest in anatomy, which he went on to study in Amsterdam and Paris. In Paris he met and worked for Thomas Hobbes, whose empiricism was a deep influence. Collecting data and making real-world observations became central to his work.

Back in England from 1646, Petty continued his medical studies at Oxford, rising to become professor of anatomy at Brasenose College by the time he was 27. Then came the second upheaval. After witnessing a bungled hanging Petty appeared to bring the criminal, a woman, back to life. She was pardoned, his reputation soared and he received a lucrative post, as physician general, in Ireland. His travels explain why Petty's economics are full of international comparisons: stagnant Ireland, more prosperous England and its great rival at the time, the Netherlands.

Success in Ireland meant Petty was granted an estate. He puzzled over how to value it. He first calculated its benefits: if cattle grazing in a field put on a certain amount of weight each year, the market price of the extra meat was a logical measure. Next he needed to work out how many years' income to tally. Men cared about their children and grandchildren, he reasoned, but concerns for the future were finite. Using data on the extent to which generations overlapped, Petty reckoned 21 years was right. He had jumped from a blank sheet of paper to an embryonic version of the "present value" calculation at the heart of modern finance.

Petty's landholding also provided the spur for his most important invention, GDP. England fought the Dutch three times between 1652 and 1674, and landowners faced high taxes. Petty thought this unjust and, to explain why, he set out the first set of national accounts for England and Wales. First, he asserted that total income must equal total spending. Since 4.5 pence a day was needed for food, housing, clothing and "all other necessities", and the population was 6 million, spending was £40 million a year. Next he tallied the income from a long list of assets – land, houses in London, ships – for a sum of £16 million. If £16 million of the £40 million in spending was income from assets, the remaining £26 million must be wages. The tax burden, he argued, should be shifted accordingly.

Other ideas were less self-serving. Out of concern that high interest rates were holding back trade in Ireland, Petty developed a sophisticated monetary theory, according to James Ullmer of Western Carolina University. He calculated the cash needed for all the transactions in Ireland each year, and how quickly it circulated, to derive an estimate of the amount of money needed to keep a lid on interest rates. This "quantity theory of money" is core to monetary economics, and Petty's version of it came a century before the one published by David Hume in 1752 that is usually credited as the first proper treatment.

Petty's monetary theories prompted him to contest criticism of England's fledgling banking system. Take, he argued, the problem of an economy that needs a money supply of £100,000 but has only £60,000 in cash. It could keep £20,000 as currency, with £40,000 put into banks. Because banks could lend the money out, loans and deposits would run close to £80,000. Add back the coins, and you have £100,000. Since such "fractional reserve" banking could help multiply money, Petty was a supporter: banks could help England compete with the Dutch.

Pyramid schemer

Petty also drew conclusions from his national accounts, which pointed to the importance of income from labour. He worried that unemployment would reduce men's facility to work – precisely the job-market scarring or "hysteresis" modern economists fret about. He pre-empted a rhetorical proposal made centuries later by John Maynard Keynes: since pointless work was better than none, the unemployed could be paid to build a pyramid on Salisbury Plain, or transport Stonehenge to London. Petty's real point was that deficient demand was a threat, and that in times of slump public investment could help offset it.

Various hues of academic snobbery explain why Petty is little known. That he included data with everything he wrote put him at risk: later studies found different results. In the century after his death his data-first approach fell out of favour; it seemed purer to construct theories first, then test them against data. Worse, Petty did not seek an all-encompassing theory of the world; because he lacked a model that joined up all markets, he was labelled an "anticipator", but not a founder, of economics.

Today these complaints seem flimsy. The economists toiling in central banks have ditched their overarching models and now run lots of little ones. At firms like Google and eBay data mining is no longer a sin but a lucrative skill. Petty's economics have triumphed again. Like his catamaran, his motorboat and his proto-photocopier, his economic ideas have stood the test of time.

December 2013

Post-crisis economics: Keynes's new heirs

Britain leads a global push to rethink the way economics is taught

FOR ECONOMISTS 2008 was a nightmare. The people who teach and research the discipline mocked by Thomas Carlyle, a 19th-century polemicist, as "the dismal science", not only failed to spot the precipice, many forecast exactly the opposite – a tranquil stability they called the "Great Moderation". While the global economy is slowly healing, the subject is still in a state of flux, with students eager to learn what went wrong, but frustrated by what they are taught. Some bold new projects to retune economics aim to change this.

Britain has form here. In the early 1930s economics was in a terrible state. The global economy was stuck in a rut, and economists could not explain why. Two Britons changed things. In 1933, John Maynard Keynes, an economist at Cambridge University, supplied the raw ingredients: a new theory that explained how deficient demand could lead to persistent recessions and long-term unemployment. The ideas were radical but technical. They really took off when John Hicks, then also at Cambridge, distilled Keynes's ideas into a simple model which quickly became the backbone of undergraduate teaching.

Now that the conditions for change are ripe again, Britain is well placed to take a lead. For a start there is fresh blood coming into the subject. The numbers taking economics A-level – over 26,000 in June 2013 – are at an all-time high. Many university students, however, are disappointed by what follows. At Manchester University, a student society has been set up to challenge the current syllabus. Among the demands are fewer lectures bogged down in detailed maths, and more time discussing important historical thinkers.

This is not just student grumbling. Many tutors bemoan the fact that the history of economic thought is now rarely taught. This does not mean a shift left to Karl Marx's communism or right to Friedrich Hayek's libertarianism, but equipping students with the tools to use historical thinkers as a source of new ideas.

To see why this matters, take banking. Irving Fisher and Milton Friedman were both sceptical of fractional reserve banking (the fact that banks' deposits are turned into loans, not safe assets) and wrote about it extensively. For the few who knew about them, their proposals were helpful in designing the "ring-fence" being used to protect retail deposits today. If more regulators had been taught about their work at university, perhaps the idea would have come before the crash, rather than after it.

It is not just students who are dissatisfied with economics. Professional economists can spot easy wins too. Many think economic history should be more widely taught, citing the fact that Ben Bernanke's Federal Reserve, influenced by his knowledge of the Great Depression and of Japan's slump in the 1990s, outperformed rich-world peers. It is not merely American financial history that matters, either. Stanley Fischer, governor of Israel's central bank between 2005 and 2013, says he found economic history (including Walter Bagehot's famous rule – to provide generous amounts of cash to troubled banks, but to charge them for it) useful in combating the 2008 crisis. This material had long fallen off the syllabus in most universities before the crash.

A new group of teachers is now listening. Led by Wendy Carlin, an economist at University College London, they are designing a new university-level curriculum. The project, which aims to launch for the 2014–15 academic year, will change things in a number of ways. Students' views are being heeded, with outfits like Rethinking Economics, a London-based student outfit, given the chance to comment on the new curriculum. It is also plugged in to the world of policy. A conference to launch Ms Carlin's project, held on November 11th 2013, was held at HM Treasury, and included economists from the Bank of England.

From Bloomsbury to Bangalore

It will also be more international. Before the crash, students could graduate with little knowledge of any economy other than America's. The academic contributors to Ms Carlin's project are spread across nine countries, including emerging markets like Chile, Colombia,

India and Russia. They have learned Hicks's lesson on presentation, with smart-looking online materials being designed by Azim Premji University in Bangalore. No one following the course will have to buy expensive books: the materials will be distributed to university departments without charge.

All this is possible because of another big change in British economics. Ever since Britain's post-Keynesian heyday in the 1950s a steady stream of economists have moved to America, in part tempted by the higher salaries there. But the cash constraint is easing as hedge funds pump cash into the subject. Brevan Howard, a hedge fund with assets of $40 billion, has founded a new financial stability research centre at Imperial College. In November 2013 it announced that Franklin Allen and Douglas Gale, professors at Wharton business school and New York University respectively, would be co-heads. The brain drain may be starting to reverse.

Ms Carlin's project has benefited from hedge fund money too, with cash coming from the Institute for New Economic Thinking (INET), a think-tank set up by George Soros, an investor, in 2009. INET now funds $4 million in economics projects per year, including a new research centre at Oxford University. Keynes too was an active investor who thought the role of economics was to protect the good things in life – music, art and intellectual life. He would have thoroughly approved.

November 2013

How GDP is measured: boundary problems

America has changed the way it measures GDP

ECONOMICS IS A MESSY DISCIPLINE: too fluid to be a science, too rigorous to be an art. Perhaps it is fitting that economists' most-used measure, gross domestic product (GDP), is a tangle too. GDP measures the total value of output in an economic territory. Its apparent simplicity explains why it is scrutinised down to tenths of a percentage point every month. But as a foundation for analysis it is highly subjective: it rests on difficult decisions about what counts as a territory, what counts as output and how to value it. Indeed, economists are still tweaking it. In December 2014 America's GDP rose by $560 billion, or 3.6%, mainly because the "boundary" that defines what counts as an economic asset was moved.

The modern history of GDP starts with America's Depression. The set of measures available to those battling the slump that started in 1929 was scarily narrow. Policymakers used stock prices, industrial production and transport data, and little else. The detail needed to diagnose economic problems properly was provided in a 1934 report by Simon Kuznets. The new national-income and product accounts that resulted measured income by industry and production by sector; they also introduced lots of new measurements, including GDP. Richard Stone of Cambridge University developed a similar system for Britain, adopted by the UN in 1947 as the first "System of National Accounts" (SNA), a set of international standards for measuring economic activity.

Since these first big steps to make GDP measurement systematic and international, improvements have been more gradual. The big problems are what to measure and how to measure it. Answering the first question involves defining a set of "boundaries": activities inside the ropes are included, those outside are not. Even the geographical boundary – how to define a nation – can be thorny. A country's territorial waters are within its national boundary, but foreign crews of ships working in those waters contribute to their home country's output. Smugglers, whose activity crosses borders and is hard to track, are a real headache.

Defining other boundaries is even harder. Since investment (activity that creates assets) is part of GDP, it is vital to define "assets". Here practicalities can trump principles. Economists have long thought of spending on research and development, or on making artwork, as types of investment. These efforts create things – patents, for example – that are a lot like fixed assets. They are durable, they give rise to a future stream of income and they help generate future output. But the previous SNA system, set up in 1993, regarded such assets as too difficult to measure. For this reason they were set outside the asset boundary. And so spending to produce them did not count as investment, part of GDP.

But the latest SNA system, agreed upon in 2008, shifted the asset boundary to include these innovative activities, prompting the recent changes to America's statistics. A new investment class called "intellectual-property products" has been created by America's Bureau of Economic Analysis (BEA). Ideally, the value of private firms' R&D would be based on the future income it generates, discounted to today's values. But since future products, and their related prices, are unobservable, those calculations are tricky. So the BEA is measuring R&D investment using firms' innovation-related costs. Government R&D, mainly spending on health, defence and aerospace, is now measured in the same way.

The BEA faces an even fiddlier task with original artwork, a category that includes films, books, music and TV shows. (Newspaper articles have no lasting value, according to the BEA, but what do they know?) The problem is that there is scant information on investment costs. Moreover, the asset – the right to the music, manuscript or TV format – is rarely sold. Rather it is used to create a future stream of products, like books and TV shows. So the BEA must estimate likely future royalty fees, and translate them into today's money to value the investment. Since artistic assets can last a long time (*The Simpsons* has been running since 1989) that is a tough task.

In the short term America's new GDP measure makes international comparisons more difficult. The BEA is not the first mover: Australia made the change in 2009, leapfrogging Canada in the OECD's country rankings of GDP per person. Canada switched in 2012, making back some of the ground. For the moment, America, Australia and Canada are the only G20 countries on the new system. By 2014 many other countries, including those in the EU, will have joined them.

Carrots and statistics

But GDP is still far from perfect. One problem is how to treat goods and services that are produced and consumed in the home. To do this the SNA defines another boundary. All goods produced and consumed at home are included in GDP: if more fruit and vegetables are grown in the garden the economy gets bigger. The logic is that home-grown produce could be sold at a market, obtain a price and be measurable. But services – cleaning a home, caring for a relative – are excluded from GDP. The logic is that services are produced as they are consumed: since they could not be sold they are outside the market.

But the assumption that there are no market prices for services delivered at home is 1940s thinking. It is easy to put a price on cleaning and caring – far simpler than working out how to price future film royalties. And excluding home-provided health care and education creates an ever-widening faultline under GDP. The market values of these services are rising much more quickly than the general rate of inflation. That means the value of the activity outside the boundary is changing rapidly over time. To stay relevant national accounts may have to change again.

August 2013

Joy to the world: is GDP growth the right goal?

What Ebenezer Scrooge and Tiny Tim can tell us about economics

WHAT IS THE POINT OF ECONOMICS? It often seems that the objective is to make the world richer. When global GDP is growing quickly, dismal scientists rejoice; their only misgiving is that growth might slow. Yet this is the season when, for devout Christians at least, the ineffable supplants the material (and the other way around for most folk). That makes it a good time to ponder whether maximising income should really be the be-all and end-all of economic policy.

Few people consider a big income as an end in itself – with the notable exception of Ebenezer Scrooge, the "squeezing, wrenching, grasping, scraping" anti-hero of Charles Dickens's *A Christmas Carol*. But we do sense that income helps people to lead more comfortable lives. Indeed, people in the ten richest countries in the world have a life expectancy 25 years higher than people in the ten poorest. People with more cash can afford better education, more varied leisure activities and healthier food, all of which improve the quality of life.

Income is not the only thing that matters, however. A paper from 1999 by William Easterly of New York University used data from 1960 to 1990 to see how close the correlation was between economic growth and 81 different indicators of quality of life. He found that it outweighed other factors (technological change, say, or changing social mores) for only 32 of them. A survey of 43 countries, published in October 2014, found that people in emerging markets are within a whisker of expressing the same level of satisfaction with their lives as people in rich countries.

If income is an imperfect proxy for quality of life, are there any plausible alternatives? In recent years many have instead focused on happiness. The United Nations has been publishing an annual "World

Happiness Report" since 2012. The British government measures "personal well-being" across the country on an annual basis. Yet happiness has its own shortcomings, argues Martha Nussbaum of the University of Chicago. While Scrooge found it easy to count his riches, happiness is harder to pin down. People are prone to what philosophers call "adaptive preferences", meaning that they may fail to report their "true" happiness. "Tiny Tim" Cratchit, the annoyingly saintly hero of A Christmas Carol, should not, by rights, be happy: he is crippled and desperately poor. Scrooge, despite his fabulous wealth and good health (Yuletide hallucinations aside), is miserable. Yet it would seem odd to conclude that Tiny Tim is better off.

If measuring happiness is so difficult, what else could economists look at? Amartya Sen of Harvard University argues that "capabilities" are the way to go. The definition of a capability is a bit fuzzy: at its simplest, a capability is something that people have reason to value. The list of potential capabilities is endless: the opportunity to live a long and healthy life, the freedom to take part in political life or to be well nourished. Capabilities, says Mr Sen, are ends that economists should strive to maximise: income is just one of the many means by which we get there.

That raises the question of which capabilities a society should maximise. Some worry that the capability approach is deeply paternalistic, with governments deciding what is best for their citizens. Leading theorists have reinforced that perception: Ms Nussbaum goes so far as to recommend "ten central capabilities" that are essential for a good life. For economists, who tend to be lovers of freedom, this is controversial stuff.

But the capability approach may be less illiberal than it seems. Insisting that GDP is the true measure of economic progress is itself a value-judgment. What is more, according to Mr Sen and Ms Nussbaum, people must have the freedom to select which capabilities they ultimately pursue. Freedom of choice has an impact on well-being; if you give people decent opportunities, what they ultimately decide to do gets less important. Someone who chooses to forgo a Christmas dinner with family and friends (as Scrooge does) is better off than someone who does not have any invitations to turn down, even though both people seem to end up in the same position.

Everyone need not go to a Christmas dinner, even though many people get a lot from it.

Life, liberty and the pursuit of capabilities

Measuring capabilities may be even more difficult than measuring GDP or happiness. There are, though, decent proxies. A country with a high life expectancy probably offers its citizens things like good health care and helps to shield them from pollution, which makes it easier for them to live a long, healthy life. A country where girls miss out on schooling or women are not allowed to drive is presumably failing to give them the opportunity to participate fully in civic life.

Some measures of economic success use such data. The Human Development Index (HDI), which Mr Sen helped to devise in 1990, considers not only income, but also life expectancy and schooling, as elements of development (by GDP per person, Norway is the sixth-richest country in the world, but according to the HDI its inhabitants are the world's best-off). On December 10th 2014 the UN released the latest version of its "inclusive-wealth index", which puts a dollar value on things like education and health.

It is no easier to raise capabilities, however, than it is to increase income. Bhutan, where the concept has driven government policy, still does not rank that highly on the HDI. Moreover, the capability approach has spawned so many measures, each more complicated than the last, that GDP starts to look appealing again. What other single number can give a decent approximation of quality of life? And yet, by the end of A Christmas Carol, even Scrooge realised that there was more to life than GDP.

December 2014

11 New firms, new economics

Silicon Valley economists: micro stars, macro effects

Meet the economists who are making markets work better

ON THE FACE OF IT, economics has had a dreadful decade: it offered no prediction of the subprime or euro crises, and only bitter arguments over how to solve them. But alongside these failures, a small group of the world's top microeconomists are quietly revolutionising the discipline. Working for big technology firms such as Google, Microsoft and eBay, they are changing the way business decisions are made and markets work.

Take, for example, the challenge of keeping costs down. An important input for a company like Yahoo! is internet bandwidth, which is bought at group level and distributed via an internal market. Demand for bandwidth is quite lumpy, with peaks and troughs at different times of the day. This creates a problem: because spikes in demand must be met, firms run with costly spare capacity much of the time.

This was one of the first questions that Preston McAfee, a former California Institute of Technology professor, looked at when he arrived at Yahoo! in 2007. Mr McAfee, who now works for Google, found that uses of bandwidth fall into two categories: urgent (displaying a web page) and delayable (backups and archiving). He showed how a two-part tariff (high prices when demand peaks, low ones otherwise) could shift less time-sensitive tasks to night-time, allowing Yahoo! to use costly bandwidth more efficiently.

The solution – two types of task, two prices – has intuitive appeal. But economists' ideas on how to design markets can seem puzzling at first. One example is the question of how much detail an online car auctioneer should reveal about the condition of the vehicles on offer. Common sense would suggest some information – a car's age and mileage – is essential, but that total transparency about other things (precise details on subpar paintwork) might deter buyers, lowering the auctioneer's commissions. Academic theory suggests otherwise: in some types of auction more information always raises revenues.

To test the idea, Steve Tadelis of the University of California at Berkeley (now also working for eBay) and Florian Zettelmeyer of Northwestern University set up a trial, randomly splitting 8,000 cars into two groups. The first group were auctioned with standard information, including age and mileage. The second had a detailed report on the car's paintwork. The results were striking: cars in the second group had better chances of a sale and sold for higher prices. This effect was most pronounced for cars in poorer condition: the probability of a sale rose by 23%, with prices up by 5%. The extra information meant that buyers were able to spot the type of car they wanted. Competition for cars rose, even the scruffier ones.

But more information is not always better. Studies show that shoppers overwhelmed by choice may simply walk away. Mr Tadelis tested whether it would be better to tailor eBay's auctions to users' experience level. The options for new users were narrowed, by removing sellers who are more difficult to assess (for example, those who had less-than-perfect feedback on things like shipping times). When new users had a simpler list of sellers to choose from, the number of successful auctions rose and buyers were more likely to use eBay again. Tailoring the market meant gains for buyers, sellers and eBay.

The desire to use theory to challenge conventional thinking is one reason economists are valuable to firms, says Susan Athey of Stanford University and Microsoft. When Ms Athey arrived at the software giant in 2007 it faced what was seen as an unavoidable trade-off: online advertising was good for revenues, but too much would deter users. If advertisers gained, users would lose. But economic theory challenges this, showing that if firms are dealing with two groups (advertisers

FIG 11.1 **Instant feedback**
US, standard deviations from the mean

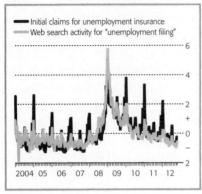

Sources: Google Correlate; US Department of Labour

and users, say), making one better off often benefits the other too.

Ms Athey and Microsoft's computer scientists put that theory to work. One idea was to toughen the algorithm that determines whether an ad is shown. This means ads are displayed fewer times, so advertisers lose out in the short term. But in the longer run, other forces come into play. More relevant ads improve the user experience, so user numbers rise. And better-targeted ads mean more users click on the advert, even if it is shown less often. Empirical evidence showed that although advertisers would respond only after some time, the eventual gain was worth the wait. Microsoft made the change.

Microeconomists have their sights on problems outside their home turf too. At the moment the policies picked by central banks and finance ministries are based on old news, since things like GDP, inflation and unemployment are measured with long lags. A team at Google headed by its chief economist, Hal Varian, is using search-engine data to provide more timely measures. Search terms like "job", "benefits" and "solitaire" are closely correlated with unemployment claims (see Figure 11.1). These types of relationship help construct new indexes that offer a real-time picture of the economy. If policymakers start to use these in a systematic way, their decisions could be based on how the economy looked yesterday, rather than months ago.

November 2012

The cutting edge: meet the market shapers

A new breed of high-tech economist is helping firms crack new markets

MOCKING ECONOMISTS is easy sport. They try to predict the future yet missed the 2008 crash, and make bizarre assumptions that cannot hold true. Other offences on the checklist include their narrow academic outlook and lack of exposure to the "real world" of business. The onslaught is common, and hard to refute. But at a turning point the herd tends to be wrong. Economics is evolving, with a mission to solve firms' real-life problems at its heart. Not unusually, the innovation is most obvious – for now – in Silicon Valley.

For Bryan Balin of SmarterTravel, a subsidiary of TripAdvisor, a travel website, economics has to be lightning quick. Only 1% of a typical travel site's visitors buy a flight, hotel or holiday before browsing away. Popular vendors can have a lot of viewer flow, but take revenues from only a tiny fraction of them. It is paramount to sift the buying wheat – to be guided as quickly as possible to the product they want – from the window-shopping chaff, who can be bombarded with advertising for other products, lifting the website's profit.

Mr Balin helps crack that problem. In the first few seconds a visitor spends on SmarterTravel's site an algorithm builds a picture of them. Click speed helps: window-shoppers tend to skip quickly between pages, serious buyers ponder for longer. Other data including the time of day, number of previous visits and location are important. The algorithm spits out the probability that the user is a potential buyer. With that, it calculates the revenue gains and risks (of distracting shoppers) associated with showing adverts. The site is adjusted in a few milliseconds.

Spotting helpful patterns when you are swimming in data is tough, explains Genevieve Graves, an astrophysicist turned data scientist. Her training put her in a good place: while doing research at Princeton University Ms Graves toiled with the Sloan Digital Sky Survey, a vast data set containing information on the location of stars and galaxies. Today she analyses something much more down to earth: human resources. The empirical technique she employs at hiQ Labs, a start-up based in San Francisco, known as "machine learning", is at the core of the new world of business economics.

Machine learning is not as scary as generations of science-fiction writers have made it sound. The basic aim, set out by Arthur Samuel in 1959, is to get computers to teach themselves. To do this a programmer tells a machine to perform a task repeatedly, measuring its success against some yardstick. Next the computer changes tack slightly, measuring whether it did better or worse, repeating this loop until it "learns" how to complete the task well. Run through enough attempts and a computer can set spam filters, turn voice recordings into text and fly a helicopter.

The data team at hiQ Labs reckons machine learning can revolutionise business. For most firms the cost of losing a senior employee is far greater than keeping existing workers happy. Leavers take knowledge and contacts with them and often induce loyal underlings to follow them out the door. In response big firms try to identify angst building in the workforce, using staff-wide surveys and blanket interviews to spot dissatisfaction. The result of this approach – a pay rise here, tax-free bikes or child-care vouchers there – are then rolled out across all staff.

This blanket approach could be improved if firms knew who was most at risk of leaving, says Ms Graves. Algorithms devised by hiQ Labs solve this. Using a firm's in-house data – from pay scales to organograms and job titles – and comparing it with information on pay and vacancies in competitor firms, it can predict who might defect, and for what reason. Managers then hone in on the potential deserters, offering a tailored solution, which often turns out to be something other than a pay rise.

Divining hidden "types" – the buyer and the browsers, the content and the disgruntled – is a common challenge in the new realm of economics, says Scott Nicholson, a Stanford University economics PhD advising hiQ. The reason is that new firms are often platforms on which buyers and sellers meet. His previous employers, LinkedIn (workers and employers) and Accretive Heath (doctors and patients), did a similar thing. In all these outfits, knowing more about a customer's type can help the platform suggest a better link.

Poynt, a cashless payment terminal (and Mr Nicholson's latest employer), also follows this model. Beyond accepting credit-card payments, Poynt hopes to provide a better connection between shopkeepers and their customers, and between the shops themselves. Linking together tills, for example, will in theory enable stores to compare themselves to anonymised local rivals (and so answer the retailer's perennial question: are all local shops doing badly, or is it just me?) A more mundane use would be to track sales and customer retention, potentially against peers. This sort of benchmarking was once firmly the preserve of blue-chip companies.

A better broker

Helping to get a new platform off the ground is a challenge, explains Riley Newman, head of economics at Airbnb. The specific challenge faced by his firm, which links "hosts" (property owners wanting to let their home) and "guests" (those looking for a place to stay), was getting supply and demand lined up. New York and San Francisco were so popular with visitors that the supply of hosts fell short. Facebook ads, which can be locally targeted, boosted supply. Boston and Portland had plenty of willing hosts but little demand. Google ads, targeted at people thought likely to visit these cities, lifted demand.

With the platform up and running Mr Newman and his team tried to make it work better. Its hosts – homeowners rather than professional hoteliers – are playing an unfamiliar role. Early on it became clear that some hosts were doing better than others. Crunching through data, it found the quality of photos of a host's abode was a key factor in their hit-rate. So Airbnb tested providing a free photography service to those offering accommodation, reasoning that better demand might offset the cost. The results were positive and Airbnb now offers free professional photos to most hosts.

In adapting products to match supply and demand, this new breed is injecting economics into the structure of Silicon Valley firms.

Although they are too busy to realise it, such firms are also providing the best defence of economics against its critics. Far from being unrealistic and out of touch, the role of chief economist will design the way that the firm works.

January 2015

Uber's economics: pricing the surge

The microeconomics of Uber's attempt to revolutionise taxi markets

NEW COMPETITORS always ruffle a few feathers. The unique thing about Uber, a new taxi-market player, is that it seems to have annoyed some of its customers as much as the incumbent cabbies it threatens. The problem is its "surge pricing", which can make the cost of Uber rides jump to many times the normal fare at weekends and on holidays. Gouging customers like this, critics reckon, will eventually make them flee, denting Uber's business. Microeconomics suggests that although Uber's model does have a flaw, its dynamic pricing should be welcomed.

Taxi markets have long needed a shake-up. In theory, entry should be easy – all that is needed is a car and a driving licence – with new drivers keeping cab fares close to costs. Yet in many cities, cabs are far from that competitive ideal. Decades of regulation conspire to keep entrants out. In New York a pair of taxi medallions sold at a 2013 auction for $2.6 million; many other cities have similar schemes. In London "the knowledge", a test of familiarity with the city's streets which GPS has made redundant but drivers still have to pass, can take four years to complete. Taxi markets often end up suspiciously clubby, with cabs in short supply and fat profits for the vehicle owners. Antitrust concerns have been raised in Australia, Ireland and Bulgaria, among others.

Uber aims to change all this. Launched in San Francisco in 2010 it lets passengers hail drivers from their smartphones – a move requiring even less effort than extending your arm. Some vehicles are not so much taxis as private cars that Uber has vetted. The convenience of hailing a cab from the comfort of a sofa or bar stool has given the service a loyal fan base, but it comes at a cost. Most of Uber's prices are slightly cheaper than a street-hailed cab. But when demand spikes, the surge prices kick in: rates during the busiest times, such as New Year's Eve, can be seven times normal levels, and minimum fares of up to $175 apply.

Critics of Uber's pricing are treading a well-worn path: setting tailored prices for the same good – price discrimination – often causes howls from consumer groups. It seems unfair when the charges for drugs vary across countries, the price of train tickets varies with the buyer's age, or, as in Uber's case, the price varies depending on the time that the journey is booked.

But price discrimination is not necessarily a bad thing, as a 2006 paper by Mark Armstrong of Oxford University explained. A firm offering a single price to all customers faces a trade-off: lowering prices raises sales but means offering a cut to customers prepared to pay more. Maximising profits can often mean lowering supply: goods are not provided to cheapskate shoppers so that more can be made from high-rollers. Customers who value the good at more than it costs to produce might miss out in a one-price-fits-all system – as many punters who have tried to find a regular cab on New Year's Eve will know.

Uber's price surge aims to solve this. Like many technology companies Uber is a middleman. It links independent cab drivers with customers wanting a ride in the same way that Google links searchers and advertisers or eBay links sellers and bidders. The business model only works when successful matches are made. Because price spikes raise the pay Uber's drivers receive (they get 80% of any fare, if they drive their own car) more cars are tempted onto the roads at times of high demand. Prices are high at 2am at the weekend not just because punters are willing to pay more, but also because drivers don't want to work then.

This strategy is common for firms that operate platforms or "two-sided" markets which link buyers and sellers, according to a 2006 paper by Jean-Charles Rochet and Jean Tirole of Toulouse University. Firms often tilt the market to give one side a particularly sweet deal: nightclubs let women in free to justify charging men a hefty fee; telephone directories are given away to create a readership which advertisers pay to access. The theory predicts each side's deal depends on two things: price sensitivity and how well stocked each side of the market is. Uber's price surge fits perfectly: Friday-night revellers are hit by a double whammy since they are willing to pay up precisely when the pool of cabs is low.

The real pricing problem

There is some evidence Uber's surge pricing is improving taxi markets. The firm says drivers are sensitive to price, so that the temptation to earn more is getting more Uber drivers onto the roads at antisocial hours. In San Francisco the number of private cars for hire has shot up, Uber says. This suggests surge pricing has encouraged the number of taxis to vary with demand, with the market getting bigger during peak hours.

However, the inflexibility of Uber's matchmaking fee, a fixed 20% of the fare, means that it may fail to optimise the matching of demand and supply. In quiet times, when fares are low, it may work well. Suppose it links lots of potential passengers willing to pay $20 for a journey with drivers happy to travel for $15. A 20% ($4) fee leaves both sides content. But now imagine a Friday night, with punters willing to pay $100 for a ride, and drivers happy to take $90: there should be scope for a deal, but Uber's $20 fee means such journeys won't happen.

Despite the revenues a matchmaking fee generates, it may not be Uber's best strategy. A fixed membership charge is often firms' best option in two-sided markets. By charging drivers a flat monthly fee Uber would generate revenue without creating a price wedge that gets in the way of matches. Since stumping up cash might put infrequent divers off, they could be offered a cheaper category of membership. Uber should keep its surge pricing in place. But to make the market as big as possible, and really revolutionise taxi travel, it might need to retune its fees.

March 2014

Hidden in the long tail: the boost from e-commerce

Consumers reap the benefits of e-commerce in surprising ways

WHEN COMMERCE BEGAN to move online, economists predicted two big benefits for consumers. Prices would become lower and more uniform. And the selection available to consumers would increase.

Identifying those benefits has been challenging. Online prices have proved to be surprisingly diverse. And while the selection of products online is indeed vast, many are niche products such as self-published books for which demand is scant to non-existent. E-commerce is still a net plus. But papers presented at the 2015 meeting of the American Economic Association demonstrate that its value arises in ways that economists did not foresee, and that are not easily captured by measures such as GDP.

Consider used books. Glenn Ellison and Sara Ellison of the Massachusetts Institute of Technology (MIT) collected prices on 335 titles and found that on average, the typical title sold for $17.80 online, 50% more than in stores. Paying more for an identical product would normally leave you worse off, not better. But in this case, the Ellisons argue the opposite is true: higher prices are a sign that buyers are being better matched to books they want.

For example, only a few bookshops might carry an out-of-print title such as *The Reign of George III, 1760–1815*, published in 1960 by Oxford University Press. They may never be visited by the readers most keenly interested in that book, who are scattered around the country (or beyond). By posting its inventory online, all those readers are now added to the potential demand for a store's copy. Higher demand translates into higher prices, which clearly makes the bookseller better off. But so is the reader since without the internet he would not have found the book. One of the authors some years ago bought a 30-year-old academic tome on pharmaceuticals online that the MIT library didn't have. She paid $20 and upon arrival saw that it had $.75 written in pencil inside the front cover, then erased. It had "evidently been languishing on the shelf of some used book store for years, and not a single customer ... was willing to pay even $.75".

These benefits are less likely to hold for easy-to-find, commoditised products; online prices of popular, usually in-print, books were less dispersed and closer to offline prices.

Rare used books are an example of a "long tail": a vast expansion in variety. But since the newly available products are often of niche interest only, the aggregate benefit to consumers is small. For example, since a minority of artists account for the vast majority of music sales, the fact that songs available for digital download tripled between 2000 and 2010 might not be a big deal: most of those new songs may be by marginal artists of no great interest.

Joel Waldfogel of the University of Minnesota believes this understates the internet's contribution. The demand for cultural products is much harder to predict than for conventional products such as shoes or soda. Seasoned publishers have only a vague idea what book, film or song will be a hit. A major record label can sign only a fraction of the artists available, knowing full well it will unwittingly reject a future superstar.

Thanks to cheap digital recording technology, file sharing, YouTube, streaming music and social media, however, barriers to entry have been dismantled. Artists can now record and distribute a song without signing to a major label. Independent labels have proliferated, and they are taking on the artists passed over by major labels. Hit songs are still a lottery, but the public gets three times as many lottery tickets.

This seems at odds with the collapse in recorded music revenue since 2000 which suggests declining, not rising, music industry output. Mr Waldfogel says that is misleading: because of piracy, revenue understates how much music the public has really consumed. He calculates the quality of songs recorded since then has been either stable (based on the number that made it onto critics' "best-of" lists) or significantly improved (based on the pattern of sales and airplay). This is corroborated by the success of indie-affiliated bands such as Arcade Fire and Mumford & Sons. Indie labels' share of the Billboard top 200 selling albums grew from 13% in 2001 to 35% in 2010. Mr

Waldfogel and a co-author reckon that tripling the selection of songs available has produced 15 times as much benefit for consumers than tripling the selection of a more predictable product.

That prices do not properly capture the benefits of online commerce is reinforced by a paper examining the search behaviour of users on eBay. Such people are often assumed to know what they want and ruthlessly pursue the lowest possible price for it. But a 2013 paper by Tom Blake of eBay, Chris Nosko of the University of Chicago and Steve Tadelis of the University of California, Berkeley, paints a more nuanced picture. They followed 500,000 eBay users chosen randomly on one particular day, and found just 16% of their searches resulted in a purchase. Users seemed to find browsing almost costless, since they were willing to conduct an additional search to achieve an average saving of just 25 cents. Moreover, many searchers were not trying to get a better price for one product but to explore different products. A user who typed in "opera DVDs" examined offers of Puccini, Verdi, Wagner and Bizet before returning and purchasing the Puccini.

This, the authors reckon, suggests price savings are but a small part of the value users derive from search; some of the value comes from what they learn while searching. Mr Tadelis speculates many users actually enjoy online searching, much as many people enjoy window-shopping at bricks-and-mortar outlets. This is clearly a problem for mainstream economics, which generally assumes search costs make people worse off, not better. It also underlines how far away measures like GDP are from capturing the benefits of the internet.

January 2015

12 The economics of behaviour

Crime: fine and punishment

The economics of crime suggests that corporate fines should be even higher

THE SUMMER OF 2012 was a bumper one for corporate fines and settlements. In just three months firms in Britain and America agreed to pay out over $10 billion because of wrongdoing. But the economics of crime suggests that fines imposed by regulators may need to rise still further if they are to offset the rewards from lawbreaking.

The latest allegations of bad behaviour are a familiar brew of overcharging, mis-selling and price-fixing. Banks have been the worst offenders. Barclays was fined $450 million for its part in the Libor price-fixing scandal; other big banks involved in the cartel followed. HSBC received a hefty fine for allegedly flouting money-laundering regulations. Two pharmaceuticals firms, GlaxoSmithKline and Abbott Laboratories, were stung for illegal marketing.

That some firms behave badly is nothing new, but the response of the authorities has changed. Take cartels. Internationally, fines rose by a factor of one thousand between the 1990s and 2000s. Data from America suggest this is not because there are more cartel cases, which have shown no upward trend since the late 1980s. Rather, the average level of fines has risen (see Figure 12.1, left side). Penalties have smashed records. The Barclays fine includes the largest ever levied by Britain's financial regulator and America's Commodity Futures Trading Commission, for instance. Even so, are fines high enough to work?

FIG 12.1 **Penalty kicked**

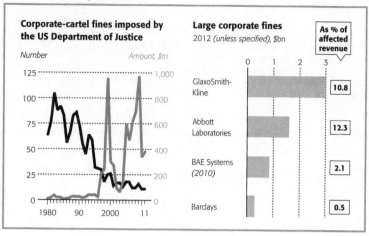

*At time of fine
Sources: US Department of Justice; *The Economist*

The economics of crime prevention starts with a depressing assumption: executives simply weigh up all their options, including the illegal ones. Given a risk-free opportunity to mis-sell a product, or form a cartel, they will grab it. Most businesspeople are not this calculating, of course, but the assumption of harsh rationality is a useful way to work out how to deter rule-breakers.

In an influential 1968 paper on the economics of crime, Gary Becker of the University of Chicago set out a framework in which criminals weigh up the expected costs and benefits of breaking the law. The expected cost of lawless behaviour is the product of two things: the chance of being caught and the severity of the punishment if caught. This framework can be used to examine the appropriate level of fines, and to see if there are ever reasons to exempt companies from fines.

In thinking about how to set fines, it helps to start from the extremes. One option is to have no fines at all for corporate wrongdoing, and to rely instead on market forces to impose the costs that keep firms in line. The market-based approach to antitrust regulation, popularised by Aaron Director of the University of Chicago, holds that antitrust violations must be ripping someone off, whether a customer or a supplier. The same is true of mis-selling cases. In time a firm acting in this way will lose business, meaning that crime will not pay.

The problem with this view is that frictions – the costs to customers of switching, say, or the barriers to entry for competitors – can allow exploitative firms to escape punishment. Market constraints alone are not always enough to ensure good behaviour. In a 2007 paper, John Connor and Gustav Helmers of Purdue University examined 283 international cartels that operated between 1990 and 2005. The aggregate revenue increase these cartels achieved by acting as they did was over $300 billion.

At the other extreme is a system of very high fines. Indeed, Mr Becker's crime calculus might lead to the conclusion that fines should be as draconian as possible – seizing all a wrongdoer's assets, for example. Anything lower reduces the expected cost of criminality, without doing anything to improve the probability of detection. (Treating whistleblowers leniently is consistent with this logic: letting them off punishment raises the odds of truth-telling, and therefore of detection.) There are plenty of arguments against ultra-high fines, however. One is that false convictions carry too high a cost. Another is that fines of this sort could cripple firms, reducing competition.

A middle way might be for regulators to levy penalties that offset the benefits of crime. Data on cartels supply useful guidance on how to go about calculating these fines. The first step is to measure the expected gain from crime which fines need to offset. In the study by Messrs Connor and Helmers, the median amount that cartel members overcharged was just over 20% of revenue in affected markets. Next, you need an assumption about the chances of being found out: a detection rate of one cartel in three would mean trustbusters were doing well. In this example, that would mean a fine of 60% of revenue is needed to offset an expected benefit of 20% of revenue – far higher than the fines in the study, which were between 1.4% and 4.9%.

The calculus of crime

Assessed against this methodology, even apparently hefty fines look pretty weak. Recent big penalties (see Figure 12.1, right side) have been far lower than a crime calculus of this sort would suggest is needed, even allowing for the fact that some firms, like Barclays, get discounts for co-operating with the authorities. Britain looks particularly lenient. Its antitrust laws impose fines of up to 10% of revenues; American regulators levy penalties of up to 40%, and the European Commission goes up to 30%.

Disgruntled customers may later bring private lawsuits, which can further raise the cost of crime. Here crime economics would suggest the American "class action" system, bunching many customers' complaints into a single lawsuit, is an asset Europe lacks. In July 2012 MasterCard and Visa agreed to a $7.3 billion settlement to resolve retailers' lawsuits alleging collusion (which the two firms deny) over credit-card fees. Criminal charges against individuals can also focus minds. Yet litigation and criminal charges tend to take years to emerge; many wrongdoers are able to avoid court. To deter bad behaviour fines need to rise. The watchdogs are biting, but some need sharper teeth.

July 2012

Noise pollution: shhhh!

Why quiet carriages don't work, and how they might be made to

QUIET CARRIAGES ON TRAINS are a nice idea: travellers voluntarily switch phones to silent, turn stereos off and keep chatter to a minimum. In reality, there is usually at least one inane babbler to break the silence.

A couple of problems prevent peaceful trips. First, there is a sorting problem: some passengers end up in the quiet carriage by accident and are not aware of the rules. Second, there is a commitment problem: noise is sometimes made by travellers who choose the quiet carriage but find an important call hard to ignore.

The train operators are trying to find answers. Trains in Queensland, Australia, are having permanent signs added to show exactly what is expected; a British operator has invested in signal-jamming technology to prevent phone calls. Microeconomics suggests another approach: putting a price on noise.

Fining people for making a din would surely dissuade the polluter and is a neat solution in theory, but it requires costly monitoring and enforcement. Another tack would be to use prices to separate quiet and noisy passengers – in effect, creating a market for silence. A simple idea would be to sell access to the quiet carriage as an optional extra when the ticket is bought. Making the quiet coach both an active choice and a costly one would dissuade many of those who do not value a peaceful ride.

Charging may also solve the commitment problem. This is particularly tricky, as attitudes to noise can change during the journey. Some passengers would pay the quiet premium but still chatter away when some vital news arrives. Schemes that reward the silent – a ratings system among fellow passengers, for example – could help. The idea is that losing your hard-won reputation offsets the short-term gain from using the phone. But such a system also fails the simplicity test.

In a 2010 book, *Identity Economics*, George Akerlof and Rachel

Kranton argue that "norms" – feelings about how everyone should behave – also play a role in decision-making. Charging a price, even if just a token amount, means the quiet carriage becomes a service that fellow passengers have bought, not just a preference they have expressed. Perhaps different norms would come into play, encouraging calm. If not, a personal bubble is always an option: noise-cancelling headphones start at around $50.

May 2012

Shaping behaviour: nudge nudge, think think

Behavioural economics is changing regulation. Payday lending is a target

IN 2010 BRITAIN'S Conservative-led government established a team – known affectionately as the "nudge unit" – to investigate how behavioural economics could be used to improve policy. Behavioural economists argue that consumers are not hyper-rational but have predictable biases, and they use insights from experiments to make models imitate reality more closely. The nudge unit was so successful at finding clever policy insights that it was part-privatised and has been advising other governments. Now, behavioural economics is changing the way Britain's regulators think about the markets they regulate.

The keenest wonks are found at the Financial Conduct Authority (FCA), which has been scrutinising the controversial payday lending market. Payday lenders offer short-term loans at astronomical interest rates. One problem with this market, says the FCA, is that borrowers may suffer from "present bias". It is not just that people prefer jam today to jam tomorrow; they also fail to foresee that when tomorrow comes, they will have the same skewed preference. This leads to optimism about future behaviour. Consumers take out expensive loans expecting to repay them quickly. Instead, they spend more than planned and end up in financial trouble. The FCA has found that some borrowers are worse off six months to a year after taking out a loan; they have lower credit scores, for instance, and are more likely to default on other debts.

The FCA has made multiple interventions in the market. In April 2012, it introduced tough new affordability checks and limited lenders' access to borrowers' bank accounts. In July, it proposed a cap on interest rates. On October 2nd, Wonga, a payday lender, announced that it would write off £220 million ($350 million), which the FCA says it lent without adequate affordability checks. The Competition and

Markets Authority is also intervening to establish a price comparison website. But soon there might not be many offers to compare; experts predict that following the introduction of a tight price cap in January 2015, many of Britain's payday lenders will exit the market.

Canny firms in many markets appear to understand behavioural economics. In March 2012, the Office of Fair Trading (OFT) intervened to prevent six furniture and carpet retailers from claiming shoppers were benefiting from big discounts when hardly any sales had been made at the undiscounted price. As it is easy for companies to claim they are offering discounts, traditional economics suggests the consumer will anticipate their trickery and ignore the "reference price". But, in an experiment, the OFT found that reference prices lead to less shopping around, benefiting traders who deploy them. A race-to-the-bottom can result. Competition is normally a good thing but, with behavioural economics in hand, British trustbusters argue that rivalry can sometimes be harmful, as scrupulous firms will fall behind their crafty rivals.

In many markets consumers fail to switch supplier to take advantage of better deals. This can be partly explained by present bias; consumers endlessly postpone the paperwork. Another contributing phenomenon is "loss aversion"; people dislike losses more than they like equivalent gains. This makes them assign disproportionate value to services they already have. Such inertia on the part of consumers gives firms more leeway to raise prices. That worries Ofgem, Britain's energy regulator. The average British consumer on a single fuel energy tariff would save nearly £100 a year by switching supplier, yet in the second quarter of 2012 only 2% did so. Ofgem wants firms to simplify their tariffs, making them easier to compare, hoping that will nudge consumers towards action.

As a result of all this, an OECD report in January 2014 declared Britain a world leader in applying behavioural economics to regulation. But not everyone is celebrating. Stephen Littlechild, a professor at Cambridge University and a former regulator, says that even if consumers make mistakes, regulators – who are human too – should not always assume they know better. Behavioural economics is controversial because it can suggest interfering with personal choices. Some might prefer to learn from their own mistakes. Yet, so far, most regulatory interventions have focused on improving consumers' access to clear information. That must be good.

October 2014

The lottery: herd mentality

Britons love gambling – and are rubbish at it

SINCE IT BEGAN IN 1994, Britain's national lottery has created over 3,200 millionaires. It is the country's most popular form of gambling, played by rich and poor alike. A plan to double the ticket price, currently £1 ($1.51), during 2013 caused howls from players. Yet many can get better value simply by picking better numbers.

One fact is all-important when it comes to lottery strategy: the numbers really are random. The game's regulator, the National Lottery Commission, conducts regular checks; independent boffins confirm that the balls are unbiased. The odds of picking the correct six numbers from 49 are the same every week: one in 13,983,816. Setting aside lesser prizes, this means that the probability-adjusted value of a ticket to win a £7 million jackpot is close to 50p.

Because each draw is independent, the past is no guide to the future. Books and websites nonetheless try to identify "hot" or "cold" balls. Many scorn unlucky number 13, which, as it happens, has appeared just 189 times (only number 20 has been rarer). Some say the hottest numbers (23, 38 and 44 have all appeared 246 times) should be picked as they are the most likely to come up; others avoid them, on the basis that a winning streak is bound to end. More sophisticated but equally daft advice comes from tipsters who add together the numbers in previous winning sets and plot the results on a chart. A bell-shaped curve appears: sensible choices must produce a sum that lies in this range, the experts say. But the curve merely results from the fact that there are more ways to end up with a central sum than an extreme one.

The only really sound strategy is to avoid numbers that others pick, since shared numbers mean shared prizes. A 1995 jackpot of £16 million was spread between 133 people, all of whom had picked a set of numbers that sat in central columns on the ticket. Research has shown that multiples of numbers, particularly "lucky" number seven, are popular with Britons. So are geometric patterns on the ticket, straight or diagonal lines. Such clustering is common in other countries, too. A German study showed that 12,000 players were picking the previous week's numbers; thousands of others were adding or subtracting one from them.

A little understanding of probability can be especially damaging. Knowing the truth of the saying that the numbers 1, 2, 3, 4, 5 and 6 are as likely to come up as any other combination, an army of some 10,000 Britons chooses them each week. If those numbers ever come up, each player would receive £700.

Higher numbers may be better than lower ones, because so many people use birth dates to guide their choices. But true randomness is best of all. Best to let the computer decide, and try a lucky dip.

March 2013

The economics of meetings: meeting up

New research hints at ways of making meetings more effective

WORKING LIFE often seems like an endless sequence of tiresome meetings. Catch-ups, kick-offs and reviews litter the calendars of most professionals. Effectiveness around the conference table can determine success in almost every career. Chief executives spend a third of their time in pow-wows of one sort or another, by one estimate. Monetary policy is usually set by committee; juries deliberate behind closed doors before voting. Yet despite our reliance on meetings, most decisions made by committee are subject to serious and pervasive bias.

In 1785 the Marquis de Condorcet, a French mathematician and philosopher, noted that if every voter in a group has a better-than-even chance of choosing the preferable of two options, and if voters do not influence each other, then large groups of voters are very likely to make the right choice. The bigger and more diverse the group the better: more people bring more information to the table which, if properly harnessed, leads to improved decisions. But ever-bigger meetings imply more time spent in them: few workers would welcome that. And even with more people in the room, all manner of behavioural flaws stand in the way.

One problem that obstructs sensible decision-making is the "halo effect" – "owning the room" in the parlance of Silicon Valley. If one aspect of an idea or argument seems appealing, people tend to judge its other features more favourably too. Polished slides, for example, will make a presentation seem more compelling. Good-looking speakers win audiences over more easily.

A second problem is called "anchoring". In a classic study Amos Tversky and Daniel Kahneman secretly fixed a roulette wheel to land on either 10 or 65. The researchers spun the wheel before their subjects, who were then asked to guess the percentage of members of the United Nations that were in Africa. Participants were influenced by irrelevant information: the average guess after a spin of 10 was

25%; for a spin of 65, it was 45%. In meetings, anchoring leads to a first-mover advantage. Discussions will focus on the first suggestions (especially if early speakers benefit from a halo effect, too). Mr Kahneman recommends that to overcome this, every participant should write a brief summary of their position and circulate it prior to the discussion.

Even this cumbersome procedure may not prevent bias if members are more worried about their reputations than about making good choices. Participants may want to avoid disagreement, lest others interpret their qualms as a personal slight. Similarly, the desire to look competent may cause people to suppress comments they fear others will think foolish.

A preference for agreement can lead to a bias towards the obvious. Suppose a panel is rating an applicant for a job before discussing her. Some of the candidate's merits – such as the extent of her experience – will be clear to all. Others, such as her personal appeal, will be more subjective. The best way for panellists to be confident of aligning their views with those of others is to concentrate on objective traits, and to discard their private insights. Panellists seeking agreement will thus put too much weight on what is public knowledge, whether or not there is any discussion.

Until now, this was just a theory. But new research has documented the phenomenon. In a 2014 paper Tom Gole of the Boston Consulting Group and Simon Quinn of Oxford University studied the votes of judges at international school debating tournaments. In these tournaments, three judges are randomly assigned to each debate (with some controls to ensure each panel has a mixture of experience, gender and so on). Judges watch the debate, then immediately vote on the winner before conferring. Crucially for the experiment, the participating teams are seeded. Using some whizzy statistical modelling, the authors find that if a judge disagrees with her fellow panellists in a given round, she is more likely to vote for the pre-tournament favourite – the higher-seeded team – in later debates. That suggests, say the authors, an unspoken desire to avoid "too much" disagreement.

Career concerns may distort incentives even if votes are secret. In a 2007 paper Gilat Levy of the London School of Economics noted that observers can work out how likely it is that committee members have voted one way or another from ballot rules. If unanimity is required for a measure to pass, and it does, then outsiders will know with certainty how every member has voted. A simple majority rule means that observers can assign at least a 50% probability to any one committee member having given their assent; if a majority of two-thirds is required, the probability that any given member has supported the proposal goes up. The incentive to vote against controversial measures rises the greater the likelihood that each member will be blamed for its passage.

Meet market

That makes designing an ideal procedure hard. Yet Condorcet's basic insight rings true: committees work best when they harness and combine the unique insights of every member. To that end, chairmen might do several things. First, they should follow Mr Kahneman's advice, and have every participant note their views in advance. Second, they should pick at random who will speak first. This would not prevent anchoring, but would at least stop any one individual from repeatedly dominating. Alternatively, members could be called on in reverse order of seniority (justices in America's Supreme Court used to vote this way). Finally, they should encourage and reward disagreement, to offset the personal costs of discord. Given the time and energy invested in meetings, the returns to running them better are high. And if calling a meeting required more effort from the person convening it, workers might find their calendars a little less crowded.

April 2014

13 Tomorrow's economic challenges

Health-care costs: an incurable disease

How health care can become both more expensive and more affordable

HEALTH-CARE EXPENDITURE IN AMERICA is growing at a disturbing rate: in 1960 it was just over 5% of GDP, in 2011 almost 18%. By 2105 the number could reach 60%, according to William Baumol of New York University's Stern School of Business. Incredible? It is simply the result of extrapolating the impact of a phenomenon Mr Baumol has become famous for identifying: the "cost disease". His 2012 book gives a nuanced diagnosis, offering both a vision of a high-cost future and a large dose of optimism. The cost disease may be incurable, but it is also survivable – if treated correctly.

To understand the cost disease, start with a simple observation: whatever the economy's average rate of productivity growth, some industries outpace others. Take car manufacturing. In 1913 Ford introduced assembly lines to move cars between workstations. This allowed workers, and their tools, to stay in one place, which cut the time to build a Model T car from 12 hours to less than two. As output per worker grows in such "progressive" sectors, firms can afford to increase wages.

In some sectors of the economy, however, such productivity gains are much harder to come by – if not impossible. Performing a Mozart quartet takes just as long in 2012 as it did in the late 18th century. Mr Baumol calls industries in which productivity growth is low or even non-existent "stagnant".

Employers in such sectors face a problem: they also need to increase their wages so workers don't defect. The result is that, although output per worker rises only slowly or not at all, wages go up as fast as they do in the rest of the economy. As the costs of production in stagnant sectors rise, firms are forced to raise prices. These increases are faster than those in sectors where productivity is improving, and faster than inflation (which blends together all the prices in the economy). So prices of goods from stagnant sectors must rise in real terms. Hence "cost disease".

The disease is most virulent in industries where standardisation and automation are hard. The best examples are goods tailored to meet customer-specific demands, such as bespoke suits and haircuts. But Mr Baumol focuses on industries in which the cost disease is rife because human interaction is important, such as health care, education and the performing arts. Because it is often human input that makes the products of these industries valuable, cutting labour would be self-defeating.

Historical data confirm that the cost disease is real. Since the 1980s the price of university education in America has risen by 440% and the cost of medical care by 250%. For the economy as a whole, the average price and wage increases were only 110% and 150% respectively (see Figure 13.1, left side). Mr Baumol's theory makes for scary extrapolations. America's health-care spending as a share of GDP, for instance, is growing by around 1.4% a year. If it continued to expand at this rate for a century, it would rise to that eye-popping figure of 60% in 2105.

Although America leads the pack in medical inflation, it is not the only country that is infected. In Japan health-care spending per person grew by 5.7% a year in real terms between 1960 and 2006; in Britain it rose by 3.5% a year over the same period. Applying Mr Baumol's logic, health-care spending in both countries could, if nothing was done about it, rise from around 10% of GDP to more than 50% in the next 100 years.

Fortunately, possibilities abound to mitigate the impact of the cost disease. Cutting waste in health care can shift down the level of spending. Though this is no cure, it does mean costs grow from a lower base when the disease inevitably takes hold. And innovation

FIG 13.1 **The cost of progress**

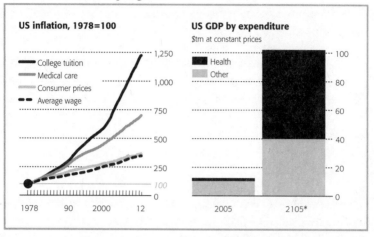

US inflation, 1978=100

- College tuition
- Medical care
- Consumer prices
- Average wage

1,250
1,000
750
500
250
100
0

1978   90   2000   12

US GDP by expenditure
$trn at constant prices

- Health
- Other

100
80
60
40
20
0

2005   2105*

*Based on an extrapolation of current trends
Sources: Thomson Reuters; *The Cost Disease* by William Baumol, 2012; *The Economist*

will mean that activities within the stagnant sector, like hand-delivered post, can be replaced by alternatives where productivity improvements are more likely, like texts and e-mail.

Rising costs will also encourage hard thinking about whether a personal and tailored touch is needed. If not, productivity gains are easier to find. In some areas of medicine computers now have better diagnostic skills than humans. In education lectures can be recorded, allowing star academics to teach millions. In the arts live opera performances are beamed to audiences in cinemas across the world.

A bigger slice of a much bigger pie

But that still leaves a rump of services within medicine, education and the arts that are resistant to productivity gains. For these, Mr Baumol offers his most intriguing prediction: although their costs will grow alarmingly high, they will remain affordable. In a way, the disease produces its own cure. If America's economy grows by 2% per year (its long-term rate), it will be eight times bigger in 100 years. In addition, goods and services in innovative sectors will become much cheaper. In 1908 the average American had to work for around 4,700 hours to earn enough to buy a Model T Ford. A century later, a typical car can be had for only 1,365 hours of labour. This means that, even if health care really did eat up 60% of the pie, there would still be much more to spend on everything else (see Figure 13.1, right side).

The real problem is not the cost disease, Mr Baumol argues, but knee-jerk reactions to it. The most likely response to spiralling budgets for publicly provided medicine and education is to shift provision to the private sector. But that will not cure the underlying disease. High costs could also lead to excessive rationing, slowing development over the long term.

If it happens, such a reaction rests on a mistaken premise: that the rising costs in the stagnant sectors make people poorer. In fact, buying power is growing much faster than medicine, education and the arts are becoming dearer. Mr Baumol's crystal ball says that in 100 years a live performance of a Mozart quartet will be vastly more expensive, but people will still be able to afford it.

September 2012

Dwindling R&D: arrested development

America and Europe are relying on private firms in the global R&D race

IT IS A FONT OF ECONOMIC GROWTH. Research and development (R&D), the hunt for new ideas, products and processes, enhances productivity and generates well-paid jobs. It plays an important role in keeping economies growing after they have industrialised. It has positive spillover effects on the number of employees firms hire, and on the wages of low-skilled workers in high-tech sectors. These public benefits help explain why R&D activity has historically been supported by large amounts of government cash. But public spending on research is in secular decline, leaving private firms to pick up the slack. This funding switch has already left Britain lagging in the global R&D race, and may yet put America at risk, too.

Private firms have plenty of incentive to shell out, of course. The companies that spend most on R&D tend to be in computing, cars and drugs. Top of their respective industries in 2010, according to Booz, a consultancy, were Microsoft, a software firm; Toyota, a car manufacturer; and Roche, a pharmaceuticals firm. In 2011 Microsoft spent $9 billion on R&D. Its 850 PhD scientists and 40,000 developers are mainly preoccupied by cloud computing. Toyota spent ¥730 billion ($9.2 billion); its hybrid cars trace their origins to 15 research centres which investigate new materials and fuels. Roche, which has over 330,000 patients enrolled in clinical trials, spent SFr8 billion ($9 billion).

Nonetheless, ensuring that private firms do enough R&D is a problem because its public benefits are likely to be higher than the private benefits (ie, profits) that go to firms. Even with patent systems to protect innovators, genuinely new inventions diffuse so that copycats and competitors benefit. These knowledge spillovers are good for the economy as a whole, but may be bad for the firm that made the original discovery. In a 2012 paper that looked at data from American firms, Nicholas Bloom of Stanford University and Mark Schankerman and John Van Reenen of the London School of Economics found that the public benefits of R&D were roughly double the private benefits. The data also suggested that the optimal rate of R&D would be twice as high as the actual rate, and possibly higher.

The simplest response to this problem is direct government funding. This was the favoured post-war model, especially in America during the space race. In the mid-1960s space exploration received around $25 billion a year from the taxpayer, measured in today's dollars. Public funding for military research was also buoyant. At its 1964 peak federal R&D hit close to 2% of American GDP. But the share of publicly funded research has since fallen sharply in some countries. In America the ratio of public R&D to GDP has fallen by half since the 1960s. In Britain the ratio fell by the same amount over a shorter period, dropping from 0.31% in 1986 to just 0.17% in 2009, the lowest level in the G7 group of advanced economies. This contrasts with sharp growth in public R&D spending in Japan, Germany and South Korea.

A fall in government spending places the onus squarely back on firms' private R&D efforts. In America this public-to-private switch has been relatively successful. Firms have increased their R&D spending faster than GDP, so that they have offset the reduction in government support (see Figure 13.2, left side). Even so America's overall R&D-to-GDP ratio has fallen behind South Korea's; China is catching up fast (see Figure 13.2, right side). Europe as a whole has a weak R&D-to-GDP ratio, despite German efforts. It currently stands at around 1.9%, far below a European Union target of 3%. Britain's position is particularly poor. Unlike in America, business R&D has fallen in tandem with public spending, dropping from 1.5% of GDP in 1986 to 1.1% in 2009. Of rich countries, only Italy looks worse.

Three things in particular help influence firms' R&D spending. The first is tax treatment. America was quick to offer tax breaks, introducing "research and experimentation" tax credits in 1981. This reduced firms' tax liability by 20% of their R&D costs, so $100 million spent on research in effect cost only $80 million. In a 2002 paper Mr Bloom, Mr Van Reenen and Rachel Griffith of Manchester University looked at R&D tax credits in nine advanced economies between 1979 and 1997, finding that a 10% fall in R&D costs produces a long-run 10% increase in R&D spending.

FIG 13.2 **Inventiveness quotient**
R&D spending as % of GDP

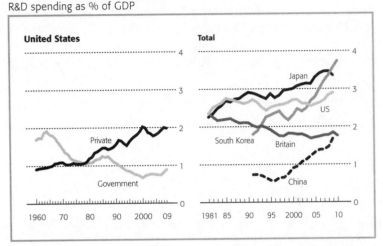

Sources: National Science Foundation; OECD

Merger policy is the second thing that can influence R&D. Competing firms race to be the first to invent new products; one of the rationales for merging with a rival can be to dull this competition. The pharmaceuticals industry has seen massive consolidation, for example: of 42 American drugs firms that existed in 1988, only 11 remained in 2012. Case studies suggest this may reduce R&D growth rates. In the six years before their 1999 merger, Astra and Zeneca increased R&D by an average of 19% a year. In the six years after AstraZeneca's R&D growth was just 1% a year.

Third, firms may face pressure from shareholders to rein in R&D budgets. Research is a current cost that delivers benefits in the distant future (although the drugs industry shows that pay-offs can disappoint). There is survey evidence that bosses choose to scrimp on R&D in order to hit earnings targets or to pay larger dividends to investors.

Britain's listless performance in private R&D spending is explained by all three of these factors. Britain was a tax laggard, introducing credits only in 2000. Much of its private R&D spending is down to drugs and services industries, where mergers are rife. And a 2012 government-sponsored report on equity markets found a lack of long-term decision-making by investors. But America should not relax. It looks increasingly stingy in its tax treatment of R&D as other countries catch up; mergers and short-termism are a concern in America, too. Relying on private firms to power R&D should mean giving them every incentive to do so.

August 2012

Big Pharma: zombie patents

Drug companies are adept at extending the lifespan of patents, at consumers' expense

IT IS HARD TO THINK of an industry in which competition is more important than pharmaceuticals. As health-care costs rocket, the price cuts – often of 85% or more – that generic drugs offer are one easy way to economise. Ibuprofen is a good example. In the early 1980s the drug, which soothes both pain and inflammation, was a costly patented product. Today Boots, a British chemist, sells 16 generic tablets for 40 pence (68 cents), just 2.5 pence per pill. In America, the drug can be bought in bulk for a penny a pop. Indeed, competition from generics is so painful to drug companies that they have invented a series of ingenious palliatives, exploiting patent laws to help maintain high prices.

Patents create short-term monopolies. The deal is simple: the drug inventor makes its formula public and in exchange is granted a competition-free run at the market, lasting up to 20 years. This gives pioneers time to recoup the costs of researching and developing new compounds, vital when creating a new medicine can cost up to $5 billion. The patent guarantees a decent return, meaning companies have both the means and the incentive to keep innovating.

When the patent reaches its expiry date, the comfortable monopoly evaporates, and is replaced by cut-throat competition. Incumbents have three ways of defending themselves. Marketing can create brand-specific demand, dulling the temptation to switch to low-price products. Ibuprofen illustrates this. Developed by the chemists at Boots itself in the 1960s, the patent expired in 1984. But a year earlier Boots had created Nurofen, branded ibuprofen. The clever mix of packaging and advertising protected its profits. The lucrative Nurofen brand was sold in 2006; Boots still stocks the product, which costs five times more than its generic equivalent.

A second strategy nudges customers towards newer drugs that are still protected by patent. Omeprazole, a drug to reduce stomach acid developed by AstraZeneca in the 1980s, shows how it works. Branded as Losec in Britain and Prilosec in America, it became one of the world's bestselling drugs in the mid-1990s. With the patent set to expire in 2001 AstraZeneca faced a drop in profits. So the company took its drug and adapted it, creating a closely related compound, esomeprazole, which it sold as Nexium. Though a clear offshoot of the original medicine, this counted as a new drug and was given a patent. A big marketing campaign and attractive pricing helped shift demand away from Losec and towards Nexium. With the help of this strategy, sales between 2006 and 2013 amounted to almost $40 billion.

This sort of "follow on" patenting is common. In a 2014 paper Sotiris Vandoros of the London School of Economics looks at what happens when patents expire in two important classes of drugs: ACE inhibitors, used to treat blood pressure, and proton-pump inhibitors, such as omeprazole. He tracked sales of these drugs after patents expired in six European countries between 1991 and 2006, measuring the switch both to generic drugs and to related but still patented compounds. Mr Vandoros's findings are worrying. When patents expired on Captopril, a leading ACE inhibitor, cheap generic versions became available. But the total volume of sales of all versions of the drug went down rather than up as demand shifted to more expensive patented products. Other drugs showed similar patterns, meaning that competition from generics was failing to cut costs.

Even more troubling than fending off competition with marketing nous and chemical tinkering is drug companies' third option: pay the makers of generics not to compete. Since the early 2000s "pay for delay" agreements have become more common. A company with a patent due to expire strikes a deal: it pays potential entrants a fee not to compete, preserving its monopoly. A pay-for-delay deal between AstraZeneca and three big generic manufacturers helped to protect Nexium from competition between 2008 and May 2014.

The economic costs of these three strategies vary hugely. Marketing is a decent way to compete. Purists may wish that firms would try to outdo each other by devoting more cash to genuine research and economists may bemoan the irrationality of those who buy branded drugs at ten times the price of an identical generic. But despite the quibbles, the market works: there is a choice, including a low-cost option.

Giving competition an adrenalin shot

Follow-on drugs are a greyer area. Some believe that many are genuinely new inventions, different enough to justify a fresh patent. Big drugmakers' defenders argue that product redesign is a symptom of a healthy and innovative market. Yet America's competition watchdog, the Federal Trade Commission (FTC), decided that normal rules of thumb do not apply: new products can harm competition in this market. It filed a legal brief to that effect in 2012 regarding Warner Chilcott, a pharmaceutical firm which had reformulated an antibiotic three times. The firm's strategy, which the FTC calls "product hopping", offered little in the way of genuinely new medicine, but helped keep generics out of the market, sustaining a monopoly.

If product hopping suggests sickly competition, pay-for-delay deals are a terminal illness. They impose huge, unnecessary costs on consumers: the 40 deals struck in 2012 cover annual drug sales of $8.1 billion; pay-for-delay costs an estimated $3.5 billion a year, according to FTC reports. Happily, pay-for-delay may itself be on the verge of losing protection. A ruling by America's Supreme Court in 2013 should make it easier to challenge such deals under competition laws.

June 2014

Innovation: has the ideas machine broken down?

The idea that innovation and new technology have stopped driving growth is getting increasing attention. But it is not well founded

BOOM TIMES ARE BACK in Silicon Valley. Office parks along Highway 101 are once again adorned with the insignia of hopeful start-ups. Rents are soaring, as is the demand for fancy vacation homes in resort towns like Lake Tahoe, a sign of fortunes being amassed. The Bay Area was the birthplace of the semiconductor industry and the computer and internet companies that have grown up in its wake. Its wizards provided many of the marvels that make the world feel futuristic, from touch-screen phones to the instantaneous searching of great libraries to the power to pilot a drone thousands of miles away. The revival in its business activity since 2010 suggests progress is motoring on.

So it may come as a surprise that some in Silicon Valley think the place is stagnant, and that the rate of innovation has been slackening for decades. Peter Thiel, a founder of PayPal, an internet payment company, and the first outside investor in Facebook, a social network, says that innovation in America is "somewhere between dire straits and dead". Engineers in all sorts of areas share similar feelings of disappointment. And a small but growing group of economists reckon the economic impact of the innovations of today may pale in comparison with those of the past.

Some suspect that the rich world's economic doldrums may be rooted in a long-term technological stasis. In a 2011 e-book Tyler Cowen, an economist at George Mason University, argued that the financial crisis was masking a deeper and more disturbing "Great Stagnation". It was this which explained why growth in rich-world real incomes and employment had long been slowing and, since 2000, had hardly risen at all (see Figure 13.3). The various motors of

FIG 13.3 **Flattened out**
Real hourly earnings in manufacturing sector

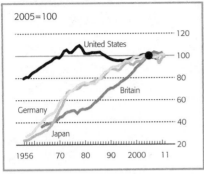

Sources: OECD; *The Economist*

20th-century growth – some technological, some not – had played themselves out, and new technologies were not going to have the same invigorating effect on the economies of the future. For all its flat-screen dazzle and high-bandwidth pizzazz, it seemed the world had run out of ideas.

Glide path

The argument that the world is on a technological plateau runs along three lines. The first comes from growth statistics. Economists divide growth into two different types: "extensive" and "intensive". Extensive growth is a matter of adding more and/or better labour, capital and resources. These are the sort of gains that countries saw from adding women to the labour force in greater numbers and increasing workers' education. And, as Mr Cowen notes, this sort of growth is subject to diminishing returns: the first addition will be used where it can do most good, the tenth where it can do the tenth-most good, and so on. If this were the only sort of growth there was, it would end up leaving incomes just above the subsistence level.

Intensive growth is powered by the discovery of ever-better ways to use workers and resources. This is the sort of growth that allows continuous improvement in incomes and welfare, and enables an economy to grow even as its population decreases. Economists label the all-purpose improvement factor responsible for such growth "technology" – though it includes things like better laws and regulations as well as technical advance – and measure it using a technique called "growth accounting". In this accounting, "technology" is the bit left over after calculating the effect on GDP of things like labour, capital and education. And at the moment, in the rich world, it looks like there is less of it about. Emerging markets still manage fast growth,

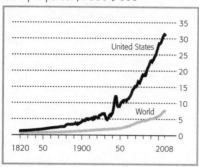

FIG 13.4 **Rising tide**
GDP per person, 1990 $'000*

*At purchasing-power parity
Source: Angus Maddison, University of Groningen

and should be able to do so for some time, because they are catching up with technologies already used elsewhere. The rich world has no such engine to pull it along, and it shows.

This is hardly unusual. For most of human history, growth in output and overall economic welfare has been slow and halting. Over the past two centuries, first in Britain, Europe and America, then elsewhere, it took off. In the 19th century growth in output per person – a useful general measure of an economy's productivity, and a good guide to growth in incomes – accelerated steadily in Britain. By 1906 it was more than 1% a year. By the middle of the 20th century, real output per person in America was growing at a scorching 2.5% a year, a pace at which productivity and incomes double once a generation (see Figure 13.4). More than a century of increasingly powerful and sophisticated machines were obviously a part of that story, as was the rising amount of fossil-fuel energy available to drive them.

But in the 1970s America's growth in real output per person dropped from its post-second-world-war peak of over 3% a year to just over 2% a year. In the 2000s it tumbled below 1%. Output per worker per hour shows a similar pattern, according to Robert Gordon, an economist at Northwestern University: it is pretty good for most of the 20th century, then slumps in the 1970s. It bounced back between 1996 and 2004, but since 2004 the annual rate has fallen to 1.33%, which is as low as it was from 1972 to 1996. Mr Gordon muses that the past two centuries of economic growth might actually amount to just "one big wave" of dramatic change rather than a new era of uninterrupted progress, and that the world is returning to a regime in which growth is mostly of the extensive sort (see Figure 13.5).

Mr Gordon sees it as possible that there were only a few truly fundamental innovations – the ability to use power on a large scale,

FIG 13.5 **One big wave**
GDP per person, % increase on previous year

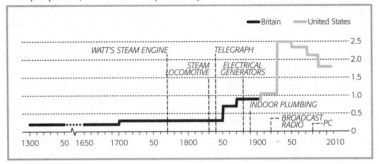

Sources: "Is US Economic Growth Over?" by Robert Gordon, NBER Working Paper, 2012; *The Economist*

to keep houses comfortable regardless of outside temperature, to get from any A to any B, to talk to anyone you need to – and that they have mostly been made. There will be more innovation – but it will not change the way the world works in the way electricity, internal-combustion engines, plumbing, petrochemicals and the telephone have. Mr Cowen is more willing to imagine big technological gains ahead, but he thinks there are no more low-hanging fruit. Turning terabytes of genomic knowledge into medical benefit is a lot harder than discovering and mass producing antibiotics.

The pessimists' second line of argument is based on how much invention is going on. Amid unconvincing appeals to the number of patents filed and databases of "innovations" put together quite subjectively, Mr Cowen cites interesting work by Charles Jones, an economist at Stanford University. In a 2002 paper Mr Jones studied the contribution of different factors to growth in American per-head incomes in the period 1950–93. His work indicated that some 80% of income growth was due to rising educational attainment and greater "research intensity" (the share of the workforce labouring in idea-generating industries). Because neither factor can continue growing ceaselessly, in the absence of some new factor coming into play growth is likely to slow.

The growth in the number of people working in research and development might seem to contradict this picture of a less inventive economy: the share of the American economy given over to R&D has expanded by a third since 1975, to almost 3%. But Pierre Azoulay of MIT and Benjamin Jones of Northwestern University find that, though there are more people in research, they are doing less good. They reckon that in 1950 an average R&D worker in America contributed almost seven times more to "total factor productivity" – essentially, the contribution of technology and innovation to growth – that an R&D worker in 2000 did. One factor in this may be the "burden of knowledge": as ideas accumulate it takes ever longer for new thinkers to catch up with the frontier of their scientific or technical speciality. Mr Jones says that from 1985 to 1997 alone the typical "age at first innovation" rose by about one year.

A fall of moondust

The third argument is the simplest: the evidence of your senses. The recent rate of progress seems slow compared with that of the early and mid-20th century. Take kitchens. In 1900 kitchens in even the poshest of households were primitive things. Perishables were kept cool in ice boxes, fed by blocks of ice delivered on horse-drawn wagons. Most households lacked electric lighting and running water. Fast forward to 1970 and middle-class kitchens in America and Europe feature gas and electric hobs and ovens, fridges, food processors, microwaves and dishwashers. Move forward another 40 years, though, and things scarcely change. The gizmos are more numerous and digital displays ubiquitous, but cooking is done much as it was by grandma.

Or take speed. In the 19th century horses and sailboats were replaced by railways and steamships. Internal-combustion engines and jet turbines made it possible to move more and more things faster and faster. But since the 1970s humanity has been coasting. Highway travel is little faster than it was 50 years ago; indeed, endemic congestion has many cities now investing in trams and bicycle lanes. Supersonic passenger travel has been abandoned. So, for the past 40 years, has the moon.

Medicine offers another example. Life expectancy at birth in America soared from 49 years at the turn of the 20th century to 74 years in 1980. Enormous technical advances have occurred since that time. Yet as of 2011 life expectancy rested at just 78.7 years. Despite hundreds of billions of dollars spent on research, people continue to fall to cancer, heart disease, stroke and organ failure. Molecular medicine has come nowhere close to matching the effects of improved sanitation.

To those fortunate enough to benefit from the best that the world has to offer, the fact that it offers no more can disappoint. As Mr Thiel and his colleagues at the Founders Fund, a venture-capital company, put it: "We wanted flying cars, instead we got 140 characters." A world where all can use Twitter but hardly any can commute by air is less impressive than the futures dreamed of in the past.

The first thing to point out about this appeal to experience and expectation is that the science fiction of the mid-20th century, important as it may have been to people who became entrepreneurs or economists with a taste for the big picture, constituted neither serious technological forecasting nor a binding commitment. It was a celebration through extrapolation of then current progress in speed, power and distance. For cars read flying cars; for battlecruisers read space cruisers.

Technological progress does not require all technologies to move forward in lock step, merely that some important technologies are always moving forward. Passenger aeroplanes have not improved much over the past 40 years in terms of their speed. Computers have sped up immeasurably. Unless you can show that planes matter more, to stress the stasis over the progress is simply a matter of taste.

Mr Gordon and Mr Cowen do think that now-mature technologies such as air transport have mattered more, and play down the economic importance of recent innovations. If computers and the internet mattered to the economy – rather than merely as rich resources for intellectual and cultural exchange, as experienced on Mr Cowen's popular blog, Marginal Revolution – their effect would be seen in the figures. And it hasn't been.

As early as 1987 Robert Solow, a growth theorist, had been asking why "you can see the computer age everywhere but in the productivity statistics". A surge in productivity growth that began in the mid-1990s was seen as an encouraging sign that the computers were at last becoming visible; but it faltered, and some, such as Mr

Gordon, reckon that the benefits of information technology have largely run their course. He notes that, for all its inhabitants' Googling and Skypeing, America's productivity performance since 2004 has been worse than that of the doldrums from the early 1970s to the early 1990s.

The fountains of paradise

Closer analysis of recent figures, though, suggests reason for optimism. Across the economy as a whole productivity did slow in 2005 and 2006 – but productivity growth in manufacturing fared better. The global financial crisis and its aftermath make more recent data hard to interpret. As for the strong productivity growth in the late 1990s, it may have been premature to see it as the effect of information technology making all sorts of sectors more productive. It now looks as though it was driven just by the industries actually making the computers, mobile phones and the like. The effects on the productivity of people and companies buying the new technology seem to have begun appearing in the 2000s, but may not yet have come into their own. Research by Susanto Basu of Boston College and John Fernald of the San Francisco Federal Reserve suggests that the lag between investments in information-and-communication technologies and improvements in productivity is between five and 15 years. The drop in productivity in 2004, on that reckoning, reflected a state of technology definitely pre-Google, and quite possibly pre-web.

Full exploitation of a technology can take far longer than that. Innovation and technology, though talked of almost interchangeably, are not the same thing. Innovation is what people newly know how to do. Technology is what they are actually doing; and that is what matters to the economy. Steel boxes and diesel engines have been around since the 1900s, and their use together in containerised shipping goes back to the 1950s. But their great impact as the backbone of global trade did not come for decades after that.

Roughly a century elapsed between the first commercial deployments of James Watt's steam engine and steam's peak contribution to British growth. Some four decades separated the critical innovations in electrical engineering of the 1880s and the broad influence of electrification on economic growth. Mr Gordon himself notes that the innovations of the late 19th century drove productivity growth until the early 1970s; it is rather uncharitable of him to assume that the post-2004 slump represents the full exhaustion of potential gains from information technology.

And information innovation is still in its infancy. Ray Kurzweil, a pioneer of computer science and a devotee of exponential technological extrapolation, likes to talk of "the second half of the chess board". There is an old fable in which a gullible king is tricked into paying an obligation in grains of rice, one on the first square of a chessboard, two on the second, four on the third, the payment doubling with every square. Along the first row, the obligation is minuscule. With half the chessboard covered, the king is out only about 100 tonnes of rice. But a square before reaching the end of the seventh row he has laid out 500 million tonnes in total – the whole world's annual rice production. He will have to put more or less the same amount again on the next square. And there will still be a row to go.

Erik Brynjolfsson and Andrew McAfee of MIT make use of this image in their e-book *Race Against the Machine*. By the measure known as Moore's law, the ability to get calculations out of a piece of silicon doubles every 18 months. That growth rate will not last forever; but other aspects of computation, such as the capacity of algorithms to handle data, are also growing exponentially. When such a capacity is low, that doubling does not matter. As soon as it matters at all, though, it can quickly start to matter a lot. On the second half of the chessboard not only has the cumulative effect of innovations become large, but each new iteration of innovation delivers a technological jolt as powerful as all previous rounds combined.

The other side of the sky

As an example of this acceleration-of-effect they offer autonomous vehicles. In 2004 the Defence Advanced Research Projects Agency (DARPA), a branch of America's Department of Defence, set up a race for driverless cars that promised $1 million to the team whose vehicle finished the 240km (150-mile) route fastest. Not one of the robotic entrants completed the course. In August 2012 Google announced that its fleet of autonomous vehicles had completed some half a million kilometres of accident-free test runs. Several American states have passed or are weighing regulations for driverless cars; a robotic-transport revolution that seemed impossible ten years ago may be here in ten more.

That only scratches the surface. Across the board, innovations fuelled by cheap processing power are taking off. Computers are beginning to understand natural language. People are controlling video games through body movement alone – a technology that may soon find application in much of the business world. Three-dimensional printing is capable of churning out an increasingly complex array of objects, and may soon move on to human tissues and other organic material.

An innovation pessimist could dismiss this as "jam tomorrow". But the idea that technology-led growth must either continue unabated or steadily decline, rather than ebbing and flowing, is at odds with history. Chad Syverson of the University of Chicago points out that productivity growth during the age of electrification was lumpy. Growth was slow during a period of important electrical innovations in the late 19th and early 20th centuries; then it surged. The information-age trajectory looks pretty similar (see Figure 13.6).

It may be that the 1970s-and-after slowdown in which the technological pessimists set such store can be understood in this way – as a pause, rather than a permanent inflection. The period from the early 1970s to the mid-1990s may simply represent one in which the contributions of earlier major innovations were exhausted while computing, biotechnology, personal communication and the rest of the technologies of today and tomorrow

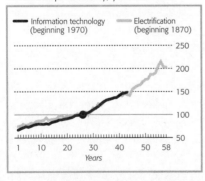

FIG 13.6 **Echoing electrification**
US labour productivity, year 26=100

Source: Chad Syverson, University of Chicago

remained too small a part of the economy to influence overall growth.

Other potential culprits loom, however – some of which, worryingly, might be permanent in their effects. Much of the economy is more heavily regulated than it was a century ago. Environmental protection has provided cleaner air and water, which improve people's lives. Indeed, to the extent that such gains are not captured in measurements of GDP, the slowdown in progress from the 1970s is overstated. But if that is so, it will probably continue to be so for future technological change. And poorly crafted regulations may unduly raise the cost of new research, discouraging further innovation.

Another thing which may have changed permanently is the role of government. Technology pessimists rarely miss an opportunity to point to the Apollo programme, crowning glory of a time in which government did not simply facilitate new innovation but provided continuing demand for talent and invention. This it did most reliably through the military-industrial complex of which Apollo was a spectacular and peculiarly inspirational outgrowth. Mr Thiel is often critical of the venture-capital industry for its lack of interest in big, world-changing ideas. Yet this is mostly a response to market realities. Private investors rationally prefer modest business models with a reasonably short time to profit and cash out.

A third factor which might have been at play in both the 1970s and the 2000s is energy. William Nordhaus of Yale University has found that the productivity slowdown which started in the 1970s radiated outwards from the most energy-intensive sectors, a product of the decade's oil shocks. Dear energy may help explain the productivity slowdown of the 2000s as well. But this is a trend that one can hope to see reversed. In America, at least, new technologies are eating into those high prices. Mr Thiel is right to reserve some of his harshest criticism for the energy sector's lacklustre record on innovation; but given the right market conditions it is not entirely hopeless.

Perhaps the most radical answer to the problem of the 1970s slowdown is that it was due to globalisation. In a 1987 paper Paul Romer, then at the University of Rochester, sketched the possibility that, with more workers available in developing countries, cutting labour costs in rich ones became less important. Investment in productivity was thus sidelined. The idea was heretical among macroeconomists, as it dispensed with much of the careful theoretical machinery then being used to analyse growth. But as Mr Romer noted, economic historians comparing 19th-century Britain with America commonly credit relative labour scarcity in America with driving forward the capital-intense and highly productive "American system" of manufacturing.

The view from Serendip

Some economists are considering how Mr Romer's heresy might apply today. Daron Acemoglu of MIT, Gino Gancia of the Centre de Recerca en Economia Internacional in Barcelona and Fabrizio Zilibotti of the University of Zurich have built a model to study this. It shows firms in rich countries shipping low-skill tasks abroad when offshoring costs little, thus driving apart the wages of skilled and unskilled workers at home. Over time, though, offshoring raises wages in less-skilled countries; that makes innovation at home more enticing. Workers are in greater demand, the income distribution narrows, and the economy comes to look more like the post-second-world-war period than the 1970s and their aftermath.

Even if that model is mistaken, the rise of the emerging world is among the biggest reasons for optimism. The larger the size of the global market, the more the world benefits from a given new idea, since it can then be applied across more activities and more people. Raising Asia's poor billions into the middle class will mean that millions of great minds that might otherwise have toiled at subsistence farming can instead join the modern economy and share the burden of knowledge with rich-world researchers – a sharing that information technology makes ever easier.

It may still be the case that some parts of the economy are immune, or at least resistant, to some of the productivity improvement that information technology can offer. Sectors like health care, education and government, in which productivity has proved hard to increase, loom larger within the economy than in the past. The frequent absence of market pressure in such areas reduces the pressure for cost savings – and for innovation.

For some, though, the opposite outcome is the one to worry about. Messrs Brynjolfsson and McAfee fear that the technological advances of the second half of the chessboard could be disturbingly rapid, leaving a scourge of technological unemployment in their wake. They argue that new technologies and the globalisation that they allow have already contributed to stagnant incomes and a decline in jobs that require moderate levels of skill. Further progress could threaten jobs higher up and lower down the skill spectrum that had, until now, seemed safe.

Pattern-recognition software is increasingly good at performing the tasks of entry-level lawyers, scanning thousands of legal documents for relevant passages. Algorithms are used to write basic newspaper articles on sporting outcomes and financial reports. In time, they may move to analysis. Manual tasks are also vulnerable. In Japan, where labour to care for an ageing population is scarce, innovation in robotics is proceeding by leaps and bounds. The rising cost of looking after people across the rich world will only encourage further development.

Such productivity advances should generate enormous welfare gains. Yet the adjustment period could be difficult. In the end, the main risk to advanced economies may not be that the pace of innovation is too slow, but that institutions have become too rigid to accommodate truly revolutionary changes – which could be a lot more likely than flying cars.

January 2013

Demography: the age invaders

A generation of old people is about to change the global economy. They will not all do so in the same way

IN THE 20TH CENTURY the planet's population doubled twice. It will not double even once in the current century, because birth rates in much of the world have declined steeply. But the number of people over 65 is set to double within just 25 years. This shift in the structure of the population is not as momentous as the expansion that came before. But it is more than enough to reshape the world economy.

According to the UN's population projections, the standard source for demographic estimates, there are around 600 million people aged 65 or older alive today. That is in itself remarkable; Fred Pearce, an author, claims it is possible that half of all the humans who have ever been over 65 are alive today. But as a share of the total population, at 8%, it is not that different from what it was a few decades ago.

By 2035, however, more than 1.1 billion people – 13% of the population – will be above the age of 65. This is a natural corollary of the dropping birth rates that are slowing overall population growth; they mean there are proportionally fewer young people around. The "old-age dependency ratio" – the ratio of old people to those of working age – will grow even faster. In 2010 the world had 16 people aged 65 and over for every 100 adults between the ages of 25 and 64, almost the same ratio it had in 1980. By 2035 the UN expects that number to have risen to 26.

In rich countries it will be much higher (see Figure 13.7). Japan will have 69 old people for every 100 of working age by 2035 (up from 43 in 2010), Germany 66 (from 38). Even America, which has a relatively high fertility rate, will see its old-age dependency rate rise by more than 70%, to 44. Developing countries, where today's ratio is much lower, will not see absolute levels rise that high; but the proportional growth will be higher. Over the same time period the old-age dependency rate in China will more than double from 15 to 36. Latin America will see a shift from 14 to 27.

FIG 13.7 **The big shift**
Old-age dependency, population aged 65
and over per 100 people aged 25–64

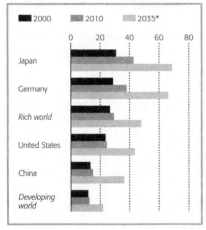

■ 2000 ■ 2010 ▨ 2035*

Japan

Germany

Rich world

United States

China

Developing
world

*Forecast
Source: UN Population Division

Three ways forward

The big exceptions to this general greying are south Asia and Africa, where fertility is still high. Since these places are home to almost 3 billion people, rising to 5 billion by mid-century, their youth could be a powerful counter to the greying elsewhere. But they will slow the change, not reverse it. The emerging world as a whole will see its collective old-age dependency rate almost double, to 22 per 100, by 2035.

The received wisdom is that a larger proportion of old people means slower growth and, because the old need to draw down their wealth to live, less saving; that leads to higher interest rates and falling asset prices. Some economists are more sanguine, arguing that people will adapt and work longer, rendering moot measures of dependency which assume no one works after the age of 65. A third group harks back to the work of Alvin Hansen, known as the "American Keynes", who argued in 1938 that a shrinking population in America would bring with it diminished incentives for companies to invest – a smaller workforce needs less investment – and hence persistent stagnation.

The unexpected baby boom of 1946–64 messed up Hansen's predictions, and unforeseen events could undermine today's demographic projections, too – though bearing in mind that the baby boom required a world war to set the stage, that should not be seen as a source of hope. But if older people work longer and thus save longer, while slowing population growth means firms have less incentive to invest, something close to what Hansen envisaged could come about even without the sort of overall population decline he foresaw. Recently Larry Summers, a Harvard professor and former treasury secretary, argued that America's economy appeared already to be suffering this sort of "secular stagnation" – a phrase taken directly from Hansen.

Who is right? The answer depends on examining the three main channels through which demography influences the economy: changes in the size of the workforce; changes in the rate of productivity growth; and changes in the pattern of savings. The result of such examination is not conclusive. But, for the next few years at least, Hansen's worries seem most relevant, not least because of a previously unexpected effect: the tendency of those with higher skills to work for longer, and more productively, than they have done to date.

The first obvious implication of a population that is getting a lot older without growing much is that, unless the retirement age changes, there will be fewer workers. That means less output, unless productivity rises to compensate. Under the UN's standard assumption that a working life ends at 65, and with no increases in productivity, ageing populations could cut growth rates in parts of the rich world by between one-third and one-half over the coming years.

Have skills, will work

Amlan Roy, an economist at Credit Suisse, has calculated that the shrinking working-age population dragged down Japan's GDP growth by an average of just over 0.6 percentage points a year between 2000 and 2013, and that by 2017 that will increase to 1 percentage point a year. Germany's shrinking workforce could reduce GDP growth by almost half a point. In America, under the same assumptions, the retirement of the baby-boomers would be expected to reduce the economy's potential growth rate by 0.7 percentage points.

The real size of the workforce, though, depends on more than the age structure of the population; it depends on who else works (women who currently do not, perhaps, or immigrants) and how long people work. In the late 20th century that last factor changed little. An analysis of 43 mostly rich countries by David Bloom, David Canning and Günther Fink, all of Harvard University, found that between 1965 and 2005 the average legal retirement age rose by less than six months. During that time male life expectancy rose by nine years.

Since the turn of the century that trend has reversed. Almost 20% of Americans aged over 65 are now in the labour force, compared with 13% in 2000. Nearly half of all Germans in their early 60s are employed today, compared with a quarter a decade ago.

This is in part due to policy. Debt-laden governments in Europe have cut back their pension promises and raised the retirement age. Half a dozen European countries, including Italy, Spain and the Netherlands, have linked the statutory retirement age to life expectancy. Personal financial circumstances have played a part, too. In most countries the shift was strongest in the wake of the 2008 financial crisis, which hit the savings of many near-retirees. The move away from corporate pension plans that provided a fraction of the recipient's final salary in perpetuity will also have kept some people working longer.

But an even more important factor is education. Better-educated older people are far more likely to work for longer. Gary Burtless of the Brookings Institution has calculated that, in America, only 32% of male high-school graduates with no further formal education are in the workforce between the ages of 62 and 74. For men with a professional degree the figure is 65% (though the overall number of such men is obviously smaller). For women the ratios are one-quarter versus one-half, with the share of highly educated women working into their 60s soaring (see Figure 13.8). In Europe, where workers of all sorts are soldiering on into their 60s more than they

FIG 13.8 **Cognitive affluence**
American labour force participation rate for men and women aged 62–74 by level of education, %

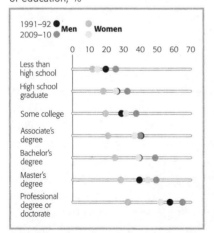

Source: Gary Burtless, Brookings Institution

used to, the effect is not quite as marked, but still striking. Only a quarter of the least-educated Europeans aged 60–64 still work; half of those with a degree do.

It is not a hard pattern to explain. Less-skilled workers often have manual jobs that get harder as you get older. The relative pay of the less-skilled has fallen, making retirement on a public pension more attractive; for the unemployed, who are also likely to be less skilled, retirement is a terrific option. Research by German economists Clemens Hetschko, Andreas Knabe and Ronnie Schöb shows that people who go straight from unemployment to retirement experience a startling increase in their sense of well-being.

Higher-skilled workers, on the other hand, tend to be paid more, which gives them an incentive to keep working. They are also on average healthier and longer-lived, so they can work and earn past 65 and still expect to enjoy the fruits of that extra labour later on.

This does not mean the workforce will grow. Overall work rates among the over-60s will still be lower than they were for the same cohort when it was younger. And even as more educated old folk are working, fewer less-skilled young people are. In Europe, jobless rates are highest among the least-educated young. In America, where the labour participation rate (at 63%) is close to a three-decade low, employment has dropped most sharply for less-skilled men. With no surge in employment among women, and little appetite for mass immigration, in most of the rich world the workforce looks likely to shrink even if skilled oldies stay employed.

Legacy of the void

A smaller workforce need not dampen growth, though, if productivity surges. This is not something most would expect to come about as a result of an ageing population. Plenty of studies and bitter experience show that most physical and many cognitive capacities decline with age. An analysis by a trio of Canadian academics based on the video game "StarCraft II", for instance, suggests that raw brainpower peaks at 24. And ageing societies may ossify. Alfred Sauvy, a French thinker who coined the term "third world", was prone to worry that the first world would become "a society of old people, living in old houses, ruminating about old ideas". Japan's productivity growth slowed sharply in the 1990s when its working-age population began to shrink; Germany's productivity performance has become lacklustre as its population ages.

But Japan's slowed productivity growth can also be ascribed to its burst asset bubble, and Germany's to reforms meant to reduce unemployment; both countries, ageing as they are, score better in the World Economic Forum's ranking for innovation than America. A dearth of workers might prompt the invention of labour-saving capital-intensive technology, just as Japanese firms are pioneering the use of robots to look after old people. And a wealth of job experience can counter slower cognitive speed. In an age of ever-smarter machines, the attributes that enhance productivity may have less to do with pure cognitive oomph than motivation, people skills and managerial experience.

Perhaps most important, better education leads to higher productivity at any age. For all these reasons, a growing group of highly educated older folk could increase productivity, offsetting much of the effect of a smaller workforce.

Evidence on both sides of the Atlantic bears this out. A clutch of studies suggests that older workers are disproportionately more productive – as you would expect if they are disproportionately better educated. Laura Romeu Gordo of the German Centre of Gerontology and Vegard Skirbekk of the International Institute for Applied Systems Analysis in Austria have shown that in Germany, older workers who stayed in the labour force have tended to move into jobs which demanded more cognitive skill. Perhaps because of such effects, the earnings of those over 50 have risen relative to younger workers.

Saving graces

This could be good news for countries with well-educated people currently entering old age – but less so in places that are less developed. Nearly half of China's workers aged between 50 and 64 have not completed primary school. As these unskilled people age, their productivity is likely to fall. Working with his International Institute for Applied Systems Analysis (IIASA) colleagues Elke Loichinger and

Daniela Weber, Mr Skirbekk tried to gauge this effect by creating a "cognition-adjusted dependency ratio". They compared the cognitive ability of people aged 50 and over across rich and emerging economies by means of an experiment which tested their ability to recall words, and used the results to weight dependency ratios. This cognition-adjusted ratio is lower in northern Europe than it is in China, even though the age-based ratio is far higher in Europe, because the elderly in Europe score much more strongly on the cognitive-skill test. Similarly adjusted, America's dependency ratio is better than India's.

If skill and education determine how long and how well older people work, they also have big implications for saving, the third channel through which ageing affects growth. A larger group of well-educated older people will earn a larger share of overall income. In America the share of male earnings going to those aged 60–74 rose from 7.3% in 2000 to 12.7% in 2014 as well-educated baby-boomers moved into their 60s. Some of these earnings will finance retirement, when those concerned finally decide to take it; more savings by people in their 60s will be matched by more spending when they reach their 80s. But many of the educated elderly are likely to accumulate far more than they will draw down towards the end of life. Circumstantial evidence supports this argument. Thomas Piketty, a French economist, calculates that the average wealth of French 80-year-olds is 134% that of 50- to 59-year-olds, the highest gap since the 1930s. For the next few years at least, skill-skewed ageing is likely to mean both more inequality and more private saving.

At the same time governments across the rich world (and particularly in Europe) are trimming their pension promises and cutting their budget deficits, both of which add to national saving. Reforms designed to trim future pensions mean that, regardless of their skill level, those close to retirement are likely to save more and that governments will spend less per old person. The European Commission's forecasts suggest overall pension spending in the EU will fall by 0.1% of GDP between 2010 and 2020, before rising by 0.6% in the subsequent decade. That is not insignificant, but it is far less than some of the breathless commentary about the "burden" of ageing implies.

Taken together, the net effect of high saving by educated older workers and less-generous pensions is likely to be an unexpected degree of thrift in the rich world, at least for the next few years. If the money saved finds productive investment opportunities, it has the potential to boost long-run growth. But where will these opportunities be? In principle, two possibilities stand out. One is rapid innovation in advanced economies. The second is fast growth in emerging economies – especially younger, poorer ones.

Unfortunately, more capital currently flows out of emerging economies into the rich world than the other way. The most successful emerging economies have built up huge stashes of foreign currency; many are leery of depending too much on foreign borrowing. Even if that were to change, the youthful economies of south Asia and Africa are too small to absorb huge flows of capital from those countries that are ageing fast.

And in the rich world, despite lots of obvious innovation, particularly in computer technology, both productivity growth and investment have been tepid of late. That may be a hangover from the financial crisis. But it could also be a structural change. The price of capital goods, notably anything to do with computers, has fallen sharply; it may be that today's innovation is simply less investment-intensive than it was in the manufacturing age. And the ageing population itself may deter investment. Fewer workers, other things being equal, means the economy needs a smaller capital stock, even if some of those workers are clever old sticks. And an ageing population spends differently. Old people buy fewer things that require heavy investment – notably houses – and more services, whether in health care or tourism.

Not destiny, but not nothing

Demographic trends will shape the future, but they do not render particular outcomes inevitable. The evolution of the economy will depend on the way policymakers respond to the new situation. But those policy reactions will themselves be shaped by the priorities of older people to a greater extent than has previously been the case; they will be a bigger share of the population and in democracies they tend to vote more than younger people do.

On both sides of the Atlantic, recent budget decisions appear to reflect the priorities of the ageing and affluent. Annuities reform in Britain increased people's freedom to spend their pension pots; the disappearance of property-tax reform spared homeowning older Italians a new burden; America's budget slashed spending on the young and poor while failing to make government health and pension spending any less generous to the well-off. Few rich-country governments have shown any appetite for large-scale investment, despite low interest rates.

A set of forces pushing investment down and pushing saving up, with no countervailing policy response, makes the impact of ageing over the next few years look like the world that Hansen described: one of slower growth (albeit not as slow as it would have been if older folk were not working more), a surfeit of saving and very low interest rates. It will be a world in which ageing reinforces the changes in income distribution that new technology has brought with it: the skilled old earn more; the less-skilled of all ages are squeezed. The less-educated and jobless young will be particularly poorly served, never building up the skills to enable them to become productive older workers.

Compared with the dire warnings about the bankrupting consequences of a "grey tsunami", this is good news. But not as good as all that.

April 2014

14 Robot economics

Machines and work: robocolleague

Robots are getting more powerful. That need not be bad news for workers

WATSON, AN IBM SUPERCOMPUTER, spectacularly beat its human rivals in a 2011 edition of *Jeopardy!*, an American quiz show. It has got smarter since then. Its components have shrunk from room-size to briefcase-size; its processing speed has more than tripled. The sleeker, faster Watson is now being put to commercial use: its first application is suggesting treatments in cancer clinics. Many people fear that Watson exemplifies a trend toward the displacement of human workers by machines.

In a 2011 e-book called *Race against the Machine*, Erik Brynjolfsson and Andrew McAfee of the Massachusetts Institute of Technology (MIT) worried that human workers would fail to adapt to the quickening pace of technological change. *The Lights in the Tunnel*, a 2009 book by Martin Ford, a software entrepreneur, painted a bleaker picture still. Mr Ford noted that about 40% of Americans work in old-fashioned occupations – as nurses, book-keepers and the like. He argued that innovation will soon allow firms to eliminate millions of jobs, like the 3 million-plus cashiers whose positions are threatened by automated cash registers, but will create few new opportunities for displaced workers.

But plenty of research suggests that innovation need not translate into a shrinking role for human labour. In a 2013 paper David Autor, also of MIT, argues that the standard "production functions" used by economists to describe how things get made need sprucing up. These functions treat labour and capital like separate elements in a recipe: mix a tablespoon of skilled work with a dose of capital to produce a helping of GDP. In the real world, however, the distinction is blurred.

Mr Autor describes an alternative approach in which production is modelled as a series of tasks. A firm's challenge is to decide how to allocate them between capital and workers of varying skills, according to their respective comparative advantages. Assignments evolve over time as costs and technologies shift: an innovation may displace humans from some jobs, for instance, but make them more productive in others.

As technology improves, Mr Autor writes, a pattern emerges. Machines take over routine tasks like repeated number-crunching or the welding of car parts. Such jobs can be programmed into machines using detailed, specific instructions. Displaced human workers are then reassigned to do more improvisational or intuitive work. At airline check-in counters, say, computers are displacing employees from mundane tasks like printing boarding passes. That makes it easier for the humans to respond to unexpected problems like cancelled flights or changed itineraries.

Machines serve as both a substitute for, and a complement to, labour in other industries. Watson is initially assisting doctors to make cancer-treatment decisions, by providing options along with the associated degrees of confidence; it may eventually replace doctors in some diagnostic work. In other cases, robots may raise demand for doctors' services. A 2013 article in the *Journal of the American Medical Association* notes that though robotically assisted surgeries do not necessarily bring better results than minimally invasive human-only surgeries, it is much easier for doctors to learn and master robotically assisted techniques. Robot-aided surgery could therefore make some procedures cheaper and more widely available.

Historically, technological advances have been relatively benign for workers. Labour-market trends through the 19th and 20th centuries show surprising continuity, according to Lawrence Katz of Harvard University and Robert Margo of Boston University. In recent decades, for example, computerisation and automation have displaced "middle-skilled" workers at the same time as employment among high- and low-skilled workers has increased. This "hollowing out" is not new, Messrs Katz and Margo note. Early industrialisation had similar effects. Middle-skilled artisans, like trained weavers, were put out of work by industrial textile production, but the fortunes of less-skilled factory workers and white-collar factory managers steadily improved. Mechanisation's insatiable appetite for routine work of all types has yet to create mass unemployment. Quite the opposite.

The worry is that technology now has its sights set on non-routine tasks as well as mundane ones. Yet Mr Autor notes that just because a skilled job can be automated does not mean it will be. The number of workers used to build Nissan vehicles varies a lot between Japan, where labour is expensive, and India, where it is abundant and cheap. The relative cost of different types of workers matters for firms as they choose how to deploy new technologies.

The road to HAL

The incentives facing firms may also be changing, according to Daron Acemoglu of MIT, Gino Gancia of the Centre de Recerca en Economia Internacional in Barcelona and Fabrizio Zilibotti of the University of Zurich. They reckon that rich-world firms reacted to globalisation by using cheap labour abroad and investing in technologies that helped skilled workers at home. Apple, for example, has used skilled American engineers to design its products and low-cost foreign workers to make them.

Rising wages in emerging markets are now making it less attractive to send unskilled work abroad. The authors suggest this could mean a sharp change in the influence of innovation on labour markets. Firms may find it more attractive to invest in technologies that boost the productivity of less-skilled domestic labour, pushing up their wages. One day, clever robots may change this. But as long as humans retain the edge on cognitive flexibility, firms will keep putting willing workers to good use.

March 2013

The future of jobs: the onrushing wave

Previous technological innovation has always delivered more long-run employment, not less. But things can change

IN 1930, when the world was "suffering ... from a bad attack of economic pessimism", John Maynard Keynes wrote a broadly optimistic essay, "Economic Possibilities for our Grandchildren". It imagined a middle way between revolution and stagnation that would leave the said grandchildren a great deal richer than their grandparents. But the path was not without dangers.

One of the worries Keynes admitted was a "new disease": "technological unemployment ... due to our discovery of means of economising the use of labour outrunning the pace at which we can find new uses for labour." His readers might not have heard of the problem, he suggested – but they were certain to hear a lot more about it in the years to come.

For the most part, they did not. Nowadays, the majority of economists confidently wave such worries away. By raising productivity, they argue, any automation which economises on the use of labour will increase incomes. That will generate demand for new products and services, which will in turn create new jobs for displaced workers. To think otherwise has meant being tarred a Luddite – the name taken by 19th-century textile workers who smashed the machines taking their jobs.

For much of the 20th century, those arguing that technology brought ever more jobs and prosperity looked to have the better of the debate. Real incomes in Britain scarcely doubled between the beginning of the common era and 1570. They then tripled from 1570 to 1875. And they more than tripled from 1875 to 1975. Industrialisation did not end up eliminating the need for human workers. On the contrary, it created employment opportunities sufficient to soak up the 20th century's exploding population. Keynes's vision of everyone in the 2030s being a lot richer is largely achieved. His belief they would work just 15 hours or so a week has not come to pass.

When the sleeper wakes

Yet some now fear that a new era of automation enabled by ever more powerful and capable computers could work out differently. They start from the observation that, across the rich world, all is far from well in the world of work. The essence of what they see as a work crisis is that in rich countries the wages of the typical worker, adjusted for cost of living, are stagnant. In America the real wage has hardly budged over the past four decades. Even in places like Britain and Germany, where employment is touching new highs, wages have been flat for a decade. Recent research suggests that this is because substituting capital for labour through automation is increasingly attractive; as a result owners of capital have captured ever more of the world's income since the 1980s, while the share going to labour has fallen.

At the same time, even in relatively egalitarian places like Sweden, inequality among the employed has risen sharply, with the share going to the highest earners soaring. For those not in the elite, argues David Graeber, an anthropologist at the London School of Economics, much of modern labour consists of stultifying "bullshit jobs" – low- and mid-level screen-sitting that serves simply to occupy workers for whom the economy no longer has much use. Keeping them employed, Mr Graeber argues, is not an economic choice; it is something the ruling class does to keep control over the lives of others.

Be that as it may, drudgery may soon enough give way to frank unemployment. There is already a long-term trend towards lower levels of employment in some rich countries. In 2013 the proportion of American adults participating in the labour force hit its lowest level since 1978, and although some of that is due to the effects of ageing, some is not. In a 2013 speech that was modelled in part on Keynes's "Possibilities", Larry Summers, a former American treasury secretary, looked at employment trends among American men aged between 25 and 54. In the 1960s only one in 20 of those men was not working. According to Mr Summers's extrapolations, in ten years the number could be one in seven.

This is one indication, Mr Summers says, that technical change is increasingly taking the form of "capital that effectively substitutes for labour". There may be a lot more for such capital to do in the near future. A 2013 paper by Carl Benedikt Frey and Michael Osborne of the University of Oxford argued that jobs are at high risk of being automated in 47% of the occupational categories into which work is customarily sorted. That includes accountancy, legal work, technical writing and a lot of other white-collar occupations.

Answering the question of whether such automation could lead to prolonged pain for workers means taking a close look at past experience, theory and technological trends. The picture suggested by this evidence is a complex one. It is also more worrying than many economists and politicians have been prepared to admit.

The lathe of heaven

Economists take the relationship between innovation and higher living standards for granted in part because they believe history justifies such a view. Industrialisation clearly led to enormous rises in incomes and living standards over the long run. Yet the road to riches was rockier than is often appreciated.

In 1500 an estimated 75% of the British labour force toiled in agriculture. By 1800 that figure had fallen to 35%. When the shift to manufacturing got under way during the 18th century it was overwhelmingly done at small scale, either within the home or in a small workshop; employment in a large factory was a rarity. By the end of the 19th century huge plants in massive industrial cities were the norm. The great shift was made possible by automation and steam engines.

Industrial firms combined human labour with big, expensive capital equipment. To maximise the output of that costly machinery, factory owners reorganised the processes of production. Workers were given one or a few repetitive tasks, often making components of finished products rather than whole pieces. Bosses imposed a tight schedule and strict worker discipline to keep up the productive pace. The Industrial Revolution was not simply a matter of replacing muscle with steam; it was a matter of reshaping jobs themselves into the sort of precisely defined components that steam-driven machinery needed – cogs in a factory system.

FIG 14.1 **Long time coming**
Britain's average annual growth, %

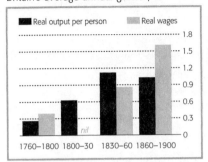

Source: "Engels' Pause: Technical Change, Capital Accumulation, and Inequality in the British Industrial Revolution" by R.C. Allen, *Explorations in Economic History*, 2009

The way old jobs were done changed; new jobs were created. Joel Mokyr, an economic historian at Northwestern University in Illinois, argues that the more intricate machines, techniques and supply chains of the period all required careful tending. The workers who provided that care were well rewarded. As research by Lawrence Katz of Harvard University and Robert Margo of Boston University shows, employment in manufacturing "hollowed out". As employment grew for highly skilled workers and unskilled workers, craft workers lost out. This was the loss to which the Luddites, understandably if not effectively, took exception.

With the low-skilled workers far more numerous, at least to begin with, the lot of the average worker during the early part of this great industrial and social upheaval was not a happy one. As Mr Mokyr notes, "life did not improve all that much between 1750 and 1850." For 60 years, from 1770 to 1830, growth in British wages, adjusted for inflation, was imperceptible because productivity growth was restricted to a few industries. Not until the late 19th century, when the gains had spread across the whole economy, did wages at last perform in line with productivity (see Figure 14.1).

Along with social reforms and new political movements that gave voice to the workers, this faster wage growth helped spread the benefits of industrialisation across wider segments of the population. New investments in education provided a supply of workers for the more skilled jobs that were by then being created in ever-greater numbers. This shift continued into the 20th century as post-secondary education became increasingly common.

Claudia Goldin, an economist at Harvard University, and Mr Katz have written that workers were in a "race between education and technology" during this period, and for the most part they won. Even so, it was not until the "golden age" after the second world war that workers in the rich world secured real prosperity, and a large, property-owning middle class came to dominate politics. At the same time communism, a legacy of industrialisation's harsh early era, kept hundreds of millions of people around the world in poverty, and the effects of the imperialism driven by European industrialisation continued to be felt by billions.

The impacts of technological change take their time appearing. They also vary hugely from industry to industry. Although in many simple economic models technology pairs neatly with capital and labour to produce output, in practice technological changes do not affect all workers the same way. Some find that their skills are complementary to new technologies. Others find themselves out of work.

Take computers. In the early 20th century a "computer" was a worker, or a room of workers, doing mathematical calculations by hand, often with the end point of one person's work the starting point for the next. The development of mechanical and electronic computing rendered these arrangements obsolete. But in time it greatly increased the productivity of those who used the new computers in their work.

Many other technical innovations had similar effects. New machinery displaced handicraft producers across numerous industries, from textiles to metalworking. At the same time it enabled vastly more output per person than craft producers could ever manage.

Player piano

For a task to be replaced by a machine, it helps a great deal if, like the work of human computers, it is already highly routine. Hence the demise of production-line jobs and some sorts of book-keeping, lost to the robot and the spreadsheet. Meanwhile work less easily broken down into a series of stereotyped tasks – whether rewarding, as the management of other workers and the teaching of toddlers can be, or more of a grind, like tidying and cleaning messy work places – has grown as a share of total employment.

But the "race" aspect of technological change means that such workers cannot rest on their pay packets. Firms are constantly experimenting with new technologies and production processes. Experimentation with different techniques and business models requires flexibility, which is one critical advantage of a human worker. Yet over time, as best practices are worked out and then codified, it becomes easier to break production down into routine components, then automate those components as technology allows.

If, that is, automation makes sense. As David Autor, an economist at the Massachusetts Institute of Technology (MIT), points out in a 2013 paper, the mere fact that a job can be automated does not mean that it will be; relative costs also matter. When Nissan produces cars in Japan, he notes, it relies heavily on robots. At plants in India, by contrast, the firm relies more heavily on cheap local labour.

Even when machine capabilities are rapidly improving, it can make sense instead to seek out ever-cheaper supplies of increasingly skilled labour. Thus since the 1980s (a time when, in America, the trend towards post-secondary education levelled off) workers there and elsewhere have found themselves facing increased competition from both machines and cheap emerging-market workers.

Such processes have steadily and relentlessly squeezed labour out of the manufacturing sector in most rich economies. The share of American employment in manufacturing has declined sharply since the 1950s, from almost 30% to less than 10%. At the same time, jobs in services soared, from less than 50% of employment to almost 70% (see Figure 14.2). It was inevitable, therefore, that firms would start to apply the same experimentation and reorganisation to service industries.

A new wave of technological progress may dramatically accelerate this automation of brainwork.

FIG 14.2 **Not what it was**
US employment by sector, % of total employment

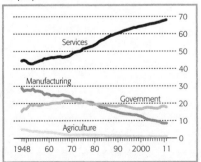

Source: US Bureau of Labour Statistics

Evidence is mounting that rapid technological progress, which accounted for the long era of rapid productivity growth from the 19th century to the 1970s, is back. The sort of advances that allow people to put in their pocket a computer that is not only more powerful than any in the world 20 years ago, but also has far better software and far greater access to useful data, as well as to other people and machines, have implications for all sorts of work.

The case for a highly disruptive period of economic growth is made by Erik Brynjolfsson and Andrew McAfee, professors at MIT, in *The Second Machine Age*, a book published in 2014. Like the first great era of industrialisation, they argue, it should deliver enormous benefits – but not without a period of disorienting and uncomfortable change. Their argument rests on an underappreciated aspect of the exponential growth in chip processing speed, memory capacity and other computer attributes: that the amount of progress computers will make in the next few years is always equal to the progress they have made since the very beginning. Mr Brynjolfsson and Mr McAfee reckon that the main bottleneck on innovation is the time it takes society to sort through the many combinations and permutations of new technologies and business models.

A startling progression of inventions seems to bear their thesis out. Ten years ago technologically minded economists pointed to driving cars in traffic as the sort of human accomplishment that computers were highly unlikely to master. Now Google cars are rolling round California driver-free no one doubts such mastery is possible, though the speed at which fully self-driving cars will come to market remains hard to guess.

Brave new world

Even after computers beat grandmasters at chess (once thought highly unlikely), nobody thought they could take on people at free-form games played in natural language. Then Watson, a pattern-recognising supercomputer developed by IBM, bested the best human competitors in America's popular and syntactically tricksy general-knowledge quiz show *Jeopardy!*. Versions of Watson are being marketed to firms across a range of industries to help with all sorts of pattern-recognition problems. Its acumen will grow, and its costs fall, as firms learn to harness its abilities.

The machines are not just cleverer, they also have access to far more data. The combination of big data and smart machines will take over some occupations wholesale; in others it will allow firms to do more with fewer workers. Text-mining programs will displace professional jobs in legal services. Biopsies will be analysed more efficiently by image-processing software than by lab technicians. Accountants may follow travel agents and tellers into the unemployment line as tax software improves. Machines are already turning basic sports results and financial data into good-enough news stories.

Jobs that are not easily automated may still be transformed. New data-processing technology could break "cognitive" jobs down into smaller and smaller tasks. As well as opening the way to eventual automation this could reduce the satisfaction from such work, just as the satisfaction of making things was reduced by deskilling and interchangeable parts in the 19th century. If such jobs persist, they may engage Mr Graeber's "bullshit" detector.

Being newly able to do brainwork will not stop computers from doing ever more formerly manual labour; it will make them better at it. The designers of the latest generation of industrial robots talk about their creations as helping workers rather than replacing them; but there is little doubt that the technology will be able to do a bit of both – probably more than a bit. A taxi driver will be a rarity in many places by the 2030s or 2040s. That sounds like bad news for journalists who rely on that most reliable source of local knowledge and prejudice – but will there be many journalists left to care? Will there be airline pilots? Or traffic cops? Or soldiers?

There will still be jobs. Even Mr Frey and Mr Osborne, whose research speaks of 47% of job categories being open to automation within two decades, accept that some jobs – especially those currently associated with high levels of education and high wages – will survive (see Figure 14.3). Tyler Cowen, an economist at George Mason University and a much-read blogger, writes in his 2013 book, *Average is Over*, that rich economies seem to be bifurcating into a small group of workers with skills highly complementary with machine intelligence, for whom he has high hopes, and the rest, for whom not so much.

FIG 14.3 **Bring on the personal trainers**

Probability that computerisation will lead to job losses within the next two decades, 2013

(1=certain)	
Job	**Probability**
Recreational therapists	0.003
Dentists	0.004
Athletic trainers	0.007
Clergy	0.008
Chemical engineers	0.02
Editors	0.06
Firefighters	0.17
Actors	0.37
Health technologists	0.40
Economists	0.43
Commercial pilots	0.55
Machinists	0.65
Word processors and typists	0.81
Real estate sales agents	0.86
Technical writers	0.89
Retail salespersons	0.92
Accountants and auditors	0.94
Telemarketers	0.99

Source: *The Future of Employment: How Susceptible are Jobs to Computerisation?* by C. Frey and M. Osborne, 2013

And although Mr Brynjolfsson and Mr McAfee rightly point out that developing the business models which make the best use of new technologies will involve trial and error and human flexibility, it is also the case that the second machine age will make such trial and error easier. It will be shockingly easy to launch a start-up, bring a new product to market and sell to billions of global consumers. Those who create or invest in blockbuster ideas may earn unprecedented returns as a result.

In his book, *Capital in the Twenty-First Century*, Thomas Piketty, an economist at the Paris School of Economics, argues along similar lines that America may be pioneering a hyper-unequal economic model in which a top 1% of capital-owners and "supermanagers" grab a growing share of national income and accumulate an increasing concentration of national wealth. The rise of the middle-class – a 20th-century innovation – was a hugely important political and social development across the world. The squeezing out of that class could generate a more antagonistic, unstable and potentially dangerous politics.

The potential for dramatic change is clear. A future of widespread technological unemployment is harder for many to accept. Every great period of innovation has produced its share of labour-market doomsayers, but technological progress has never previously failed to

FIG 14.4 **A history to repeat?**
Average real wage, year 1 = 100

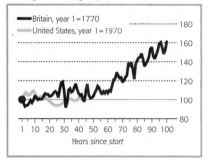

Source: *Pessimism Preserved: Real Wages in the British Industrial Revolution* by R.C. Allen, 2013; US Bureau of Labour Statistics

generate new employment opportunities.

The productivity gains from future automation will be real, even if they mostly accrue to the owners of the machines. Some will be spent on goods and services – golf instructors, household help and so on – and most of the rest invested in firms that are seeking to expand and presumably hire more labour. Though inequality could soar in such a world, unemployment would not necessarily spike. The current sluggishness in wages may, like that of the early industrial era, be a temporary matter, with the good times about to roll (see Figure 14.4).

These jobs may look distinctly different from those they replace. Just as past mechanisation freed, or forced, workers into jobs requiring more cognitive dexterity, leaps in machine intelligence could create space for people to specialise in more emotive occupations, as yet unsuited to machines: a world of artists and therapists, love counsellors and yoga instructors.

Such emotional and relational work could be as critical to the future as metal-bashing was in the past, even if it gets little respect at first. Cultural norms change slowly. Manufacturing jobs are still often treated as "better" – in some vague, non-pecuniary way – than paper-pushing is. To some 18th-century observers, working in the fields was inherently more noble than making gewgaws.

But though growth in areas of the economy that are not easily automated provides jobs, it does not necessarily help real wages. Mr Summers points out that prices of things-made-of-widgets have fallen remarkably in past decades; America's Bureau of Labour Statistics reckons that today you could get the equivalent of an early 1980s television for a twentieth of its then price, were it not that no televisions that poor are still made. However, prices of things not made of widgets, most notably college education and health care, have shot up. If people lived on widgets alone – goods whose costs have fallen because of both globalisation and technology – there would have been no pause in the increase of real wages. It is the increase in the prices of stuff that isn't mechanised (whose supply is often under the control of the state and perhaps subject to fundamental scarcity) that means a pay packet goes no further than it used to.

So technological progress squeezes some incomes in the short term before making everyone richer in the long term, and can drive up the costs of some things even more than it eventually increases earnings. As innovation continues, automation may bring down costs in some of those stubborn areas as well, though those dominated by scarcity – such as houses in desirable places – are likely to resist the trend, as may those where the state keeps market forces at bay. But if innovation does make health care or higher education cheaper, it will probably be at the cost of more jobs, and give rise to yet more concentration of income.

The machine stops

Even if the long-term outlook is rosy, with the potential for greater wealth and lots of new jobs, it does not mean that policymakers should simply sit on their hands in the meantime. Adaptation to past waves of progress rested on political and policy responses. The most obvious are the massive improvements in educational attainment brought on first by the institution of universal secondary education and then by the rise of university attendance. Policies aimed at similar gains would now seem to be in order. But as Mr Cowen has pointed out, the gains of the 19th and 20th centuries will be hard to duplicate.

Boosting the skills and earning power of the children of 19th-century farmers and labourers took little more than offering schools where they could learn to read, write and do algebra. Pushing a large proportion of college graduates to complete graduate work successfully will be harder and more expensive. Perhaps cheap and innovative online education will indeed make new attainment possible. But as Mr Cowen notes, such programmes may tend to deliver big gains only for the most conscientious students.

Another way in which previous adaptation is not necessarily a good guide to future employment is the existence of welfare. The alternative to joining the 19th-century industrial proletariat was malnourished deprivation. Today, because of measures introduced in response to, and to some extent on the proceeds of, industrialisation, people in the developed world are provided with unemployment benefits, disability allowances and other forms of welfare. They are also much more likely than a bygone peasant to have savings. This means that the "reservation wage" – the wage below which a worker will not accept a job – is now high in historical terms. If governments refuse to allow jobless workers to fall too far below the average standard of living, then this reservation wage will rise steadily, and ever more workers may find work unattractive. And the higher it rises, the greater the incentive to invest in capital that replaces labour.

Everyone should be able to benefit from productivity gains – in that, Keynes was united with his successors. His worry about technological unemployment was mainly a worry about a "temporary phase of maladjustment" as society and the economy adjusted to ever-greater levels of productivity. So it could well prove. However, society may find itself sorely tested if, as seems possible, growth and innovation deliver handsome gains to the skilled, while the rest cling to dwindling employment opportunities at stagnant wages.

January 2014

Bibliography

Part 1 Money, banks and crashes

1 Money

Anagol, S., Etang, A. and Karlan, D., "Continued Existence of Cows Disproves Central Tenets of Capitalism?", NBER Working Paper 19437, 2013.

Goodhart, C., "The two concepts of money: implications for the analysis of optimal currency areas", *European Journal of Political Economy*, August 1998.

Kiyotaki, N., "Evil is the root of all money", *American Economic Review*, Vol. 92, No. 2, 2001.

Menger, C., "On the Origins of Money", *The Economic Journal*, June 1892.

2 A short history of financial crashes

"The American President on the American Crisis", *The Economist*, December 26th 1857.

Bagehot, W., *The Works and Life of Walter Bagehot*, Vol. 2, ed. Mrs Russell Barrington, Longmans, Green, & Co., 1915.

Bruner, R.F. and Carr, S.D., *The Panic of 1907: Lessons Learned from the Market's Perfect Storm*, John Wiley & Sons, 2007.

Calomiris, C.W. and Schweikart, L., "The Panic of 1857: Origins, Transmission, and Containment", *The Journal of Economic History*, Vol. 51, No. 4, 1991.

Clapham, J.H., *The Bank of England: A History, Volume II (1797-1914)*, Cambridge University Press, 1945.

Cowen, D.J., Sylla, R. and Wright, R.E., "The U.S. Panic of 1792: Financial Crisis Management and the Lender of Last Resort", mimeo, July 2006.

Crafts, N. and Fearon, P., "Lessons from the 1930s' Great Depression", CAGEOnline Working Paper Series 23, 2010.

Davies, R., Richardson, P., Katinaite, V. and Manning, M.J., "Evolution of the UK Banking System", *Bank of England Quarterly Bulletin*, Q4, December, 2010.

Dawson, F.G., *The First Latin American Debt Crisis: The City of London and the 1822-25 Loan Bubble*, Princeton University Press, 1990.

Evans, D.M., *The History of the Commercial Crisis, 1857-1858 and the Stock Exchange Panic of 1859*, Groombridge, 1859.

Flandreau, M. and Flores, J.H., "Bonds and Brands: Intermediaries and Reputation in Sovereign Debt Markets 1820-1830", *The Journal of Economic History*, Vol. 69, No. 3, 2007.

Friedman, M. and Schwartz, A., *A Monetary History of the United States, 1867-1960*, Princeton University Press, 1963.

Galbraith, J.K., *The Great Crash 1929*, Pelican, 1961.

Kindleberger, C.P., *Manias, Panics and Crashes: A History of Financial Crises*, Basic Books, 1978.

Neal, L., "The Financial Crisis of 1825 and the Restructuring of the British Financial System", Federal Reserve Bank of St Louis, May 1998.

Sprague, O.M.W., "The American Crisis of 1907", *The Economic Journal*, Vol. 18, 1908.

Tallman, E.W. and Moen, J.R., "Lessons from the Panic of 1907", *Federal Reserve Bank of Atlanta Economic Review*, Vol. 75, May/June 1990.

3 Lessons from the financial crisis

Admati, A. and Hellwig, M., *The Bankers' New Clothes: What's Wrong with Banking and What to Do about It*, Princeton University Press, 2013.

Alesina, A. and Ardagna, S., "Large Changes in Fiscal Policy: Taxes Versus Spending", NBER Working Paper 15438, January 2010.

Borio, C., "The financial cycle and macroeconomics: what have we learnt?", Bank for International Settlements, Working Paper No. 395, December 2012.

Christiano, L., Eichenbaum, M. and Rebelo, S., "When Is the Government Spending Multiplier Large?", *Journal of Political Economy*, Vol. 119, No. 1, February 2011.

Haldane, A., "The $100 billion question", speech, Bank of England, March 2010.

Koo, R., "The world in balance sheet recession: causes, cure, and politics", *real-world economics review*, No. 58, 2011.

Miles, D., Yang. J. and Marcheggiano, G., "Optimal Bank Capital", *The Economic Journal*, March 2013.

Reinhart, C.M. and Rogoff, K.S., "Growth in a Time of Debt", *American Economic Review*, American Economic Association, Vol. 100, No. 2, May 2010.

Shin, H.S., "Global Banking Glut and Loan Risk Premium", Princeton University, 2012.

Sutherland, D. and Hoeller, P., "Debt and Macroeconomic Stability: An Overview of the Literature and Some Empirics", OECD Economics Department, Working Paper No. 1006, December 2012.

Williams, J.C., "The Federal Reserve's Unconventional Policies", *FRBSF Economic Letter*, November 2012.

Part 2 Firms, jobs and pay

5 Changing firms

"Where mergers go wrong", *McKinsey Quarterly*, May 2004.

Ali-Yrkkö, J., "Nokia and Finland in a Sea of Change", ETLA (Research Institute of the Finnish Economy), 2010.

Andrade, G., Mitchell, M. and Stafford, E., "New Evidence and Perspectives on Mergers", *Journal of Economic Perspectives*, Vol. 15, No. 2, Spring 2001.

Andrade, G. and Stafford, E., "Investigating the economic role of mergers", *Journal of Corporate Finance*, Vol. 10, 2004.

Borg, J., Borg, M. and Leeth, J., "The success of mergers in the 1920s: A stock market appraisal of the second merger wave", *International Journal of Industrial Organization*, Vol. 7, Issue 1, March 1989.

Brewer, E. and Jagtiani, J., "How much did banks pay to become too-big-to-fail and to become systemically important", Federal Reserve Bank of Philadelphia Working Paper No. 09–34, 2011.

Canals, C., Gabaix, X., Vilarrubia, J.M. and Weinstein, D., "Trade Patterns, Trade Balances and Idiosyncratic shocks", Banco de España, Documentos de Trabajo, 2007.

Coase, R.H., "The Nature of the Firm", *Economica*, New Series, Vol. 4, No. 16, November 1937.

Di Giovanni, J. and Levchenko, A., "Country Size, International Trade, and Aggregate Fluctuations in Granular Economies", *Journal of Political Economy*, 2012.

Gabaix, X., "The Granular Origins of Aggregate Fluctuations", *Econometrica*, May 2011.

Haas-Wilson, D. and Vita, M., "Mergers between Competing Hospitals: Lessons from Retrospective Analyses", in "Symposium on retrospective merger analysis in healthcare", *International Journal of the Economics of Business*, Vol. 18, No. 1, February 2011.

Harford, J., "Corporate cash reserves and acquisitions", *Journal of Finance*, Vol. 54, 1999.

Harford, J., "What drives merger waves?", *Journal of Financial Economics*, Vol. 77, 2005.

Igami, M. and Yang, N., "Cannibalization and Preemptive Entry of Multi-Product Firms", Social Science Research Network, 2013.

Lucas, R.E., "On the size distribution of business firms", *Bell Journal of Economics*, 1978.

Mosheim, R. and Lovell, C., "Scale Economies and Inefficiency of US Dairy Farms", *American Journal of Agricultural Economics*, Vol. 91, No. 3, August 2009.

Nelson, R., "The first merger wave", *Merger Movements in American Industry, 1895-1956*, Princeton University Press, 1959.

Pels, E. and Rietveld, P., "Rail cost functions and scale elasticities: a meta-analysis", Vrije Universiteit Amsterdam, 2003.

Thaler, R.H., "Anomalies: The Winner's Curse", *Journal of Economic Perspectives*, Vol. 2, No. 1, Winter 1988.

Watts, S. and Kalita, N., "Tall Buildings, A Strategic Design Guide – Cost Section" and "The Economics of High Rise", Davis Langdon Tall Buildings Research, 2010.

Wilson, N.E., "Branding, Cannibalization, and Spatial Preemption: An Application to the Hotel Industry", Working Paper No. 309, Federal Trade Commission, 2011.

6 Unemployment

Bils, M., Yongsung Chang and Sun-Bin Kim, "How sticky wages in existing jobs can affect hiring", NBER Working Paper 19821, January 2014.

Calvo, G., Coricelli, F. and Ottonello, P., "The labor market consequences of financial crises with or without inflation: jobless and wageless recoveries", NBER Working Paper 18480, October 2012.

Davis, S., Faberman, J. and Haltiwanger, J., "Recruiting Intensity During and After the Great Recession: National and Industry Evidence", NBER Working Paper, January 2012.

Lazear, E. and Spletzer, J., "Hiring, Churn and the Business Cycle", NBER Working Paper, December 2011.

Martin, B. and Rowthorn, R., "Is the British economy supply constrained II? A renewed critique of productivity pessimism", Centre for Business Research, May 2012.

Oreopoulos, P., Von Wachter, T. and Heisz, A., "The Short- and Long-Term Career Effects of Graduating in a Recession", *American Economic Journal: Applied Economics*, January 2012.

7 Pay

Ackerlof, G.A. and Kranton, R.E., "Identity, Supervision, and Work Groups", *American Economic Review*, Vol. 98, No. 2, 2008.

Aguiar, M. and Hurst, E., "A summary of trends in American time allocation: 1965-2005", Social Indicators Research, 2009.

Allegretto, S.A., Dube, A. and Reich, M., "Do minimum wages really reduce teen employment? Accounting for heterogeneity and selectivity in state panel data", *Industrial Relations*, April 2011.

Baker, G.P. "Incentive Contracts and Performance Measurement", *Journal of Political Economy*, Vol. 100, No. 3, 1992.

Becker, G.S. "Crime and Punishment: An Economic Approach", *Journal of Political Economy*, Vol. 76, No. 2, 1968.

Belot, M. and Schröder, M., "Sloppy Work, Lies and Theft: A Novel Experimental Design to Study Counterproductive Behaviour", *Journal of Economic Behavior and Organization*, 2013.

Bénabou, R. and Tirole, J., "Intrinsic and Extrinsic Motivation", *Review of Economic Studies*, Vol. 70, 2003.

Boly, A., "On the Incentive Effects of Monitoring: Evidence from the Lab and the Field", *Experimental Economics*, Vol. 14, Issue 2, May 2011.

Butcher, T., Dickens, R. and Manning, A., "Minimum wages and wage inequality: Some theory and an application to the UK", CEP Discussion Paper No. 1177, October 2012.

Deci, E., "Effects of Externally Mediated Rewards on Intrinsic Motivation", *Journal of Personality and Social Psychology*, 1971.

Dickinson, D.L. and Villeval, M.C., "Does Monitoring Decrease Work Effort? The Complementarity between Agency and Crowding-out Theories", *Games and Economic Behavior*, Vol. 63, 2008.

Dube, A., Lester, T.W. and Reich, M., "Minimum wage effects across state borders: Estimates using contiguous counties", *The Review of Economics and Statistics*, November 2010.

Falk, A. and Kosfeld, M., "The Hidden Costs of Control", *American Economic Review*, Vol. 96, No. 5, 2006.

Gershuny, J. and Fisher, K., "Post-industrious society: Why work time will not disappear for our grandchildren", Centre for Time Use Research, Department of Sociology, University of Oxford, 2014.

Hirsch, B.T., Kaufman, B.E. and Zelenska, T., "Minimum wage channels of adjustment", IZA Discussion Paper No. 6132, November 2011.

Hochschild, A.R., *The Time Bind: When home becomes work and work becomes home*, Holt Paperbacks, 2001.

Kahneman, D., *et al.*, "Would you be happier if you were richer? A focusing illusion", *Science*, June 30th 2006.

Kuhn, P. and Lozano, F., "The expanding workweek? Understanding trends in long work hours among US men, 1979–2004", National Bureau of Economic Research, 2008.

Manning, A., "Minimum wage: Maximum impact", Resolution Foundation, April 2012.

Metcalf, D., "Why has the British national minimum wage had little or no impact on employment?", CEP Discussion Paper No. 781, April 2007.

Neumark, D., Salas, J.M.I. and Wascher, W., "Revising the minimum wage-employment debate: Throwing out the baby with the bathwater?", IZA Discussion Paper No. 7166, January 2013.

Rabin, M., "Incorporating fairness into game theory and economics", *American Economic Review*, 1993.

Smith, T., "Job Satisfaction in the United States", National Opinion Research Centre, University of Chicago, 2007.

Veblen, T., *The Theory of the Leisure Class: An economic study of institutions*, Aakar Books, 1899.

Voth, H-J., "The longest years: new estimates of labor input in England, 1760–1830", *Journal of Economic History*, 2001.

8 Inequality

Ashok, V., Kuziemko, I. and Washington, E., "Support for Redistribution in an Age of Rising Inequality", Working Paper, BPEA Conference Draft, March 19–20th 2015.

Azzimonti, M., de Francisco, E. and Quadrini, V., "Financial globalization, inequality, and the raising of public debt", Federal Reserve Bank of Philadelphia Working Paper, February 2012.

Berg, A. and Ostry, J., "Inequality and unsustainable growth: Two sides of the same coin?", IMF Staff Discussion Note, April 2011.

Berg, A., Ostry, J. and Tsangarides, C., "Redistribution, inequality, and growth", IMF Staff Discussion Note, February 2014.

Bertrand, M. and Morse, A., "Trickle-down consumption", NBER Working Paper 18883, February 2012.

Bollard, A., Klenow, P. and Li, H., "Entry costs rise with development", SCID Working Paper 518, December 2014.

Bordo, M. and Meissner, C., "Does inequality lead to a financial crisis?, NBER Working Paper, March 2012.

Clark, G., "What is the true rate of social mobility in Sweden? A surname analysis, 1700–2012", mimeo, August 2012.

Clark, G., "What is the true rate of social mobility? Evidence from the information content of surnames", American Economic Association conference paper, January 2013.

Clark, G. and Cummins, N., "What is the true rate of social mobility? Surnames and social mobility in England, 1800–2012", mimeo, September 2012.

Cloyne, J. and Surico, P., "Household Debt and the Dynamic Effects of Income Tax Changes", Discussion Paper No. 9649, Centre for Economic Policy Research, 2014.

Collado, D., Ortuno-Ortin, I. and Romeu, A., "Long-run intergenerational social mobility and the distribution of surnames", American Economic Association conference paper, December 2012.

Corak, M., "Do poor children become poor adults? Lessons for public policy from a cross country comparison of generational earnings mobility", *Research on Economic Inequality*, 2006.

Cynamon, B.Z. and Fazzari, S.M., "Inequality, the Great Recession, and Slow Recovery", mimeo, October 24th 2014. Available at http://ssrn.com/abstract=2205524 or http://dx.doi.org/10.2139/ssrn.2205524

Kaplan, G., Violante, G.L. and Weidner, J., "The Wealthy Hand-to-Mouth", NBER Working Paper 20073, 2014.

Kumhof, M. and Rancière, R., "Inequality, leverage and crises", IMF Working Paper, November 2010.

Lindahl, M., Palme, M., Sandgren Massih, S. and Sjögren, A., "The intergenerational persistence of human capital: An empirical analysis of four generations", IZA discussion paper, April 2012.

Long, J. and Ferrie, J., "Grandfathers matter(ed): Occupational mobility across three generations in the U.S. and Britain, 1850–1910", American Economic Association conference paper, 2012.

Long, J. and Ferrie, J., "Intergenerational Occupational Mobility in Great Britain and the United States since 1850", *American Economic Review*, Vol. 103, No. 4, 2013.

Mare, R. and Xi Song, "Social mobility in multiple generations", Population Association of America conference paper, September 2011.

Mueller, H., Simintzi, E. and Ouimet, P., "Wage inequality and firm growth", LIS Working Paper 632, March 2015.

Pigou, A.C., *The Economics of Welfare*, Macmillan & Co, 1920.

9 Secular stagnation

Cynamon, B. and Fazzari, S., "Inequality and Household Finance During the Consumer Age", INET Research Note 23, February 2013.

Goodhart, C. and Erfurth, P., "Demography and economics: Look past the past", VoxEU.org, November 4th 2014.

Hamilton, J.D., Harris, E.S., Hatzius, J. and West, K.D., "The Equilibrium Real Funds Rate: Past, Present and Future", US Monetary Policy Forum, University of Chicago Booth School of Business, 2015.

Hansen, A., *Full Recovery or Stagnation*, W.W. Norton, 1938.

Hansen, A., "Economic Progress and Declining Population Growth", *American Economic Review*, March 1939.

Justiniano, A., Primiceri, G. and Tambalotti, A., "The effects of the saving and banking glut on the U.S. economy", NBER Working Paper 19635, November 2013.

Keynes, J.M., "Some economic consequences of a declining population", Galton Lecture, 1937.

Pinto, E. and Tevlin, S., "Perspectives on the Recent Weakness in Investment", FEDS Notes, May 21st 2014.

Reinhart, C. and Rogoff, K., "The aftermath of financial crises", NBER Working Paper 14656, January 2009.

Summers, L., "U.S. Economic Prospects: Secular Stagnation, Hysteresis, and the Zero Lower Bound", *Business Economics*, February 2014.

Teulings, C. and Baldwin, R. (eds), *Secular Stagnation: Facts, Causes and Cures*, Centre for Economic Policy Research, 2014. Published as a VoxEU.org e-book.

Part 3

10 Reinventing economics

Easterly, W., "Life during growth", *Journal of Economic Growth*, September 1999.

Gu, W., Terefe, B. and Wang, W., "The Impact of R&D Capitalization on GDP and Productivity Growth in Canada", Statistics Canada, October 2012.

Kuznets, S., "National Income 1929-1932", 1934. Senate Document No. 124, 73rd Congress, 2nd Session. Washington, DC: US Government Printing Office. Available at http://library.bea.gov

Landefeld J.S., Seskin, E.P. and Fraumeni, B.M., "Taking the Pulse of the Economy: Measuring GDP", *Journal of Economic Perspectives*, Vol. 22, No. 2, 2008.

Pew Research Centre, "People in emerging markets catch up to advanced economies in life satisfaction", October 2014.

United Nations, "Measurement of National Income and the Construction of Social Accounts", 1947.

United Nations, "System of National Accounts 2008", 2008.

US Bureau of Economic Analysis, "Results of the 2013 Comprehensive Revision of the National Income and Product Accounts", 2013.

11 New firms, new economics

Armstrong, M., "Price discrimination", MPRA Paper 4693, University Library of Munich, 2006.

Blake, T., Nosko, C. and Tadelis, S., "Consumer Search on eBay", unpublished research, June 2013.

Ellison, G. and Ellison, S.F., "Match Quality, Search, and the Internet Market for Used Books", Massachusetts Institute of Technology Working Paper, September 2014.

Rochet, J-C. and Tirole, J., "Two-Sided Markets: A Progress Report", *The RAND Journal of Economics*, Vol. 37, No. 3, Autumn 2006.

Waldfogel, J., "Copyright Protection, Technological Change, And The Quality Of New Products: Evidence From Recorded Music Since Napster", NBER Working Paper 17503, October 2011.

Waldfogel, J., "Digitization and the Quality of New Media Products: The Case of Music", in Goldfarb, A. Greenstein, S. and Tucker, C. (eds), *Economic Analysis of the Digital Economy*, National Bureau of Economic Research, 2015.

12 The economics of behaviour

Becker, G.S., "Crime and Punishment: An Economic Approach", *Journal of Political Economy*, Vol. 76, No. 2, Mar–Apr 1968.

Connor, J.M. and Helmers, C.G., "Statistics on Modern Private International Cartels, 1990–2005", American Antitrust Institute Working Paper No. 07-01, 2007.

Gole, T. and Quinn, S., "Committees and Status Quo Bias: Structural Evidence from a Randomized Field Experiment". Oxford University, 2014.

Kahneman, D. and Tversky, A., "Judgement under uncertainty: Heuristics and biases", *Science*, Vol. 185, 1974.

Levy, G., "Decision Making Procedures for Committees of Careerist Experts", London School of Economics, 2007.

OECD, "Behavioural Insights and New Approaches to Policy Design", Summary of Workshop, 2010.

Posner, R.A., "The Chicago School of Antitrust Analysis", *University of Pennsylvania Law Review*, Vol. 127, No. 4, April 1979.

13 Tomorrow's economic challenges

Acemoglu, D., Gancia, G. and Zilibotti, F., "Offshoring and Directed Technical Change", NBER Working Paper 18585, December 2012.

Azoulay, P. and Jones, B., "Generating Ideas: Academic and Applied Research", presentation at Innovation and Early Stage Ideas conference, Tinbergen Institute, 2006.

Baumol, W. et al., *The Cost Disease: Why Computers Get Cheaper and Health Care Doesn't*, Yale University Press, 2012.

Bloom, D.E., Canning, D. and Fink, G., "Implications of Population Aging for Economic Growth", NBER Working Paper 16705, 2011.

Bloom, N., Griffith, R. and Van Reenen, J., "Do R&D Tax Credits Work?", *Journal of Public Economics*, Vol. 85, 2002.

Bloom, N., Schankerman, M. and Van Reenen, J., "Identifying Technology Spillovers and Product Market Rivalry", Centre for Economic Performance, Discussion Paper No. 675, December 2012.

Department for Business, Innovation & Skills, *The Kay Review of UK Equity Markets and Long-Term Decision Making*, July 2012.

Gordo, L.R. and Skirbekk, V., "Skill demand and the comparative advantage of age: Jobs tasks and earnings from the 1980s to the 2000s in Germany", *Labour Economics*, Vol. 22, Issue C, 2013.

Graham, J., Harvey, C. and Rajgopal, S., "The Economic Implications of Corporate Financial Reporting", *Journal of Accounting and Economics*, Vol. 40, No. 1–3.

Hetschko, C., Knabe, A. and Schöb, R., "Changing Identity: Retiring From Unemployment, *The Economic Journal*, Vol. 124, 2014.

Jones, C.I., "Sources of U.S. Economic Growth in a World of Ideas", *American Economic Review*, Vol. 92, No.1, March 2002.

Romer, P.M., "Growth Based on Increasing Returns Due to Specialization", *American Economic Review*, Vol. 77, No. 2, 1987.

Vandoros, S., "Therapeutic Substitution Post-patent Expiry: The cases of ace inhibitors and proton pump inhibitors", *Health Economics*, Vol. 23, No. 5, 2014.

14 Robot economics

Acemoglu *et al.*, op. cit.

Autor, D., "The 'Task Approach' to Labor Markets: An overview", NBER Working Paper 18711, January 2013.

Brynjolfsson, E. and McAfee, A., *Race Against the Machine: How the digital revolution is accelerating innovation, driving productivity, and irreversibly transforming employment and the economy*, Digital Frontier Press, 2011.

Ford, M., *The Lights in the Tunnel: Automation, accelerating technology, and the economy of the future*, CreateSpace Independent Publishing Platform, 2009

Frey, C.B. and Osborne, M.A., "The Future of Employment: How Susceptible are Jobs to Computerisation?", Working Paper, Oxford University, 2013.

Katz, L.F. and Margo, R.A., "Technical Change and the Relative Demand for Skilled Labor: The United States in Historical Perspective", NBER Working Paper 18752, February 2013.

Summers, L., "Economic Possibilities for our Children", Martin Feldstein Lecture, NBER, 2013.

Wright, J.D., Ananth, C.V., Lewin, S.N. *et al.*, "Robotically Assisted vs Laparoscopic Hysterectomy Among Women With Benign Gynecologic Disease", *Journal of the American Medical Association*, Vol. 309 No. 7, 2013.

Index

Page numbers in *italics* indicate figures.

PublicAffairs is a publishing house founded in 1997. It is a tribute to the standards, values, and flair of three persons who have served as mentors to countless reporters, writers, editors, and book people of all kinds, including me.

I. F. STONE, proprietor of *I. F. Stone's Weekly*, combined a commitment to the First Amendment with entrepreneurial zeal and reporting skill and became one of the great independent journalists in American history. At the age of eighty, Izzy published *The Trial of Socrates*, which was a national bestseller. He wrote the book after he taught himself ancient Greek.

BENJAMIN C. BRADLEE was for nearly thirty years the charismatic editorial leader of *The Washington Post*. It was Ben who gave the *Post* the range and courage to pursue such historic issues as Watergate. He supported his reporters with a tenacity that made them fearless and it is no accident that so many became authors of influential, best-selling books.

ROBERT L. BERNSTEIN, the chief executive of Random House for more than a quarter century, guided one of the nation's premier publishing houses. Bob was personally responsible for many books of political dissent and argument that challenged tyranny around the globe. He is also the founder and longtime chair of Human Rights Watch, one of the most respected human rights organizations in the world.

·   ·   ·

For fifty years, the banner of Public Affairs Press was carried by its owner Morris B. Schnapper, who published Gandhi, Nasser, Toynbee, Truman, and about 1,500 other authors. In 1983, Schnapper was described by *The Washington Post* as "a redoubtable gadfly." His legacy will endure in the books to come.

Peter Osnos, *Founder and Editor-at-Large*